JOURNEYS

Reader's Notebook
Teacher's Edition

Grade 2

HOUGHTON MIFFLIN HARCOURT
School Publishers

Printed in the U.S.A.

ISBN: 978-0-547-86073-2

         10 0982 21 20 19 18 17 16 15 14

4500467480   A B C D E F G

Contents

Volume 2

Contents

Name _____ Date _____

Short Vowels *a, i*

Henry and Mudge
Phonics: Short Vowels *a, i*

Read each word. Draw a line to the picture that it matches.

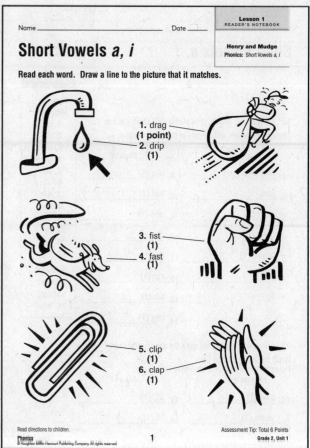

1. drag
(1 point)
2. drip
(1)

3. fist
(1)
4. fast
(1)

5. clip
(1)
6. clap
(1)

Read directions to children.

Assessment Tip: Total 6 Points
1
Grade 2, Unit 1

Name _____ Date _____

Subjects

Henry and Mudge
Grammar: Subjects and Predicates

- A **sentence** tells a complete thought. It has a naming part and an action part.
- The **subject** is the naming part of a sentence.
- The subject tells who or what does or did something. The subject tells what the sentence is about.

<u>Children</u> play spy games.

Thinking Question
Who or what does something?

✏️ Draw a line under the naming part of the sentence.

1. <u>Jason</u> sneaks around. **(1 point)**

2. <u>Kim</u> looks through windows. **(1)**

3. <u>My brother</u> writes in a notebook. **(1)**

4. <u>John</u> reads spy books. **(1)**

✏️ Write the naming part from the box to finish each sentence.

The cat	Jill

5. **Jill (1)** _____ tells spy stories.

6. **The cat (1)** _____ purrs on her lap.

Assessment Tip: Total 6 Points
2
Grade 2, Unit 1

Name _____ Date _____

Short Vowels *a, i*

Henry and Mudge
Phonics: Short Vowels *a, i*

Write labels on the groceries. Use words from the Word Bank. (1 point each)

Word Bank

milk	bran	mints
jam	yams	ham

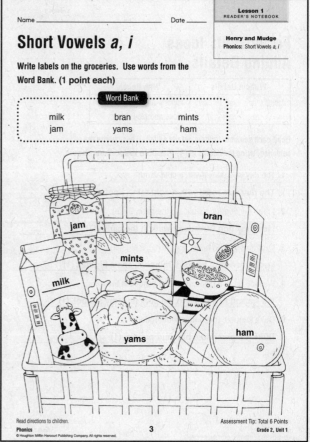

jam

bran

mints

milk

yams

ham

Read directions to children.

Assessment Tip: Total 6 Points
3
Grade 2, Unit 1

Reader's Notebook
1
Volume 1, pp. i–3

Panel 1 (top left)

Short Vowels *a, i*

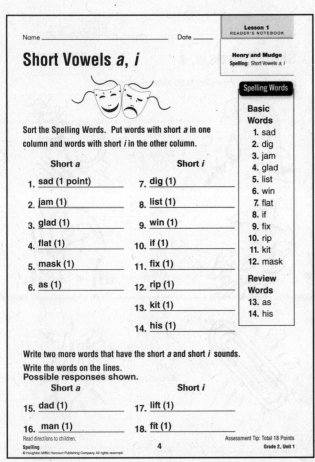

Sort the Spelling Words. Put words with short *a* in one column and words with short *i* in the other column.

Short *a*	Short *i*
1. sad (1 point)	7. dig (1)
2. jam (1)	8. list (1)
3. glad (1)	9. win (1)
4. flat (1)	10. if (1)
5. mask (1)	11. fix (1)
6. as (1)	12. rip (1)
	13. kit (1)
	14. his (1)

Spelling Words

Basic Words
1. sad
2. dig
3. jam
4. glad
5. list
6. win
7. flat
8. if
9. fix
10. rip
11. kit
12. mask

Review Words
13. as
14. his

Write two more words that have the short *a* and short *i* sounds.
Write the words on the lines.
Possible responses shown.

Short *a*	Short *i*
15. dad (1)	17. lift (1)
16. man (1)	18. fit (1)

Read directions to children.
Spelling · 4
© Houghton Mifflin Harcourt Publishing Company. All rights reserved.
Assessment Tip: Total 18 Points
Grade 2, Unit 1

Panel 2 (top right)

Predicates

- A **predicate** is the action part of a sentence.
- A predicate tells what the subject in a sentence does or did.
- The action part of a sentence uses words that show action.

David (hides toys.)

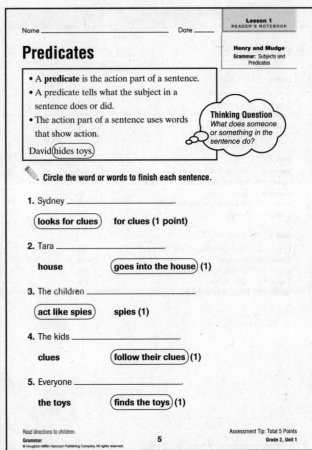

Thinking Question
What does someone or something in the sentence do?

Circle the word or words to finish each sentence.

1. Sydney _____
   (looks for clues)   for clues (1 point)

2. Tara _____
   house   (goes into the house) (1)

3. The children _____
   (act like spies)   spies (1)

4. The kids _____
   clues   (follow their clues) (1)

5. Everyone _____
   the toys   (finds the toys) (1)

Read directions to children.
Grammar · 5
© Houghton Mifflin Harcourt Publishing Company. All rights reserved.
Assessment Tip: Total 5 Points
Grade 2, Unit 1

Panel 3 (bottom left)

Focus Trait: Ideas
Adding Details

Without Details	With Details
Jackie's dog liked to play.	Jackie's dog liked to chase sticks and play catch.

Read each sentence without details added. Then rewrite the sentence, using the details in ( ). Possible responses shown.

1. The day was rainy. (with a cold wind)
   The day was rainy with a cold rain. (1 point)

2. I took my dog for a walk. (in the park, Duke)
   I took my dog Duke for a walk in the park. (1)

3. I got dressed. (in boots, a raincoat, a big hat)
   I got dressed in boots, a raincoat, and a big hat. (1)

4. We walked to a place. (near my school, in the park)
   We walked to a place in the park near my school. (1)

5. Duke jumped. (big, into a mud puddle)
   Duke jumped into a big mud puddle. (1)

Read directions to children.
Writing · 6
© Houghton Mifflin Harcourt Publishing Company. All rights reserved.
Assessment Tip: Total 5 Points
Grade 2, Unit 1

Panel 4 (bottom right)

CVC Words

Finish writing the name of the picture. One syllable is written for you.

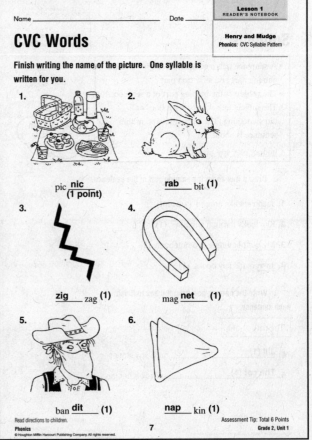

1. pic **nic** (1 point)

2. **rab** bit (1)

3. **zig** zag (1)

4. mag **net** (1)

5. ban **dit** (1)

6. **nap** kin (1)

Read directions to children.
Phonics · 7
© Houghton Mifflin Harcourt Publishing Company. All rights reserved.
Assessment Tip: Total 6 Points
Grade 2, Unit 1

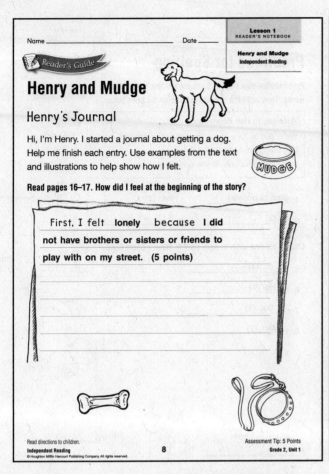

Henry and Mudge

Henry's Journal

Hi, I'm Henry. I started a journal about getting a dog. Help me finish each entry. Use examples from the text and illustrations to help show how I felt.

Read pages 16–17. How did I feel at the beginning of the story?

First, I felt **lonely** because **I did not have brothers or sisters or friends to play with on my street. (5 points)**

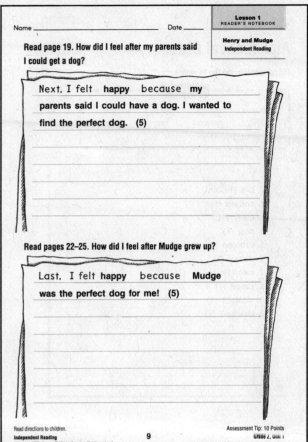

Read page 19. How did I feel after my parents said I could get a dog?

Next, I felt **happy** because **my parents said I could have a dog. I wanted to find the perfect dog. (5)**

Read pages 22–25. How did I feel after Mudge grew up?

Last, I felt **happy** because **Mudge was the perfect dog for me! (5)**

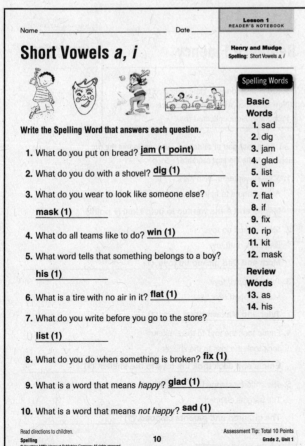

Short Vowels *a, i*

Write the Spelling Word that answers each question.

1. What do you put on bread? **jam (1 point)**

2. What do you do with a shovel? **dig (1)**

3. What do you wear to look like someone else?
   mask (1)

4. What do all teams like to do? **win (1)**

5. What word tells that something belongs to a boy?
   his (1)

6. What is a tire with no air in it? **flat (1)**

7. What do you write before you go to the store?
   list (1)

8. What do you do when something is broken? **fix (1)**

9. What is a word that means *happy*? **glad (1)**

10. What is a word that means *not happy*? **sad (1)**

Spelling Words

Basic Words
1. sad
2. dig
3. jam
4. glad
5. list
6. win
7. flat
8. if
9. fix
10. rip
11. kit
12. mask

Review Words
13. as
14. his

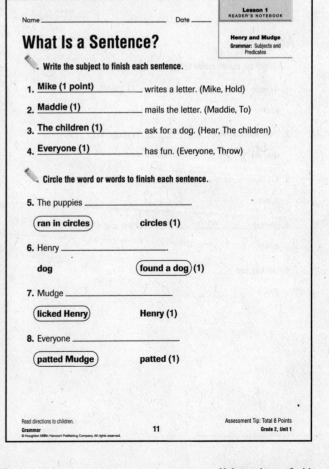

What Is a Sentence?

Write the subject to finish each sentence.

1. **Mike (1 point)** ___ writes a letter. (Mike, Hold)

2. **Maddie (1)** ___ mails the letter. (Maddie, To)

3. **The children (1)** ___ ask for a dog. (Hear, The children)

4. **Everyone (1)** ___ has fun. (Everyone, Throw)

Circle the word or words to finish each sentence.

5. The puppies ___
   (ran in circles)   circles (1)

6. Henry ___
   dog   (found a dog) (1)

7. Mudge ___
   (licked Henry)   Henry (1)

8. Everyone ___
   (patted Mudge)   patted (1)

Alphabetical Order

Henry and Mudge
Vocabulary Strategies:
Alphabetical Order

Put the words in the box in alphabetical order.

Word Bank

collars	straight	floppy	weighed
big	drooled	dog	curly
row	stood		

1. big (1 point)
2. collars (1)
3. curly (1)
4. dog (1)
5. drooled (1)
6. floppy (1)
7. row (1)
8. stood (1)
9. straight (1)
10. weighed (1)

Proofread for Spelling

Henry and Mudge
Spelling: Short Vowels a, i

Proofread the sign below. Cross out the four misspelled words. Then write the correct spellings on the lines below.

> **Welcome to Our Berry Patch!**
> We're glid to have you! You can pick your own.
> Buy our canning cit, and make your
> own jamm. Just ask iff you need help.

Spelling Words

Basic Words
1. sad
2. dig
3. jam
4. glad
5. list
6. win
7. flat
8. if
9. fix
10. rip
11. kit
12. mask

1. glad (2 points) _____ 3. jam (2) _____

2. kit (2) _____ 4. if (2) _____

Change the first letter in each word to make a Basic Word.

5. mix fix (1) _____

6. sip rip (1) _____

7. slat flat (1) _____

8. tin win (1) _____

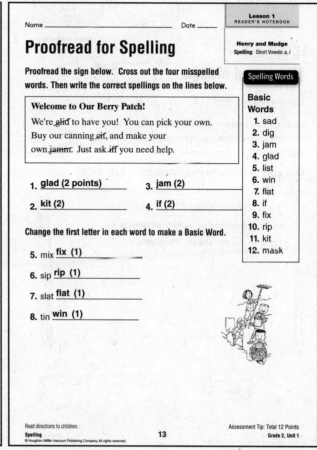

Articles

Henry and Mudge
Grammar: Spiral Review

✏ Write the correct article to complete each sentence.

1. Her dog is _____ a _____ beagle. (1 point)

   a, an

2. They fed my horse _____ the _____ carrots. (1)

   the, an

3. My favorite pet is _____ a _____ cat. (1)

   a, an

4. We saw _____ an _____ alligator at the zoo. (1)

   a, an

5. Did you see _____ the _____ parrots? (1)

   the, a

Sentence Fluency

Henry and Mudge
Grammar: Connect to Writing

> **Short Sentences**
> Pedro collected toys. Janie collected toys.
> **New Sentence with Joined Subjects**
> Pedro and Janie collected toys.

✏ Read each pair of sentences. Use *and* to join the two subjects. Write the new sentence.

1. Miguel wanted to help kids.
   Anna wanted to help kids.

   Miguel and Anna wanted to help kids. (1 point)

2. Mom picked up toys.
   Dad picked up toys.

   Mom and Dad picked up toys. (1)

3. Tyler wrapped toys.
   Max wrapped toys.

   Tyler and Max wrapped toys. (1)

4. Emma took the toys to the shelter.
   Jack took the toys to the shelter.

   Emma and Jack took the toys to the shelter. (1)

5. The children clapped.
   The parents clapped.

   The children and parents clapped. (1)

Short Vowels *o, u, e*

My Family
Phonics: Short Vowels *o, u, e*

Word Bank

tent	skunk	nest	stem
hump	frog	spot	

Write the picture names in the puzzle. **(2 points each)**

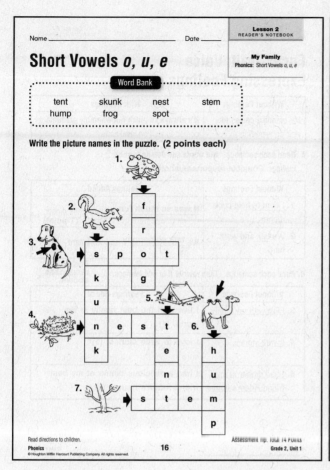

Assessment Tip: Total 14 Points
16
Grade 2, Unit 1

Is It a Sentence?

My Family
Grammar: Simple Sentences

- A sentence tells what someone or something does or did.
- A **complete simple sentence** has a subject (naming part) and a predicate (action part).

Grandma makes a soup.
Subject: Grandma
Predicate: makes a soup

Thinking Question
What is the subject, or naming part, and what is the predicate, or action part?

Underline each complete simple sentence.

1. Chops peppers.
   Harry chops peppers. **(1 point)**

2. Stirs the soup.
   Nan stirs the soup. **(1)**

3. My brother sets the table. **(1)**
   My brother.

Circle the part of the sentence that is missing.

4. Grandma and Mama _____

   subject   (**predicate**) **(1)**

5. _____ eat the soup.

   (**subject**)   **predicate (1)**

Assessment Tip: Total 5 Points
17
Grade 2, Unit 1

Short Vowels *o, u, e*

My Family
Phonics: Short Vowels *o, u,* and *e*

Word Bank

stop	bump	left
plug	step	up

Write the words on the correct signs.

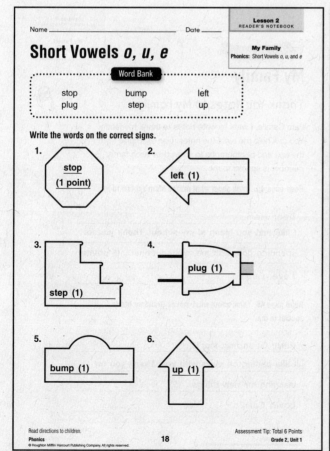

1. **stop** **(1 point)**
2. **left (1)**
3. **step (1)**
4. **plug (1)**
5. **bump (1)**
6. **up (1)**

Assessment Tip: Total 6 Points
18
Grade 2, Unit 1

Short Vowels *o, u, e*

My Family
Spelling: Short Vowels *o, u, e*

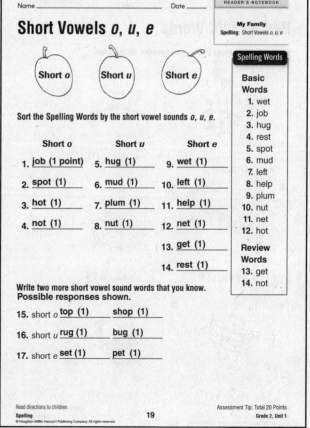

Short *o*   Short *u*   Short *e*

Spelling Words

Basic Words
1. wet
2. job
3. hug
4. rest
5. spot
6. mud
7. left
8. help
9. plum
10. nut
11. net
12. hot

Review Words
13. get
14. not

Sort the Spelling Words by the short vowel sounds *o, u, e.*

Short *o*	Short *u*	Short *e*
1. job **(1 point)**	5. hug **(1)**	9. wet **(1)**
2. spot **(1)**	6. mud **(1)**	10. left **(1)**
3. hot **(1)**	7. plum **(1)**	11. help **(1)**
4. not **(1)**	8. nut **(1)**	12. net **(1)**
		13. get **(1)**
		14. rest **(1)**

Write two more short vowel sound words that you know. **Possible responses shown.**

15. short *o* **top (1)**   **shop (1)**

16. short *u* **rug (1)**   **bug (1)**

17. short *e* **set (1)**   **pet (1)**

Assessment Tip: Total 20 Points
19
Grade 2, Unit 1

Word Order in Sentences

- When a sentence tells something, the subject comes first.
- The predicate of a sentence comes next.

> **Thinking Question**
> *Is the first part of the sentence the naming part?*

Incorrect Word Order	Correct Word Order
Told stories we.	We told stories.

✏️ Draw a line under each sentence that has the correct word order.

1. <u>The family eats snacks.</u> **(1 point)**

2. <u>Louisa baked a cake.</u> **(1)**

3. Blows out candles Nick.

4. <u>The children play games.</u> **(1)**

5. All eat together we.

6. <u>Papa opened gifts.</u> **(1)**

7. So much he enjoyed them.

8. <u>They ate dessert later.</u> **(1)**

Focus Trait: Voice
Expressing Feelings

Without Feelings	With Feelings
My grandma comes to visit on weekends.	**It's always so much fun when** my grandma comes to visit on weekends.

A. Read each sentence. Add words and details to show feelings. Possible responses shown.

Without Feelings	Feelings Added
1. I liked to help cook dinner.	**It was so much fun** to help cook dinner. **(1 point)**
2. We talk and work hard.	We **talk so happily** and work hard. **(1)**

B. Read each sentence. Then rewrite it to add feelings. Possible responses shown.

Without Feelings	Feelings Added
3. I live with my family.	I live with the best family in the world. **(1)**
4. I write stories.	I love to write stories. **(1)**
5. I had dinner at my friend Adam's house.	I had a delicious dinner at my best friend Adam's house. **(1)**

Review CVC Words

Say the picture name. Draw a line between the syllables.

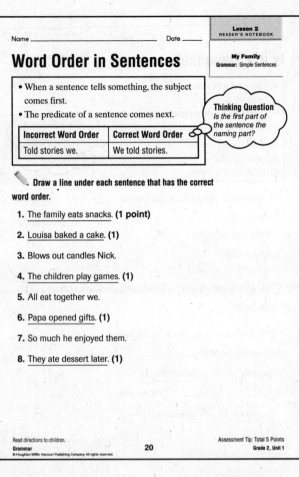

1. d e n | t i s t
(1 point)

2. b o b | c a t **(1)**

3. p e n | c i l **(1)**

4. c o b | w e b **(1)**

5. m a s | c o t **(1)**

6. l a p | t o p **(1)**

📜 **Reader's Guide**

My Family

Thank You Notes to My Family

I am Camila. I want to write notes to thank my family. You can help me write the notes. Use examples from the text and photographs to show how each family member is special to me.

Read page 45. Think about what makes Mom special to me.

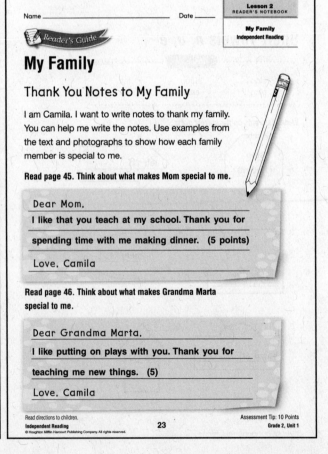

Dear Mom,

I like that you teach at my school. Thank you for

spending time with me making dinner. (5 points)

Love, Camila

Read page 46. Think about what makes Grandma Marta special to me.

Dear Grandma Marta,

I like putting on plays with you. Thank you for

teaching me new things. (5)

Love, Camila

Read page 52. Think about what makes Aunt Martica special to me.

Dear Aunt Martica,

I like when we all get together at your house to play music. Thank you for having us over on Sundays. (5)

Love, Camila

Read page 57. Think about what makes Papi special to me.

Dear Papi,

I love when we go fishing together. Thank you for taking me. (5)

Love, Camila

Short Vowels *o, u, e*

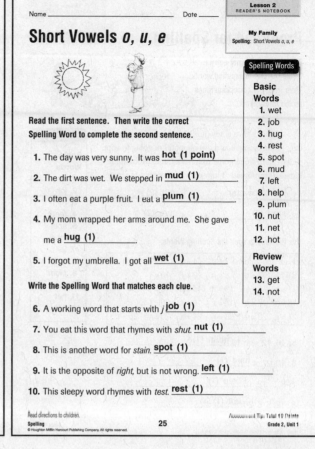

Spelling Words

Basic Words
1. wet
2. job
3. hug
4. rest
5. spot
6. mud
7. left
8. help
9. plum
10. nut
11. net
12. hot

Review Words
13. get
14. not

Read the first sentence. Then write the correct Spelling Word to complete the second sentence.

1. The day was very sunny. It was __hot (1 point)__

2. The dirt was wet. We stepped in __mud (1)__

3. I often eat a purple fruit. I eat a __plum (1)__

4. My mom wrapped her arms around me. She gave me a __hug (1)__

5. I forgot my umbrella. I got all __wet (1)__

Write the Spelling Word that matches each clue.

6. A working word that starts with *j* __job (1)__

7. You eat this word that rhymes with *shut*. __nut (1)__

8. This is another word for *stain*. __spot (1)__

9. It is the opposite of *right*, but is not wrong. __left (1)__

10. This sleepy word rhymes with *test*. __rest (1)__

Run-On Sentences

Read each sentence. Decide if it is one run-on sentence or two complete simple sentences. Circle the correct answer.

1. My cousins played soccer. Then they went swimming.

   run-on sentence (complete simple sentences) (1 point)

2. We play in the backyard we dug holes.

   (run-on sentence) complete simple sentences (1)

3. Angel and I like to play together we are best friends.

   (run-on sentence) complete simple sentences (1)

4. Uncle Manuel works long hours. He is a doctor.

   run-on sentence (complete simple sentences) (1)

Rewrite each run-on sentence as two simple complete sentences.

5. My sister learned to dance she took a class.

   __My sister learned to dance. She took a class. (2)__

6. She practices a lot every day she goes to the gym.

   __She practices a lot. Every day she goes to the gym. (2)__

7. Sometimes I like to watch her I go with her to class.

   __Sometimes I like to watch her. I go with her to class. (2)__

Name _____ Date _____

Lesson 2
READER'S NOTEBOOK

My Family
Vocabulary Strategies:
Using a Glossary

Using a Glossary

Read each glossary entry. Then use the definitions to write an example sentence for each word. Possible responses shown.

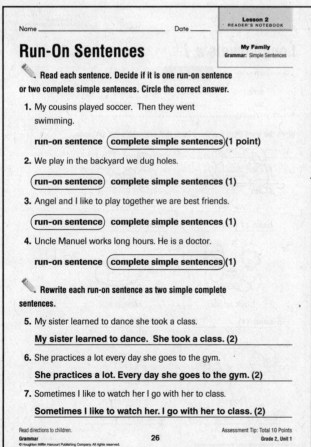

crown – a head covering made of gold or jewels
family – a group of people who are related
guitar – something you play to make music
house – a building where people live
sailor – a person who works on a ship or boat
teach – to show or tell someone how to do something

1. sailor

   __Her father is a sailor.__ (1 point)

2. house

   __Our house has six rooms.__ (1)

3. guitar

   __My sister plays the guitar.__ (1)

4. crown

   __The queen wears a crown.__ (1)

5. teach

   __I want to teach English.__ (1)

6. family

   __There are nine people in my family.__ (1)

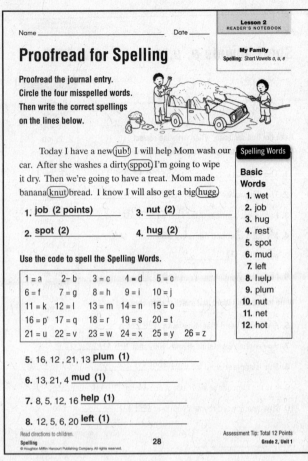

Proofread for Spelling

Lesson 2
READER'S NOTEBOOK

My Family
Spelling: Short Vowels o, u, e

Proofread the journal entry.
Circle the four misspelled words.
Then write the correct spellings
on the lines below.

Today I have a new (jub!) I will help Mom wash our
car. After she washes a dirty (sppot) I'm going to wipe
it dry. Then we're going to have a treat. Mom made
banana (knut) bread. I know I will also get a big (hugg.)

1. **job (2 points)**	3. **nut (2)**
2. **spot (2)**	4. **hug (2)**

Spelling Words

Basic Words
1. wet
2. job
3. hug
4. rest
5. spot
6. mud
7. left
8. help
9. plum
10. nut
11. net
12. hot

Use the code to spell the Spelling Words.

1 = a	2 = b	3 = c	4 = d	5 = c
6 = f	7 = g	8 = h	9 = i	10 = j
11 = k	12 = l	13 = m	14 = n	15 = o
16 = p	17 = q	18 = r	19 = s	20 = t
21 = u	22 = v	23 = w	24 = x	25 = y	26 = z

5. 16, 12 , 21, 13 **plum (1)**

6. 13, 21, 4 **mud (1)**

7. 8, 5, 12, 16 **help (1)**

8. 12, 5, 6, 20 **left (1)**

Read directions to children.
Spelling
© Houghton Mifflin Harcourt Publishing Company. All rights reserved.
28
Assessment Tip: Total 12 Points
Grade 2, Unit 1

Subjects

Lesson 2
READER'S NOTEBOOK

My Family
Grammar: Spiral Review

✎ Draw a line under the subject in each sentence.

1. <u>Grandma and Grandpa</u> came to visit. **(1 point)**

2. <u>The whole family</u> went on a picnic. **(1)**

3. <u>The park</u> was crowded. **(1)**

4. <u>The day</u> was warm and sunny. **(1)**

✎ Write a subject to complete each sentence.
(possible responses)

5. **The dog** _____ was friendly. **(1)**

6. **Alex** _____ took the bus. **(1)**

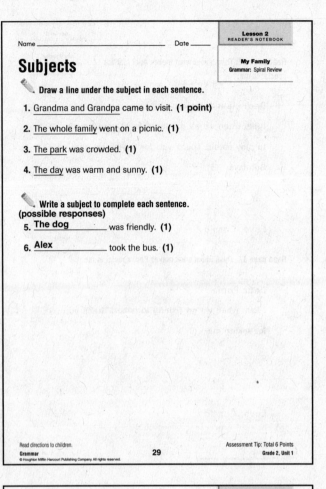

Read directions to children.
Grammar
© Houghton Mifflin Harcourt Publishing Company. All rights reserved.
29
Assessment Tip: Total 6 Points
Grade 2, Unit 1

Sentence Fluency

Lesson 2
READER'S NOTEBOOK

My Family
Grammar: Connect to Writing

Not Complete Sentences
Walks me to school. Uncle Luis.

Complete Sentences
My brother walks me to school.
Uncle Luis picks me up.

✎ Read each word group. Add a subject or a predicate to
each group to make a complete sentence. Use the words in
the box. Possible responses shown.

Mom	Aunt Rose
brings us gifts	My sister
makes me laugh	

1. Uncle Luis **makes me laugh (1 point)**

2. **Mom (1)** _____ helps me do homework.

3. **My sister (1)** _____ sings to me.

4. Papa **brings us gifts (1)**

5. **Aunt Rose (1)** _____ cooks me dinner.

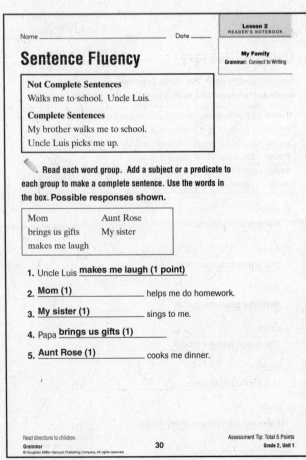

Read directions to children.
Grammar
© Houghton Mifflin Harcourt Publishing Company. All rights reserved.
30
Assessment Tip: Total 5 Points
Grade 2, Unit 1

Long Vowels a, i

Lesson 3
READER'S NOTEBOOK

Dogs
Phonics: Long Vowels a, i

Word Bank

time	nice	like
slice	cake	bake

Write the word from the Word Bank that completes the sentence.

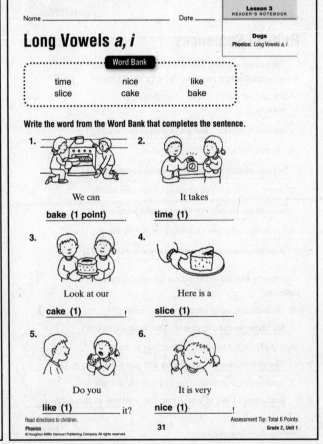

1. We can
bake (1 point)

2. It takes
time (1)

3. Look at our
cake (1) !

4. Here is a
slice (1)

5. Do you
like (1) it?

6. It is very
nice (1) !

Read directions to children.
Phonics
© Houghton Mifflin Harcourt Publishing Company. All rights reserved.
31
Assessment Tip: Total 6 Points
Grade 2, Unit 1

Statements and Questions

Dogs
Grammar: Types of Sentences

- A **statement** is a sentence that tells something. A statement begins with a capital letter and ends with a period.
- A **question** is a sentence that asks something. A question begins with a capital letter and ends with a question mark.

My dog is very big.
What is your dog's name?

Thinking Questions
Does the sentence tell something or ask something? Does it end with a period or a question mark?

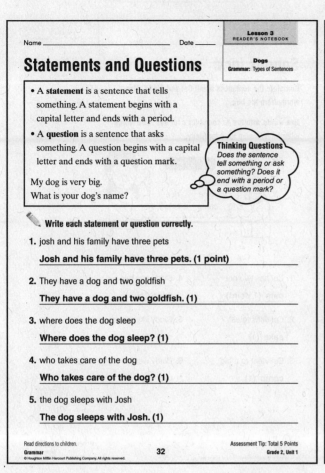 Write each statement or question correctly.

1. josh and his family have three pets

Josh and his family have three pets. (1 point)

2. They have a dog and two goldfish

They have a dog and two goldfish. (1)

3. where does the dog sleep

Where does the dog sleep? (1)

4. who takes care of the dog

Who takes care of the dog? (1)

5. the dog sleeps with Josh

The dog sleeps with Josh. (1)

Read directions to children.

Grammar   32

Assessment Tip: Total 5 Points

Grade 2, Unit 1

© Houghton Mifflin Harcourt Publishing Company. All rights reserved.

Long Vowels *a, i*

Dogs
Phonics: Long Vowels *a, i*

Write the words where they belong. Then write four more words of your own in each column. **Possible responses shown.**

```
Word Bank
grade      time      wide      gaze
mile       crate     slide     blame
```

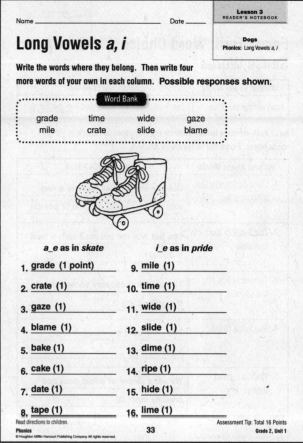

a_e as in *skate*   **i_e** as in *pride*

1. **grade (1 point)**   9. **mile (1)**

2. **crate (1)**   10. **time (1)**

3. **gaze (1)**   11. **wide (1)**

4. **blame (1)**   12. **slide (1)**

5. **bake (1)**   13. **dime (1)**

6. **cake (1)**   14. **ripe (1)**

7. **date (1)**   15. **hide (1)**

8. **tape (1)**   16. **lime (1)**

Read directions to children.

Phonics   33

Assessment Tip: Total 16 Points

Grade 2, Unit 1

© Houghton Mifflin Harcourt Publishing Company. All rights reserved.

Long Vowels *a, i*

Dogs
Spelling: Long Vowels *a, i*

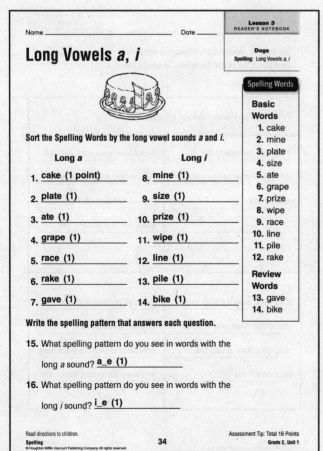

Sort the Spelling Words by the long vowel sounds *a* and *i*.

Spelling Words

Basic Words
1. cake
2. mine
3. plate
4. size
5. ate
6. grape
7. prize
8. wipe
9. race
10. line
11. pile
12. rake

Review Words
13. gave
14. bike

Long *a*

1. **cake (1 point)**

2. **plate (1)**

3. **ate (1)**

4. **grape (1)**

5. **race (1)**

6. **rake (1)**

7. **gave (1)**

Long *i*

8. **mine (1)**

9. **size (1)**

10. **prize (1)**

11. **wipe (1)**

12. **line (1)**

13. **pile (1)**

14. **bike (1)**

Write the spelling pattern that answers each question.

15. What spelling pattern do you see in words with the long *a* sound? **a_e (1)**

16. What spelling pattern do you see in words with the long *i* sound? **i_e (1)**

Read directions to children.

Spelling   34

Assessment Tip: Total 16 Points

Grade 2, Unit 1

© Houghton Mifflin Harcourt Publishing Company. All rights reserved.

Commands

Dogs
Grammar: Types of Sentences

- A **command** is a sentence that gives an order.
- A command begins with a capital letter and ends with a period.

Bring your dog to school.

Thinking Question
Does the sentence give an order, begin with a capital letter, and end with a period?

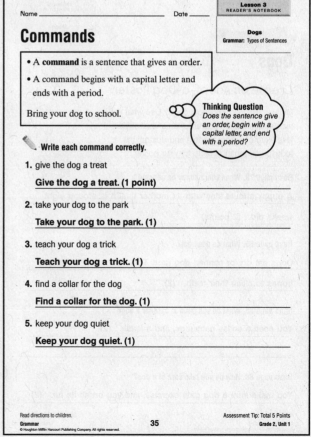 Write each command correctly.

1. give the dog a treat

Give the dog a treat. (1 point)

2. take your dog to the park

Take your dog to the park. (1)

3. teach your dog a trick

Teach your dog a trick. (1)

4. find a collar for the dog

Find a collar for the dog. (1)

5. keep your dog quiet

Keep your dog quiet. (1)

Read directions to children.

Grammar   35

Assessment Tip: Total 5 Points

Grade 2, Unit 1

© Houghton Mifflin Harcourt Publishing Company. All rights reserved.

© Houghton Mifflin Harcourt Publishing Company. All rights reserved.

9

Volume 1, pp. 32–35

Focus Trait: Word Choice
Sense Words

Without Sense Words	Sense Words Added
I run across the grass.	I run across the **wet** grass and **feel the hot sun.**

Read each sentence below. Rewrite each sentence to include sense words. **Possible responses shown.**

Without Sense Words	Sense Words Added
1. Outside my window there is a flag.	Outside my window there is a flag with red and white stripes. (2 points)
2. The bat hits the baseball.	The bat hits the baseball with a loud crack. (2)
3. The snow lies on the ground.	The cold and slippery snow lies on the ground. (2)
4. The wind blows.	The cold wind blows against my face. (2)
5. We ate a good dinner.	We ate a dinner of sweet peas and crunchy corn. (2)

Sounds for *c*

Complete the sentences about Cal and Cindy. Use words from the box.

Use words with the /k/ sound for *c* for Cal. Use words with the /s/ sound for *c* for Cindy.

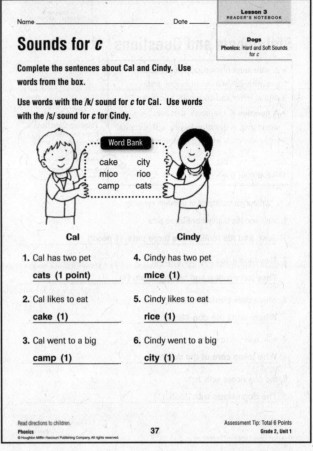

Word Bank
cake   city
mico   rico
camp   cats

Cal

1. Cal has two pet
   cats (1 point)

2. Cal likes to eat
   cake (1)

3. Cal went to a big
   camp (1)

Cindy

4. Cindy has two pet
   mice (1)

5. Cindy likes to eat
   rice (1)

6. Cindy went to a big
   city (1)

Reader's Guide

Dogs

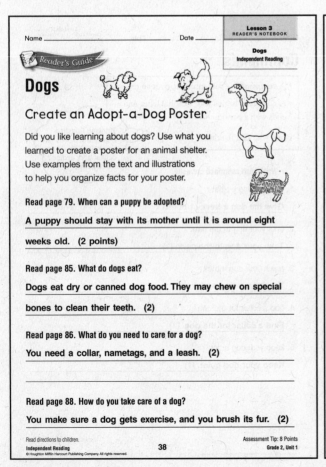

Create an Adopt-a-Dog Poster

Did you like learning about dogs? Use what you learned to create a poster for an animal shelter. Use examples from the text and illustrations to help you organize facts for your poster.

Read page 79. When can a puppy be adopted?
A puppy should stay with its mother until it is around eight weeks old. (2 points)

Read page 85. What do dogs eat?
Dogs eat dry or canned dog food. They may chew on special bones to clean their teeth. (2)

Read page 86. What do you need to care for a dog?
You need a collar, nametags, and a leash. (2)

Read page 88. How do you take care of a dog?
You make sure a dog gets exercise, and you brush its fur. (2)

Use the four questions and answers to complete each box in the poster. Remember to write a title for your poster.

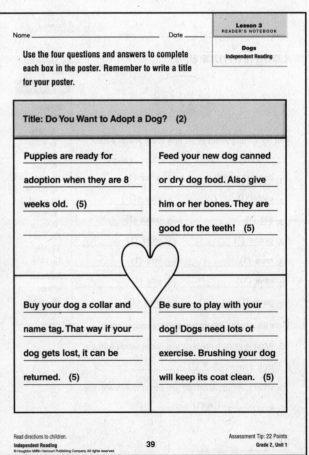

Title: Do You Want to Adopt a Dog? (2)	
Puppies are ready for adoption when they are 8 weeks old. (5)	Feed your new dog canned or dry dog food. Also give him or her bones. They are good for the teeth! (5)
Buy your dog a collar and name tag. That way if your dog gets lost, it can be returned. (5)	Be sure to play with your dog! Dogs need lots of exercise. Brushing your dog will keep its coat clean. (5)

Long Vowels *a,i*

Write a Spelling Word for each picture.

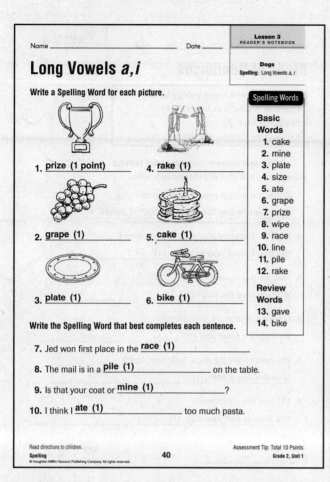

1. **prize (1 point)**

4. **rake (1)**

2. **grape (1)**

5. **cake (1)**

3. **plate (1)**

6. **bike (1)**

Write the Spelling Word that best completes each sentence.

7. Jed won first place in the **race (1)**

8. The mail is in a **pile (1)** on the table.

9. Is that your coat or **mine (1)** ?

10. I think I **ate (1)** too much pasta.

Spelling Words

Basic Words
1. cake
2. mine
3. plate
4. size
5. ate
6. grape
7. prize
8. wipe
9. race
10. line
11. pile
12. rake

Review Words
13. gave
14. bike

Exclamations

- An **exclamation** is a sentence that shows strong feeling.
- An exclamation begins with a capital letter and ends with an exclamation point.

That dog saved the day!

Thinking Questions
Does the sentence show strong feeling? Does it end with an exclamation point?

Write each exclamation correctly.

1. People like my dog
   People like my dog! (1 point)

2. he is the smartest dog I know
   He is the smartest dog I know! (1)

3. My dog chewed my friend's shoe to bits
   My dog chewed my friend's shoe to bits! (1)

4. her dog had puppies
   Her dog had puppies! (1)

5. Those dogs run so fast
   Those dogs run so fast! (1)

Multiple-Meaning Words

Read both definitions of each word. Then read the sentence. Put a checkmark next to the definition that best matches the meaning of the underlined word.

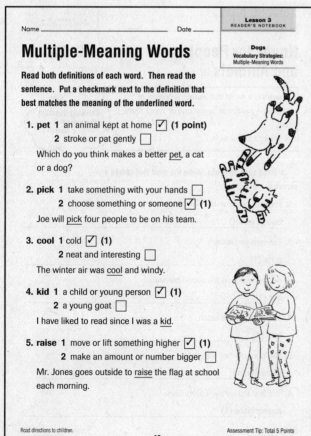

1. **pet** 1 an animal kept at home ☑ (1 point)
   2 stroke or pat gently ☐
   Which do you think makes a better pet, a cat or a dog?

2. **pick** 1 take something with your hands ☐
   2 choose something or someone ☑ (1)
   Joe will pick four people to be on his team.

3. **cool** 1 cold ☑ (1)
   2 neat and interesting ☐
   The winter air was cool and windy.

4. **kid** 1 a child or young person ☑ (1)
   2 a young goat ☐
   I have liked to read since I was a kid.

5. **raise** 1 move or lift something higher ☑ (1)
   2 make an amount or number bigger ☐
   Mr. Jones goes outside to raise the flag at school each morning.

Proofread for Spelling

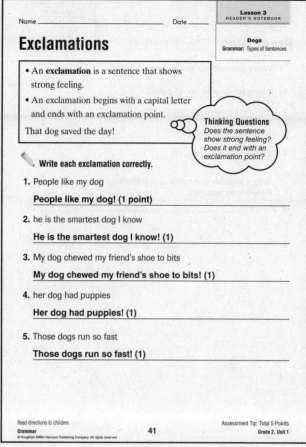

Proofread the story. Circle the six misspelled words. Then write the correct spellings on the lines below.

I was working in the yard when Jake and Ken stopped by with a new (byke.)
"Is it yours?" I asked Ken.
"No," Jake said. "It's (mien.) Do you want to (rase?)"
"Yeah, let's!" I answered. I took my (rak) and made a starting (lyne) in the dirt. "Ken, you be the judge and give the winner a (prise!)"

1. **bike (2 points)**
2. **mine (2)**
3. **race (2)**
4. **rake (2)**
5. **line (2)**
6. **prize (2)**

Change one letter in each word to make a Spelling Word.

7. ripe **wipe (1)**
8. slate **plate (1)**
9. side **size (1)**
10. ape **ate (1)**
11. lake **cake or rake (1)**
12. tile **pile (1)**

Spelling Words

Basic Words
1. cake
2. mine
3. plate
4. size
5. ate
6. grape
7. prize
8. wipe
9. race
10. line
11. pile
12. rake

Review Words
13. gave
14. bike

Predicates

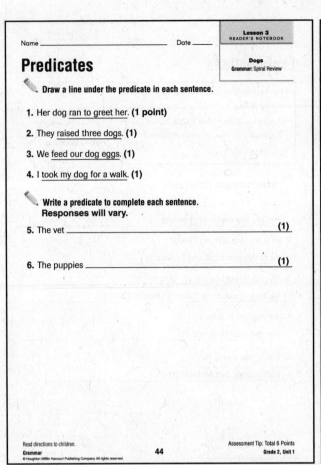

Draw a line under the predicate in each sentence.

1. Her dog ran to greet her. **(1 point)**

2. They raised three dogs. **(1)**

3. We feed our dog eggs. **(1)**

4. I took my dog for a walk. **(1)**

Write a predicate to complete each sentence.
Responses will vary.

5. The vet _____ **(1)**

6. The puppies _____ **(1)**

Kinds of Sentences

Statement: Dave is happy walking his dog.
Question: Is Dave walking his dog?
Command: Walk the dog.
Exclamation: Dave loves walking his dog!

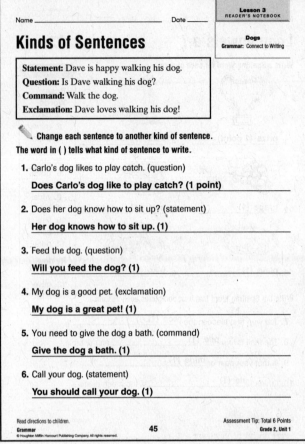

Change each sentence to another kind of sentence.
The word in ( ) tells what kind of sentence to write.

1. Carlo's dog likes to play catch. (question)
   Does Carlo's dog like to play catch? (1 point)

2. Does her dog know how to sit up? (statement)
   Her dog knows how to sit up. (1)

3. Feed the dog. (question)
   Will you feed the dog? (1)

4. My dog is a good pet. (exclamation)
   My dog is a great pet! (1)

5. You need to give the dog a bath. (command)
   Give the dog a bath. (1)

6. Call your dog. (statement)
   You should call your dog. (1)

Long Vowels *o, u, e*

Read the words in the box. Cross out the words with short vowels. Use the words that are left to complete the jokes.

mole	home	~~stamp~~
Luke	~~blend~~	~~rust~~
~~hunt~~	~~Ken~~	~~mask~~
rose	stone	nose
~~nest~~	broke	

What do you get if you toss a big s**tone (2 points)** into a little lake?

A wet stone!

What smells best at Jen's h**ome (2)** ?

Jen's n**ose (2)** !

What did the m**ole (2)** say to the r**ose (2)** ?

Hi Bud!

What did L**uke (2)** say when he b**roke (2)** his leg in two spots?

I will never go back to those two spots!

Nouns for People and Animals

A **noun** is a word that names a person or animal. A noun can name one or more than one.
A spider spins a web.

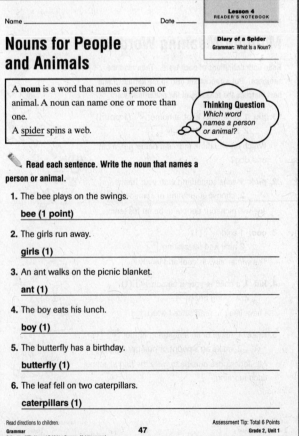

Thinking Question
Which word names a person or animal?

Read each sentence. Write the noun that names a person or animal.

1. The bee plays on the swings.
   bee (1 point)

2. The girls run away.
   girls (1)

3. An ant walks on the picnic blanket.
   ant (1)

4. The boy eats his lunch.
   boy (1)

5. The butterfly has a birthday.
   butterfly (1)

6. The leaf fell on two caterpillars.
   caterpillars (1)

Name _____ Date _____

Long Vowels *o, u, e*

Add *e* to finish each word.

Then use the words in the puzzle.

Word Bank

pol**e**   cub**e**   nos**e**   rul**e**
rud**e**   tun**e**   ston**e**   smok**e**

Across

2. what to do or not do **(1 point)**
4. rock **(1)**
5. a flag is on it **(1)**
7. can be made of ice **(1)**

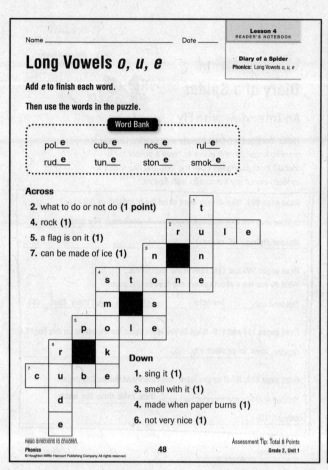

Down

1. sing it **(1)**
3. smell with it **(1)**
4. made when paper burns **(1)**
6. not very nice **(1)**

48

Long Vowels *o, u*

Sort the Spelling Words by the long vowel sounds *o* and *u*.

Spelling Words

Basic Words
1. doze
2. nose
3. use
4. rose
5. pole
6. close
7. cute
8. woke
9. mule
10. rode
11. role
12. tune

Review Words
13. home
14. joke

Long *o*

1. doze **(1 point)**
2. nose **(1)**
3. rose **(1)**
4. pole **(1)**
5. close **(1)**
6. woke **(1)**
7. rode **(1)**
8. role **(1)**
9. home **(1)**
10. joke **(1)**
11. bone **(1)**
12. spoke **(1)**

Long *u*

13. use **(1)**
14. cute **(1)**
15. mule **(1)**
16. tune **(1)**
17. tube **(1)**
18. flute **(1)**

Add two words you know with the long *o* sound to the list. Then add two words you know with the long *u* sound. **Possible responses shown.**

49

Nouns for Places and Things

- Not all nouns name people and animals.
- Nouns also name **places** and **things**.

Spider went to a <u>party</u>.

Thinking Question
Which word names a place or thing?

✏ Write the noun that names the place or thing.

1. Ladybug ate a cookie.

    cookie (1 point)

2. Beetle baked a pie.

    pie (1)

3. Ant went to the store.

    store (1)

4. Butterfly writes a song.

    song (1)

5. The soup spilled on the bees.

    soup (1)

6. Fly loves a party.

    party (1)

50

Focus Trait: Ideas
Main Idea

All of the sentences in a paragraph should be about the main idea. Below, the writer crossed out a sentence because it was not about the main idea.

Main idea: <u>I went to the park with my sister today.</u>

I went to the park with my sister today. We tried the seesaw. It didn't work. ~~Grampa says that in his day, flies and spiders did not get along.~~ We tried the tire swing. It didn't work, either.

Read the main idea and the details below it. Cross out the detail sentence that does not tell more about the main idea.

1. **Main idea:** <u>I'm sleeping over at my friend's house.</u>

    After dinner, we will watch a movie.
    We will stay up late.
    ~~I forgot my homework today.~~
    We will tell scary stories. **(2 points)**

2. **Main idea:** <u>A big storm is coming this way.</u>

    The wind is blowing things around.
    ~~My friends like to swim in a pool.~~
    The sky is getting dark.
    Cold rain has already started. **(2)**

51

Name _____ Date _____
Lesson 4
READER'S NOTEBOOK
Diary of a Spider
Phonics: Hard and Soft Sounds for g

Hard and Soft Sounds for *g*

Complete the sentences. Use words from the box.

Word Bank

garden	magic	dig	gave
gate	huge	giant	

1. Today Granny **gave (2 points)** _____ me some seeds.

2. Now we can start a **garden (2)** _____.

3. We start work next to the **gate (2)** _____.

4. We will **dig (2)** _____ before we plant the seeds.

5. Granny says seeds are like **magic (2)** _____.

6. A little seed grows into a **huge (2)** _____ plant.

7. I hope our plants grow as big as a **giant (2)** _____!

Reader's Guide

Diary of a Spider

An Interview with Fly

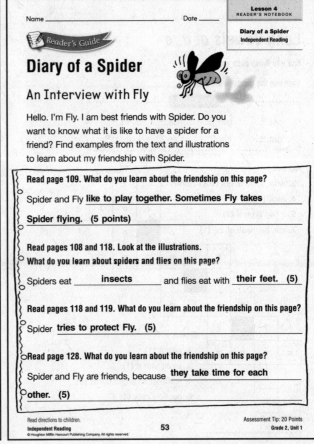

Hello. I'm Fly. I am best friends with Spider. Do you want to know what it is like to have a spider for a friend? Find examples from the text and illustrations to learn about my friendship with Spider.

Read page 109. What do you learn about the friendship on this page?

Spider and Fly **like to play together. Sometimes Fly takes**

Spider flying. (5 points) _____

Read pages 108 and 118. Look at the illustrations. What do you learn about spiders and flies on this page?

Spiders eat _____ **insects** _____ and flies eat with _____ **their feet. (5)**

Read pages 118 and 119. What do you learn about the friendship on this page?

Spider **tries to protect Fly. (5)** _____

Read page 128. What do you learn about the friendship on this page?

Spider and Fly are friends, because **they take time for each**

other. (5) _____

A newspaper is interviewing me about my friendship with Spider. Use what you learned to answer their questions.

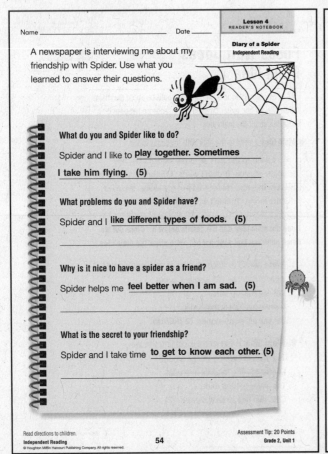

What do you and Spider like to do?

Spider and I like to **play together. Sometimes**

I take him flying. (5) _____

What problems do you and Spider have?

Spider and I **like different types of foods. (5)** _____

Why is it nice to have a spider as a friend?

Spider helps me **feel better when I am sad. (5)** _____

What is the secret to your friendship?

Spider and I take time **to get to know each other. (5)** _____

Name _____ Date _____
Lesson 4
READER'S NOTEBOOK
Diary of a Spider
Spelling: Long Vowels o, u

Long Vowels *o, u*

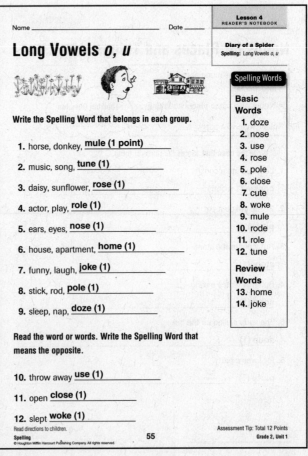

Write the Spelling Word that belongs in each group.

1. horse, donkey, **mule (1 point)** _____

2. music, song, **tune (1)** _____

3. daisy, sunflower, **rose (1)** _____

4. actor, play, **role (1)** _____

5. ears, eyes, **nose (1)** _____

6. house, apartment, **home (1)** _____

7. funny, laugh, **joke (1)** _____

8. stick, rod, **pole (1)** _____

9. sleep, nap, **doze (1)** _____

Read the word or words. Write the Spelling Word that means the opposite.

10. throw away **use (1)** _____

11. open **close (1)** _____

12. slept **woke (1)** _____

Spelling Words

Basic Words
1. doze
2. nose
3. use
4. rose
5. pole
6. close
7. cute
8. woke
9. mule
10. rode
11. role
12. tune

Review Words
13. home
14. joke

Kinds of Nouns

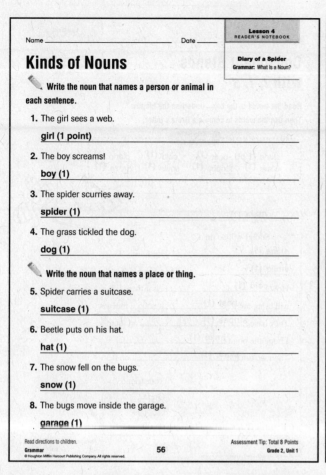

Write the noun that names a person or animal in each sentence.

1. The girl sees a web.

   girl (1 point)

2. The boy screams!

   boy (1)

3. The spider scurries away.

   spider (1)

4. The grass tickled the dog.

   dog (1)

Write the noun that names a place or thing.

5. Spider carries a suitcase.

   suitcase (1)

6. Beetle puts on his hat.

   hat (1)

7. The snow fell on the bugs.

   snow (1)

8. The bugs move inside the garage.

   garage (1)

Name _____ Date _____

Lesson 4
READER'S NOTEBOOK

Diary of a Spider
Vocabulary Strategies:
Context Clues

Context Clues

Read the sentences. Use context clues to figure out the meaning of the underlined words. Circle the definition that best matches the meaning of the word.

1. We travel to many countries. Sometimes we travel by plane. Sometimes we travel by ship. **(1 point)**
   a. to eat
   b. to go on a trip
   c. to grow

2. I want to learn how to play the piano. A piano teacher can teach me to play. **(1)**
   a. to get knowledge
   b. to read about something
   c. to see

3. Cats run away when dogs scare them. **(1)**
   a. to yell loudly
   b. to jump or skip
   c. to make someone feel afraid

4. Julio brought his folder home in his backpack. **(1)**
   a. forgot something
   b. carried something
   c. hid something

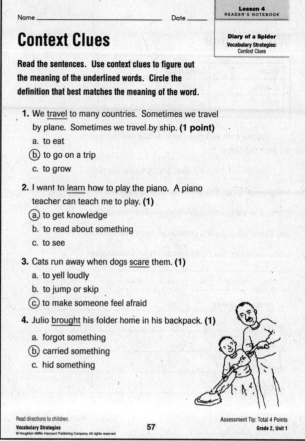

Proofread for Spelling

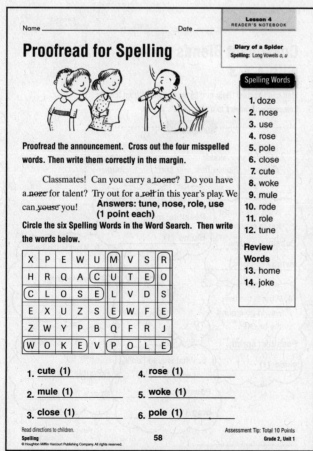

Proofread the announcement. Cross out the four misspelled words. Then write them correctly in the margin.

Classmates! Can you carry a ~~toone~~? Do you have a ~~noze~~ for talent? Try out for a ~~roll~~ in this year's play. We can ~~youse~~ you!

Answers: tune, nose, role, use (1 point each)

Circle the six Spelling Words in the Word Search. Then write the words below.

X	P	E	W	U	M	V	S	R
H	R	Q	A	C	U	T	E	O
C	L	O	S	E	L	V	D	S
E	X	U	Z	S	E	W	F	E
Z	W	Y	P	B	Q	F	R	J
W	O	K	E	V	P	O	L	E

Spelling Words

1. doze
2. nose
3. use
4. rose
5. pole
6. close
7. cute
8. woke
9. mule
10. rode
11. role
12. tune

Review Words

13. home
14. joke

1. **cute (1)**   4. **rose (1)**

2. **mule (1)**   5. **woke (1)**

3. **close (1)**   6. **pole (1)**

Statements and Questions

Write Statement or Question to identify each sentence.

1. The web is in my tree. **Statement (1 point)**

2. Did Mom say the web is hers? **Question (1)**

3. Who said the next bug is mine? **Question (1)**

4. You can share my tasty treat. **Statement (1)**

Write each statement or question correctly.

5. who likes the spider's web

   Who likes the spider's web?   (1)

6. it looks like my web

   It looks like my web.   (1)

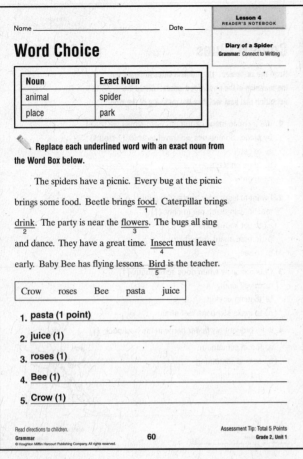

Word Choice

Noun	Exact Noun
animal	spider
place	park

Replace each underlined word with an exact noun from the Word Box below.

The spiders have a picnic. Every bug at the picnic brings some food. Beetle brings <u>food</u>. Caterpillar brings <u>drink</u>. The party is near the <u>flowers</u>. The bugs all sing and dance. They have a great time. <u>Insect</u> must leave early. Baby Bee has flying lessons. <u>Bird</u> is the teacher.

Crow	roses	Bee	pasta	juice

1. pasta (1 point) _____
2. juice (1) _____
3. roses (1) _____
4. Bee (1) _____
5. Crow (1) _____

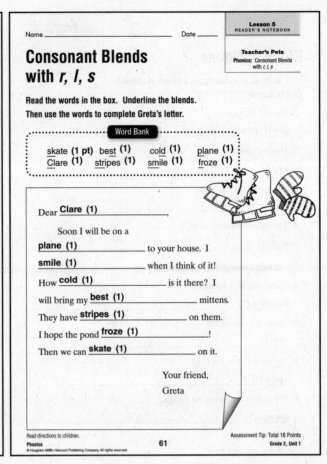

Consonant Blends with r, l, s

Read the words in the box. Underline the blends.
Then use the words to complete Greta's letter.

Word Bank

skate (1 pt) best (1) cold (1) plane (1)
Clare (1) stripes (1) smile (1) froze (1)

Dear **Clare (1)** _____

Soon I will be on a **plane (1)** _____ to your house. I **smile (1)** _____ when I think of it! How **cold (1)** _____ is it there? I will bring my **best (1)** _____ mittens. They have **stripes (1)** _____ on them. I hope the pond **froze (1)** _____! Then we can **skate (1)** _____ on it.

Your friend,
Greta

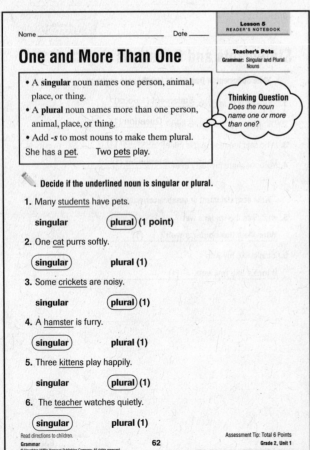

One and More Than One

- A **singular** noun names one person, animal, place, or thing.
- A **plural** noun names more than one person, animal, place, or thing.
- Add -s to most nouns to make them plural. She has a pet. Two pets play.

Thinking Question
Does the noun name one or more than one?

Decide if the underlined noun is singular or plural.

1. Many <u>students</u> have pets.
   singular (plural) (1 point)

2. One <u>cat</u> purrs softly.
   (singular) plural (1)

3. Some <u>crickets</u> are noisy.
   singular (plural) (1)

4. A <u>hamster</u> is furry.
   (singular) plural (1)

5. Three <u>kittens</u> play happily.
   singular (plural) (1)

6. The <u>teacher</u> watches quietly.
   (singular) plural (1)

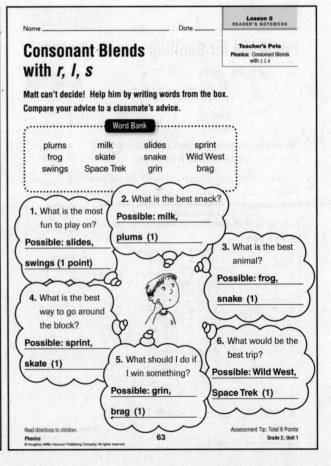

Consonant Blends with r, l, s

Matt can't decide! Help him by writing words from the box.
Compare your advice to a classmate's advice.

Word Bank

plums milk slides sprint
frog skate snake Wild West
swings Space Trek grin brag

1. What is the most fun to play on?
   Possible: slides, swings (1 point)

2. What is the best snack?
   Possible: milk, plums (1)

3. What is the best animal?
   Possible: frog, snake (1)

4. What is the best way to go around the block?
   Possible: sprint, skate (1)

5. What should I do if I win something?
   Possible: grin, brag (1)

6. What would be the best trip?
   Possible: Wild West, Space Trek (1)

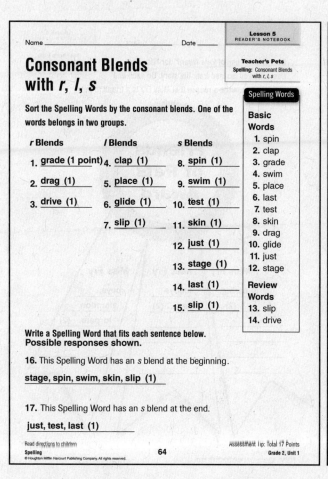

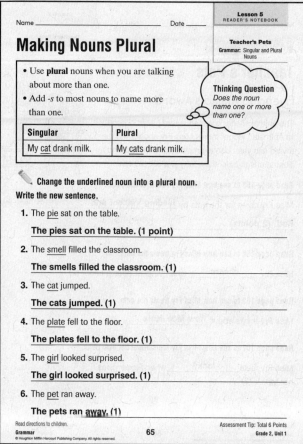

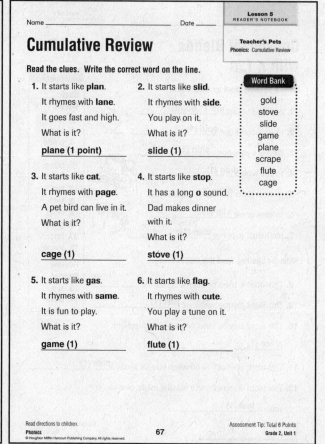

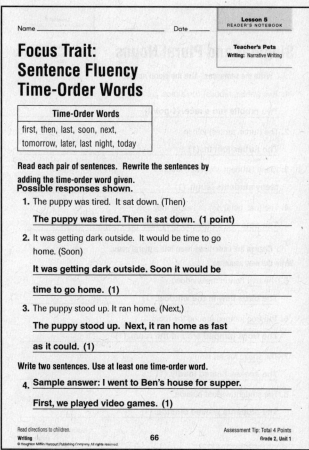

Consonant Blends with *r, l, s*

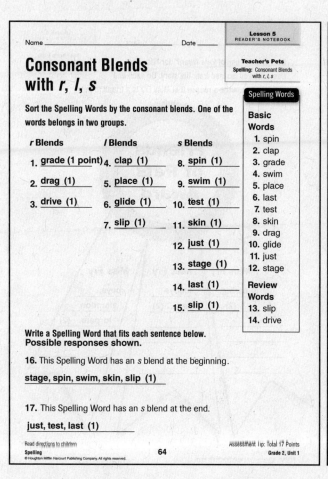

Name _____ Date _____

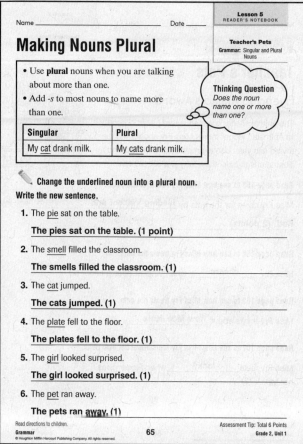

Consonant Blends with *r, l, s*

Sort the Spelling Words by the consonant blends. One of the words belongs in two groups.

r Blends	*l* Blends	*s* Blends
1. grade (1 point)	4. clap (1)	8. spin (1)
2. drag (1)	5. place (1)	9. swim (1)
3. drive (1)	6. glide (1)	10. test (1)
	7. slip (1)	11. skin (1)
		12. just (1)
		13. stage (1)
		14. last (1)
		15. slip (1)

Spelling Words

Basic Words
1. spin
2. clap
3. grade
4. swim
5. place
6. last
7. test
8. skin
9. drag
10. glide
11. just
12. stage

Review Words
13. slip
14. drive

Write a Spelling Word that fits each sentence below.
Possible responses shown.

16. This Spelling Word has an *s* blend at the beginning.

stage, spin, swim, skin, slip (1)

17. This Spelling Word has an *s* blend at the end.

just, test, last (1)

Read directions to children.
Spelling
64
Assessment Tip: Total 17 Points
Grade 2, Unit 1
© Houghton Mifflin Harcourt Publishing Company. All rights reserved.

Lesson 5
READER'S NOTEBOOK

Teacher's Pets
Grammar: Singular and Plural Nouns

Name _____ Date _____

Making Nouns Plural

- Use **plural** nouns when you are talking about more than one.
- Add *-s* to most nouns to name more than one.

Thinking Question
Does the noun name one or more than one?

Singular	Plural
My cat drank milk.	My cats drank milk.

Change the underlined noun into a plural noun. **Write the new sentence.**

1. The <u>pie</u> sat on the table.

The pies sat on the table. (1 point)

2. The <u>smell</u> filled the classroom.

The smells filled the classroom. (1)

3. The <u>cat</u> jumped.

The cats jumped. (1)

4. The <u>plate</u> fell to the floor.

The plates fell to the floor. (1)

5. The <u>girl</u> looked surprised.

The girl looked surprised. (1)

6. The <u>pet</u> ran away.

The pets ran away. (1)

Read directions to children.
Grammar
65
Assessment Tip: Total 6 Points
Grade 2, Unit 1
© Houghton Mifflin Harcourt Publishing Company. All rights reserved.

Lesson 5
READER'S NOTEBOOK

Teacher's Pets
Writing: Narrative Writing

Name _____ Date _____

Focus Trait: Sentence Fluency Time-Order Words

Time-Order Words
first, then, last, soon, next, tomorrow, later, last night, today

Read each pair of sentences. Rewrite the sentences by adding the time-order word given.
Possible responses shown.

1. The puppy was tired. It sat down. (Then)

The puppy was tired. Then it sat down. (1 point)

2. It was getting dark outside. It would be time to go home. (Soon)

It was getting dark outside. Soon it would be

time to go home. (1)

3. The puppy stood up. It ran home. (Next,)

The puppy stood up. Next, it ran home as fast

as it could. (1)

Write two sentences. Use at least one time-order word.

4. **Sample answer: I went to Ben's house for supper.**

First, we played video games. (1)

Read directions to children.
Writing
66
Assessment Tip: Total 4 Points
Grade 2, Unit 1
© Houghton Mifflin Harcourt Publishing Company. All rights reserved.

Lesson 5
READER'S NOTEBOOK

Teacher's Pets
Phonics: Cumulative Review

Name _____ Date _____

Cumulative Review

Read the clues. Write the correct word on the line.

1. It starts like **plan**.
   It rhymes with **lane**.
   It goes fast and high.
   What is it?

   plane (1 point)

2. It starts like **slid**.
   It rhymes with **side**.
   You play on it.
   What is it?

   slide (1)

3. It starts like **cat**.
   It rhymes with **page**.
   A pet bird can live in it.
   What is it?

   cage (1)

4. It starts like **stop**.
   It has a long **o** sound.
   Dad makes dinner with it.
   What is it?

   stove (1)

5. It starts like **gas**.
   It rhymes with **same**.
   It is fun to play.
   What is it?

   game (1)

6. It starts like **flag**.
   It rhymes with **cute**.
   You play a tune on it.
   What is it?

   flute (1)

Word Bank
gold
stove
slide
game
plane
scrape
flute
cage

Read directions to children.
Phonics
67
Assessment Tip: Total 6 Points
Grade 2, Unit 1
© Houghton Mifflin Harcourt Publishing Company. All rights reserved.

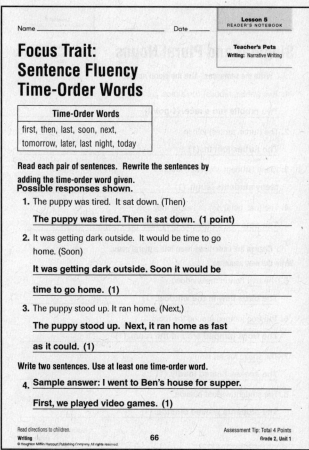
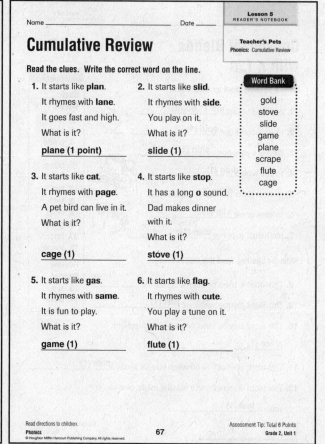

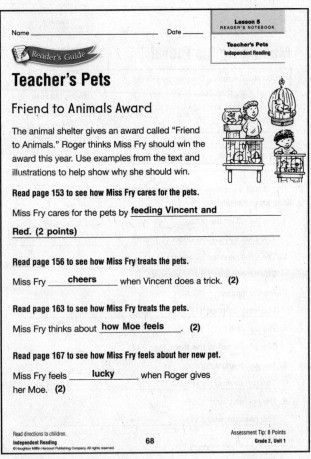

Reader's Guide

Teacher's Pets

Friend to Animals Award

The animal shelter gives an award called "Friend to Animals." Roger thinks Miss Fry should win the award this year. Use examples from the text and illustrations to help show why she should win.

Read page 153 to see how Miss Fry cares for the pets.

Miss Fry cares for the pets by __feeding Vincent and__

__Red.__ **(2 points)**

Read page 156 to see how Miss Fry treats the pets.

Miss Fry __cheers__ when Vincent does a trick. **(2)**

Read page 163 to see how Miss Fry treats the pets.

Miss Fry thinks about __how Moe feels__. **(2)**

Read page 167 to see how Miss Fry feels about her new pet.

Miss Fry feels __lucky__ when Roger gives her Moe. **(2)**

Design a "Friend of Pets Award" for Miss Fry. Use what you learned from the story. On each end of the ribbon, write a reason that Miss Fry is a friend to pets.

Friends of Pets Award

Miss Fry is caring. (2)

Miss Fry enjoys pets. (2)

Miss Fry pays attention to pets. (2)

Consonant Blends with *r, l, s*

Write a Spelling Word for each clue.

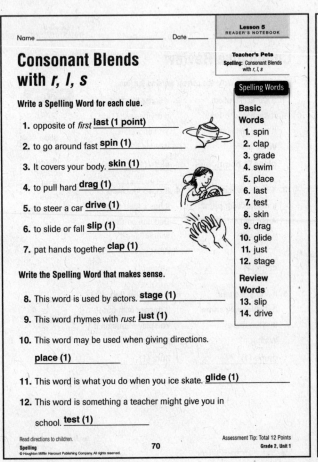

1. opposite of *first* __last__ **(1 point)**

2. to go around fast __spin__ **(1)**

3. It covers your body. __skin__ **(1)**

4. to pull hard __drag__ **(1)**

5. to steer a car __drive__ **(1)**

6. to slide or fall __slip__ **(1)**

7. pat hands together __clap__ **(1)**

Write the Spelling Word that makes sense.

8. This word is used by actors. __stage__ **(1)**

9. This word rhymes with *rust.* __just__ **(1)**

10. This word may be used when giving directions.

 __place__ **(1)**

11. This word is what you do when you ice skate. __glide__ **(1)**

12. This word is something a teacher might give you in

 school. __test__ **(1)**

Spelling Words

Basic Words
1. spin
2. clap
3. grade
4. swim
5. place
6. last
7. test
8. skin
9. drag
10. glide
11. just
12. stage

Review Words
13. slip
14. drive

Singular and Plural Nouns

Write the sentences. Use the plural nouns.

1. Two (rabbit, rabbits) run a race.

 __Two rabbits run a race.__ **(1 point)**

2. The (turtle, turtles) join in.

 __The turtles join in.__ **(1)**

3. Many (student, students) laugh.

 __Many students laugh.__ **(1)**

4. The (pet, pets) run as fast as they can.

 __The pets run as fast as they can.__ **(1)**

Change the underlined noun into a plural noun. Write the new sentence.

5. The <u>bird</u> flew in the window.

 __The birds flew in the window.__ **(1)**

6. The <u>frog</u> jumped around the room.

 __The frogs jumped around the room.__ **(1)**

7. The <u>snake</u> hissed loudly.

 __The snakes hissed loudly.__ **(1)**

8. The <u>student</u> walked outside.

 __The students walked outside.__ **(1)**

Word Endings -ed, -ing

Choose the word that best completes each sentence.
Write the word on the line.

1. Troy and Chad **walked (1 point)** to school yesterday.

   walked   **walking**

2. Vicky is **calling (1)** Tina on the phone now.

   called   **calling**

3. I see two dogs **barking (1)** at that cat.

   barked   **barking**

4. My grandma **stayed (1)** with us last summer.

   stayed   **staying**

5. Yesterday the teacher **asked (1)** us a question.

   asked   **asking**

6. Dad took the key and **locked (1)** the gate.

   locked   **locking**

Proofread for Spelling

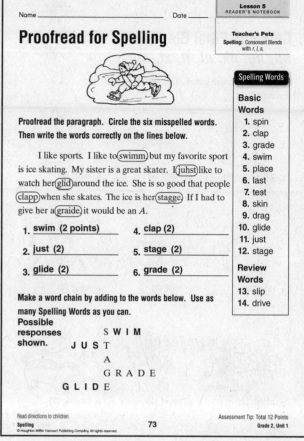

Proofread the paragraph. Circle the six misspelled words.
Then write the words correctly on the lines below.

I like sports. I like to (swimm) but my favorite sport
is ice skating. My sister is a great skater. I (juhst) like to
watch her (glid) around the ice. She is so good that people
(clapp) when she skates. The ice is her (stagge). If I had to
give her a (graide) it would be an A.

Spelling Words
Basic Words
1. spin
2. clap
3. grade
4. swim
5. place
6. last
7. test
8. skin
9. drag
10. glide
11. just
12. stage
Review Words
13. slip
14. drive

1. swim (2 points)   4. clap (2)

2. just (2)   5. stage (2)

3. glide (2)   6. grade (2)

Make a word chain by adding to the words below. Use as
many Spelling Words as you can.

Possible responses shown.

```
            S W I M
    J U S T
        A
        G R A D E
G L I D E
```

Commands and Exclamations

Write **Command** or **Exclamation** to identify each
sentence.

1. Take good care of our pet. **Command (1)**

2. Tell us about your pet. **Command (1)**

3. I can't believe how slow that snail is! **Exclamation (1)**

4. Our pet is the greatest pet in the school! **Exclamation (1)**

Write each command or exclamation correctly.

5. help me feed the pets

   Help me feed the pets. (1)

6. our new pet is terrific

   Our new pet is terrific! (1)

Conventions

Singular Nouns	Plural Nouns
one lizard	two lizards
a student	many students

Rewrite each sentence. Use the plural for each
underlined noun.

1. We saw many pet at school.

   We saw many pets at school. (1 point)

2. Two rabbit lived with the first graders.

   Two rabbits lived with the first graders. (1)

3. Some duck quacked in the second grade class.

   Some ducks quacked in the second grade class. (1)

4. Three snake hissed in the third grade class.

   Three snakes hissed in the third grade class. (1)

5. The fourth graders fed some spider.

   The fourth graders fed some spiders. (1)

6. Many animal lived at the school.

   Many animals lived at the school. (1)

Common Final Blends
nd, ng, nk, nt, ft, xt, mp

Write the name of each picture. Then circle the final consonant blend.

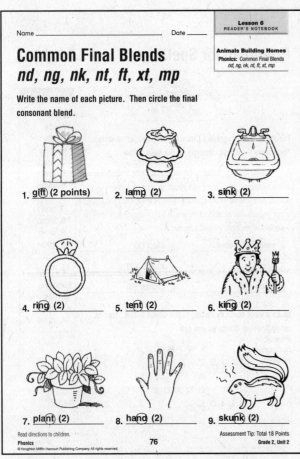

1. gift (2 points)   2. lamp (2)   3. sink (2)

4. ring (2)   5. tent (2)   6. king (2)

7. plant (2)   8. hand (2)   9. skunk (2)

Adding -es to Nouns

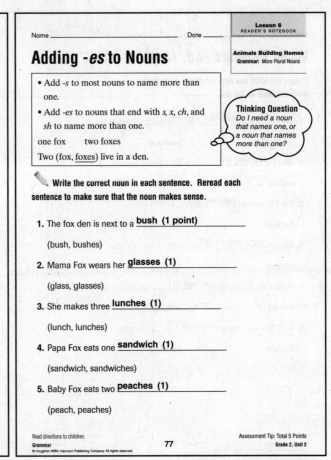

- Add -s to most nouns to name more than one.
- Add -es to nouns that end with s, x, ch, and sh to name more than one.

one fox   two foxes

Two (fox, <u>foxes</u>) live in a den.

Thinking Question
Do I need a noun that names one, or a noun that names more than one?

Write the correct noun in each sentence. Reread each sentence to make sure that the noun makes sense.

1. The fox den is next to a <u>bush (1 point)</u>

   (bush, bushes)

2. Mama Fox wears her <u>glasses (1)</u>

   (glass, glasses)

3. She makes three <u>lunches (1)</u>

   (lunch, lunches)

4. Papa Fox eats one <u>sandwich (1)</u>

   (sandwich, sandwiches)

5. Baby Fox eats two <u>peaches (1)</u>

   (peach, peaches)

Common Final Blends
nd, ng, nk, nt, ft, xt, mp

Answer each pair of clues using the words below them.

1. Coming after: <u>next (1 point)</u>

   Went away: <u>left (1)</u>

   next   **left**

2. A small lake: <u>pond (1)</u>

   To be on your feet: <u>stand (1)</u>

   stand   **pond**

3. To take a sip: <u>drink (1)</u>

   Sleep in a tent: <u>camp (1)</u>

   camp   **drink**

4. Write letters on a page: <u>print (1)</u>

   Look for something that is lost: <u>hunt (1)</u>

   print   **hunt**

5. A tune you can sing: <u>song (1)</u>

   The sound a horn makes: <u>honk (1)</u>

   honk   **song**

Final Blends nd, ng, nk, nt, ft, xt, mp

Sort the Spelling Words by their final blends.

nd blends: <u>end, stand, pond (3 points)</u>

ng blends: <u>sing, bring, long (3)</u>

nk blends: <u>drink, sank (2)</u>

nt blends: <u>hunt (1)</u>

ft blends: <u>left (1)</u>

xt blends: <u>next (1)</u>

mp blends: <u>jump, stamp, camp (3)</u>

Now add two words that you know to any of the lists.
Possible responses: *mp* blends: bump (1);
nd blends: find (1)

Spelling

Basic Words
1. next
2. end
3. camp
4. sank
5. sing
6. drink
7. hunt
8. stand
9. long
10. stamp
11. pond
12. bring

Review Words
13. jump
14. left

Nouns That Change Spelling

Some nouns change their spelling to name more than one.

one child   two children

Two (child, children) find a nest.

Thinking Question
Do I need a noun that names one, or a noun that names more than one?

✏ **Write the correct noun to finish each sentence. Reread each sentence to make sure that it makes sense.**

1. Two **children (1 point)** take a walk.

   (child, children)

2. I soaked both my **feet (1)** .

   (foot, feet)

3. One **goose (1)** is in the pond.

   (goose, geese)

4. Many **men (1)** stand near the hole.

   (man, men)

5. Two **mice (1)** ran into the hole.

   (mouse, mice)

80

Assessment Tip: Total 5 Points
Grade 2, Unit 2

Focus Trait: Ideas
Main Idea and Supporting Details

Main Idea	Supporting Details
Animals need homes.	Keep them safe from enemies
	Protect them from weather
	Help them raise babies

Read each set of sentences. Underline the sentence that contains the main idea.

1. Snakes also live in holes.
   Rabbits live underground in warrens.
   <u>Many kinds of animals live in holes.</u> **(1 point)**

2. Some people live in apartments.
   <u>People live in different kinds of houses.</u> **(1)**
   Some people live in ice houses called igloos.

3. They can protect you from harm.
   <u>Dogs make good pets.</u> **(1)**
   They are loyal.

4. <u>Some mammals live in the water.</u> **(1)**
   Dolphins look like fish, but they are mammals.
   Sea otters are mammals that live in the Pacific Ocean.

81

Assessment Tip: Total 4 Points
Grade 2, Unit 2

Cumulative Review

Read the words in the box. Write the word that completes each sentence.

Word Bank

nest	twigs	end
spring	play	branches

1. The **end (1 point)** of winter is near.

2. It is a sunny day in the **spring (1)**

3. Squirrels run and **play (1)**

4. Buds on the **branches (1)** will open soon.

5. Two robins build a **nest (1)** in the tree.

6. They use **twigs (1)** and grass to make it strong.

On the lines below, write a word that begins with the beginning blends shown. Possible responses shown.

7. br **brag (1)**   9. fr **frog (1)**   11. st **stamp (1)**

8. pr **price (1)**   10. cl **class (1)**   12. tr **tracks (1)**

82

Assessment Tip: Total 12 Points
Grade 2, Unit 2

Reader's Guide

Animals Building Homes

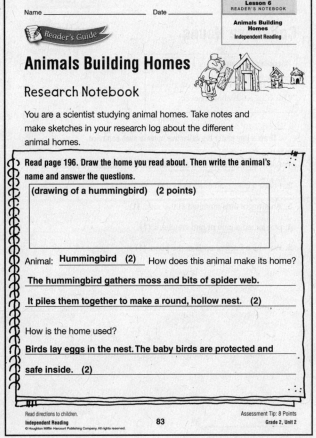

Research Notebook

You are a scientist studying animal homes. Take notes and make sketches in your research log about the different animal homes.

Read page 196. Draw the home you read about. Then write the animal's name and answer the questions.

(drawing of a hummingbird)   (2 points)

Animal: **Hummingbird (2)**   How does this animal make its home?

The hummingbird gathers moss and bits of spider web.

It piles them together to make a round, hollow nest.   (2)

How is the home used?

Birds lay eggs in the nest. The baby birds are protected and

safe inside.   (2)

83

Assessment Tip: 8 Points
Grade 2, Unit 2

Name _____ Date _____

Lesson 6
READER'S NOTEBOOK

Animals Building
Homes
Independent Reading

Read page 202. Draw the home you read about.
Write the animal's name under the drawing.
Then answer the questions.

(drawing of a gopher's room)   (2)

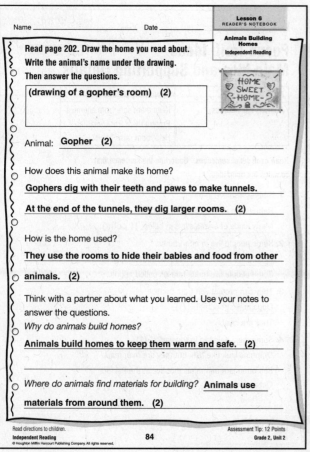

Animal: **Gopher**   (2) _____

How does this animal make its home?

Gophers dig with their teeth and paws to make tunnels.

At the end of the tunnels, they dig larger rooms.   (2)

How is the home used?

They use the rooms to hide their babies and food from other

animals.   (2)

Think with a partner about what you learned. Use your notes to
answer the questions.

Why do animals build homes?

Animals build homes to keep them warm and safe.   (2)

_____

Where do animals find materials for building? **Animals use**

materials from around them.   (2)

Name _____ Date _____

Lesson 6
READER'S NOTEBOOK

Animals Building
Homes
Spelling: Common Final Blends
nd, ng, nk, nt, ft, xt, mp

Final Blends *nd, ng, nk, nt, ft, xt, mp*

Use the Spelling Words to complete the story.

My dad and I like to (1) **camp (1 point)**

out. This year, Dad let me (2) **bring (1)**

my friend Jason. It was a (3) **long (1)**

drive. Dad stopped near a clear

(4) **pond (1)** .

We don't (5) **hunt (1)** animals,

but we do like to fish. It was hot, so we

brought a lot of water to (6) **drink (1)** .

Dad taught us to (7) **sing (1)** old songs.

We had a great time! At the (8) **end (1)** of

the weekend, we didn't want to go home. Jason and

I hope to go again (9) **next (1)** year.

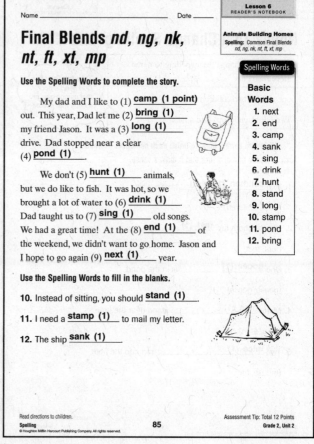

Use the Spelling Words to fill in the blanks.

10. Instead of sitting, you should **stand (1)**

11. I need a **stamp (1)** to mail my letter.

12. The ship **sank (1)** .

Spelling Words
Basic Words
1. next
2. end
3. camp
4. sank
5. sing
6. drink
7. hunt
8. stand
9. long
10. stamp
11. pond
12. bring

Collective Nouns

A **collective noun** names a group of
people or things.

Our <u>class</u> reads about beavers.

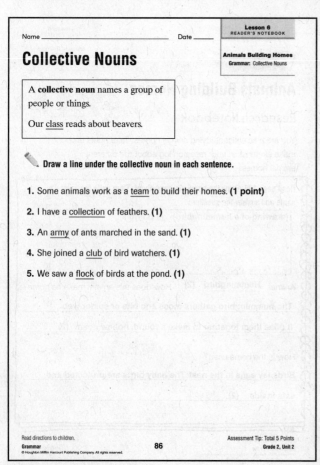 **Draw a line under the collective noun in each sentence.**

1. Some animals work as a <u>team</u> to build their homes. **(1 point)**

2. I have a <u>collection</u> of feathers. **(1)**

3. An <u>army</u> of ants marched in the sand. **(1)**

4. She joined a <u>club</u> of bird watchers. **(1)**

5. We saw a <u>flock</u> of birds at the pond. **(1)**

Name _____ Date _____

Lesson 6
READER'S NOTEBOOK

Animals Building Homes
Vocabulary Strategies:
Prefixes un- and re-

Prefixes *un-* and *re-*

**Choose the word from the box that best completes each
sentence. Write the word on the line.**

Word Bank
rehang   untie   rebuild   unreal
unfold   remake   unload

1. **untie (2 points)** my shoes before I take them off.

2. Please **unfold (2)** the blanket and put it on
the bed.

3. I know that story is true, but it is so strange that it
seems **unreal (2)** !

4. The picture fell off the wall, so I have to
rehang (2) it.

5. My little brother messed up my bed, so I had to
remake (2) it.

6. The birds used twigs to **rebuild (2)** their nest
after it fell out of the tree.

7. I helped Mom **unload (2)** all the food from
the car.

Proofread for Spelling

Proofread the story. Circle the six misspelled words.
Then write the correct spellings on the lines below.

Spelling Words

Basic Words
1. next
2. end
3. camp
4. sank
5. sing
6. drink
7. hunt
8. stand
9. long
10. stamp
11. pond
12. bring

I needed to buy a ⟨stampe⟩ to mail my letter. I was
at the end of a ⟨log⟩ line at the post office. One person
in line started to ⟨sang⟩ Another took a ⟨drenk⟩ from a
water bottle. A grandpa tugged at a child and scolded,
"⟨Stad⟩ still!" I was about to give up and go home when I
heard, "⟨Nextt⟩!" The line was finally moving.

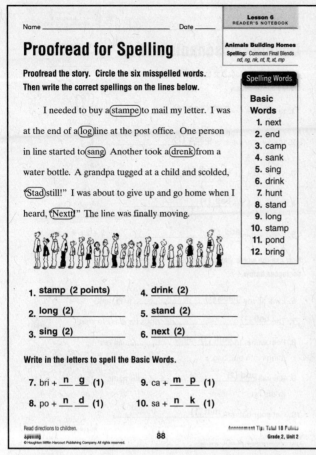

1. **stamp (2 points)**   4. **drink (2)**

2. **long (2)**   5. **stand (2)**

3. **sing (2)**   6. **next (2)**

Write in the letters to spell the Basic Words.

7. bri + **n g** (1)   9. ca + **m p** (1)

8. po + **n d** (1)   10. sa + **n k** (1)

Parts of a Sentence

Read each sentence. The action part has one line
underneath it. Draw two lines under the naming part.

1. The cat and dog live in the house. **(1 point)**

2. The puppy and kitten play together. **(1)**

3. A man and woman feed them. **(1)**

4. A boy and girl pet them. **(1)**

5. An aunt and uncle visit. **(1)**

Read each sentence. The naming part has two lines
underneath it. Draw one line under the action part.

6. Tigers and bears sleep in caves. **(1)**

7. Turtles and snails live in shells. **(1)**

8. Bees and wasps make hives. **(1)**

9. Birds and mice build nests. **(1)**

10. Gophers dig burrows. **(1)**

Sentence Fluency

Short Sentences	New Sentence with Joined Subjects
Foxes live in dens. Bears live in dens.	Foxes and bears live in dens.

Short Sentences	New Sentence with Joined Subjects
Mice make their own nests. Birds make their own nests.	Mice and birds make their own nests.

Read the sentences below. Use *and* to combine their
subjects. Write the new sentence on the line.

1. Geese fly to warm places in winter.
   Ducks fly to warm places in winter.
   Geese and ducks fly to warm places in winter. (2 points)

2. Seals live in cold places.
   Penguins live in cold places.
   Seals and penguins live in cold places. (2)

3. Squirrels use the branches of trees.
   Crows use the branches of trees.
   Squirrels and crows use the branches of trees. (2)

4. Baby finches are fed in nests.
   Baby cardinals are fed in nests.
   Baby finches and baby cardinals are fed in nests. (2)

Double Consonants and *ck*

Read the words below. Think about how the words in
each group are alike. Write the missing word that fits
in each group.

Word Bank

quack	fluff	dress	duck
mitt	kick	spill	neck

1. pants, shirt, **dress (1 point)**

2. fish, frog, **duck (1)**

3. bat, ball, **mitt (1)**

4. arm, leg, **neck (1)**

5. tip, splash, **spill (1)**

6. moo, meow, **quack (1)**

7. fur, fuzz, **fluff (1)**

8. run, jump, **kick (1)**

Write a word that rhymes with each word below.
Possible responses shown.

9. stall **wall (1)**   11. back **quack (1)**

10. mess **dress (1)**   12. will **spill (1)**

Names for People, Animals, Places, and Things

> Some **nouns** name special people, animals, places, or things. These special nouns are **proper nouns**. Proper nouns begin with capital letters.
>
> Today <u>Lanie Lin</u> plants a garden.

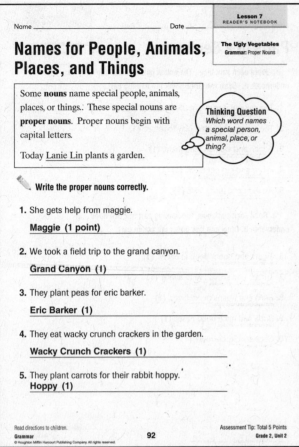

Thinking Question
Which word names a special person, animal, place, or thing?

✏ Write the proper nouns correctly.

1. She gets help from maggie.

   Maggie (1 point)

2. We took a field trip to the grand canyon.

   Grand Canyon (1)

3. They plant peas for eric barker.

   Eric Barker (1)

4. They eat wacky crunch crackers in the garden.

   Wacky Crunch Crackers (1)

5. They plant carrots for their rabbit hoppy.

   Hoppy (1)

Double Consonants and *ck*

Put these letters together to write words that end with double consonants.

1. m + i + t + t = **mitt (1 point)** _____

2. g + l + a + s + s = **glass (1)** _____

3. s + t + u + f + f = **stuff (1)** _____

4. b + e + l + l = **bell (1)** _____

5. a + d + d = **add (1)** _____ $2 + 2 = 4$

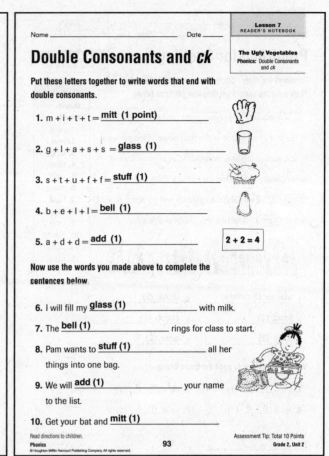

Now use the words you made above to complete the sentences below.

6. I will fill my **glass (1)** _____ with milk.

7. The **bell (1)** _____ rings for class to start.

8. Pam wants to **stuff (1)** _____ all her things into one bag.

9. We will **add (1)** _____ your name to the list.

10. Get your bat and **mitt (1)** _____

Double Consonants and *ck*

Sort the Spelling Words. Put words that end in *ck* in one list. Put words that end in double consonants in the other list.

Spelling Words

Basic Words
1. dress
2. spell
3. class
4. full
5. add
6. neck
7. stuck
8. kick
9. rock
10. black
11. trick
12. doll

Review Words
13. will
14. off

ck Words	Double Consonant Words
1. **neck (1 point)**	8. **dress (1)**
2. **stuck (1)**	9. **spell (1)**
3. **kick (1)**	10. **class (1)**
4. **rock (1)**	11. **full (1)**
5. **black (1)**	12. **add (1)**
6. **trick (1)**	13. **will (1)**
7. **sick (1)**	14. **off (1)**
	15. **doll (1)**
	16. **call (1)**

Add one more word that you know to each list.
Possible responses shown.

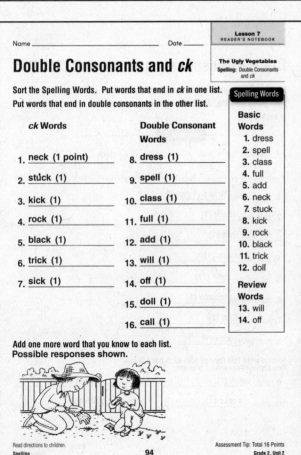

Names for Special People and Animals

> Some **nouns** name special people or animals. These are **proper nouns**. Names for people and animals begin with capital letters.
>
> <u>Grace</u> fed her cat <u>Fluffy</u>.

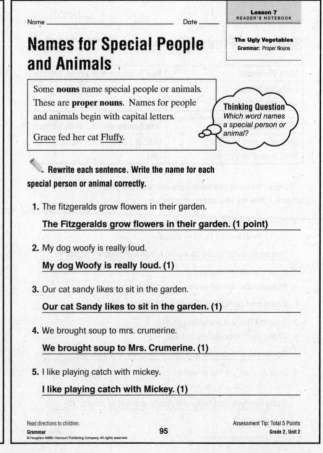

Thinking Question
Which word names a special person or animal?

✏ Rewrite each sentence. Write the name for each special person or animal correctly.

1. The fitzgeralds grow flowers in their garden.

   The Fitzgeralds grow flowers in their garden. (1 point)

2. My dog woofy is really loud.

   My dog Woofy is really loud. (1)

3. Our cat sandy likes to sit in the garden.

   Our cat Sandy likes to sit in the garden. (1)

4. We brought soup to mrs. crumerine.

   We brought soup to Mrs. Crumerine. (1)

5. I like playing catch with mickey.

   I like playing catch with Mickey. (1)

Name _____ Date _____

Focus Trait: Organization
Retelling Events in Order

Events Not in Order	Events in Order
I woke up.	1. I woke up.
I brushed my teeth.	2. I put toothpaste on my
I put toothpaste on my toothbrush.	toothbrush.
	3. I brushed my teeth.

Work with a partner. Number each set of sentences in the order that makes the most sense.

1. __2__ I put on my shoes.   2. __3__ I had dinner.

   __1__ I put on my socks.   __1__ I had breakfast.

   __3__ I tied my shoes. **(1 point)**   __2__ I had lunch. **(1)**

Work on your own. Number each set of sentences in an order that makes sense.

3. __3__ The plants started to grow.   5. __3__ I went to school.

   __2__ We planted seeds.   __1__ I woke up.

   __1__ We dug up the soil. **(1)**   __2__ I grabbed my lunch. **(1)**

4. __1__ I took out a glass.

   __2__ I poured milk.

   __3__ I drank the milk. **(1)**

Name _____ Date _____

Double Consonants (CVC)

Write a word from the box to complete each sentence below.

Word Bank

happen   bottom   button   cotton   puppet

1. The dress is made of __cotton (1 point)__

2. What will __happen (1)__ if it starts to rain?

3. The children had fun at the __puppet (1)__ show.

4. The rag doll has a __button (1)__ for a nose.

5. The prize is at the __bottom (1)__ of the sack.

Answer each clue using a word from the box.

Word Bank

rabbit   kitten   hidden   mitten   muffin

6. Something good to eat __muffin (1)__

7. Another name for a bunny __rabbit (1)__

8. It keeps your hand warm. __mitten (1)__

9. A baby cat __kitten (1)__

10. Hard to find __hidden (1)__

Name _____ Date _____

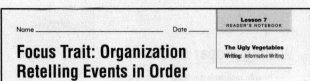

The Ugly Vegetables

E-mails to Grandma

Hi. I am e-mailing my Grandma to tell her about the garden. Help me finish each e-mail. Use examples from the text and illustrations to show how I feel about the garden.

Read page 233. What can I tell Grandma about the garden?

re: Garden

How is your garden looking?
Love, Grandma

I am __excited__ because our plants __have popped out__ __of the ground. (5 points)__

Read page 237. Now, what can I tell Grandma about the garden?

re: Garden

How is your garden looking today?
Love, Grandma

I am __disappointed__ because our garden __does not have__ __beautiful flowers like our neighbor's gardens. (5)__

Name _____ Date _____

Read page 237. What can I tell Grandma about the garden?

re: Garden

Now, are you excited about your garden?
Love, Grandma

I am __sad__ because our garden __has ugly vegetables. (5)__

Read page 242. What can I tell Grandma about the garden?

re: Garden

How is your garden looking now?
Love, Grandma

I am __excited__ because our garden __helped us make a__ __yummy soup. (5)__

Read page 243. What can I tell Grandma about the garden?

re: Garden

How are you feeling about your garden?
Love, Grandma

I am __proud__ because __our neighbors loved our__ __vegetable soup. (5)__

Double Consonants and *ck*

Write the Spelling Word for each picture.

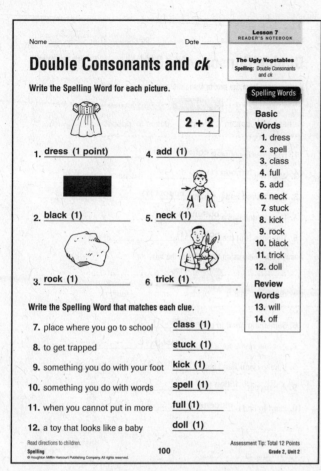

2 + 2

1. **dress (1 point)**   4. **add (1)**

2. **black (1)**   5. **neck (1)**

3. **rock (1)**   6. **trick (1)**

Write the Spelling Word that matches each clue.

7. place where you go to school   **class (1)**

8. to get trapped   **stuck (1)**

9. something you do with your foot   **kick (1)**

10. something you do with words   **spell (1)**

11. when you cannot put in more   **full (1)**

12. a toy that looks like a baby   **doll (1)**

Spelling Words

Basic Words
1. dress
2. spell
3. class
4. full
5. add
6. neck
7. stuck
8. kick
9. rock
10. black
11. trick
12. doll

Review Words
13. will
14. off

Read directions to children.
Spelling   100
© Houghton Mifflin Harcourt Publishing Company. All rights reserved.

Assessment Tip: Total 12 Points
Grade 2, Unit 2

Writing Proper Nouns

Rewrite each sentence. Write the name for each special thing correctly.

1. Sue gardens with her deep digger shovel.

   Sue gardens with her Deep Digger Shovel.   (1 point)

2. I gave my dad happy day raisins.

   I gave my dad Happy Day Raisins.   (1)

3. I drink giggly grape juice.

   I drink Giggly Grape Juice.   (1)

Rewrite each sentence. Write the name for each special place correctly.

4. Grapes grow on franklin road.

   Grapes grow on Franklin Road.   (1)

5. Olives grow in italy.

   Olives grow in Italy.   (1)

6. Apples grow in portland.

   Apples grow in Portland.   (1)

Read directions to children.
Grammar   101
© Houghton Mifflin Harcourt Publishing Company. All rights reserved.

Assessment Tip: Total 6 Points
Grade 2, Unit 2

Homophones

Word Bank

too	won	wear	plain
two	one	where	plane

Choose the word from the box that best completes the sentence. Write the word on the line.

1. The farmer has **two (1 point)** shovels.

2. **Where (1)** did you put my keys?

3. I don't like stripes or spots. I only like to wear **plain (1)** clothes.

4. I am happy because my team **won (1)** the game.

5. My sister is going to the movies. I want to go, **too (1)**

6. I have only **one (1)** flower in the vase.

7. What are you going to **wear (1)** to the party?

8. We will take a car to the airport, and then we will get on a **plane (1)**

Read directions to children.
Vocabulary Strategies   102
© Houghton Mifflin Harcourt Publishing Company. All rights reserved.

Assessment Tip: Total 8 Points
Grade 2, Unit 2

Proofread for Spelling

Proofread the journal entry. Circle the five misspelled words. Then spell the words correctly on the lines below.

Today we went on a clas trip. The first bus was ful, so we waited for the next one. After about a block, the bus ran over a big rouck. There was a loud noise and then the bus stopped. The driver said that we were stukk. He had to ad air to the tire before we could go.

1. **class (1 point)**

2. **full (1)**

3. **rock (1)**

4. **stuck (1)**

5. **add (1)**

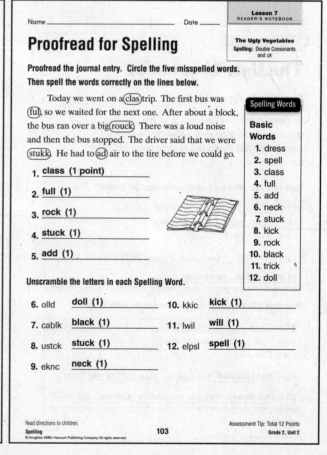

Unscramble the letters in each Spelling Word.

6. olld   **doll (1)**   10. kkic   **kick (1)**

7. cablk   **black (1)**   11. lwil   **will (1)**

8. ustck   **stuck (1)**   12. elpsl   **spell (1)**

9. eknc   **neck (1)**

Spelling Words

Basic Words
1. dress
2. spell
3. class
4. full
5. add
6. neck
7. stuck
8. kick
9. rock
10. black
11. trick
12. doll

Read directions to children.
Spelling   103
© Houghton Mifflin Harcourt Publishing Company. All rights reserved.

Assessment Tip: Total 12 Points
Grade 2, Unit 2

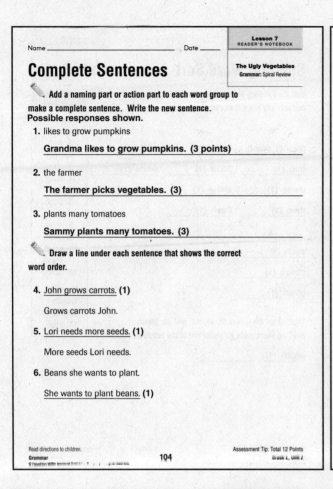

Complete Sentences

Add a naming part or action part to each word group to make a complete sentence. Write the new sentence. **Possible responses shown.**

1. likes to grow pumpkins

   Grandma likes to grow pumpkins. (3 points)

2. the farmer

   The farmer picks vegetables. (3)

3. plants many tomatoes

   Sammy plants many tomatoes. (3)

Draw a line under each sentence that shows the correct word order.

4. <u>John grows carrots.</u> **(1)**

   Grows carrots John.

5. <u>Lori needs more seeds.</u> **(1)**

   More seeds Lori needs.

6. Beans she wants to plant.

   <u>She wants to plant beans.</u> **(1)**

Read directions to children.
Grammar
© Houghton Mifflin Harcourt Publishing Company. All rights reserved.
104
Assessment Tip: Total 12 Points
Grade 2, Unit 2

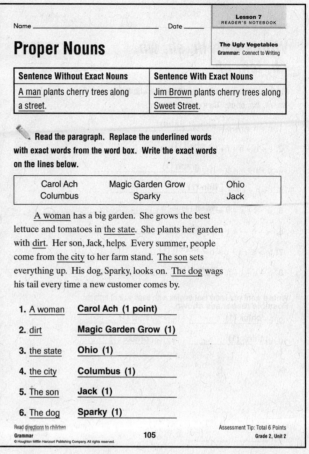

Proper Nouns

Sentence Without Exact Nouns	Sentence With Exact Nouns
A man plants cherry trees along a street.	Jim Brown plants cherry trees along Sweet Street.

Read the paragraph. Replace the underlined words with exact words from the word box. Write the exact words on the lines below.

Carol Ach	Magic Garden Grow	Ohio
Columbus	Sparky	Jack

A woman has a big garden. She grows the best lettuce and tomatoes in the state. She plants her garden with dirt. Her son, Jack, helps. Every summer, people come from the city to her farm stand. The son sets everything up. His dog, Sparky, looks on. The dog wags his tail every time a new customer comes by.

1. A woman **Carol Ach (1 point)**

2. dirt **Magic Garden Grow (1)**

3. the state **Ohio (1)**

4. the city **Columbus (1)**

5. The son **Jack (1)**

6. The dog **Sparky (1)**

Read directions to children.
Grammar
© Houghton Mifflin Harcourt Publishing Company. All rights reserved.
105
Assessment Tip: Total 6 Points
Grade 2, Unit 2

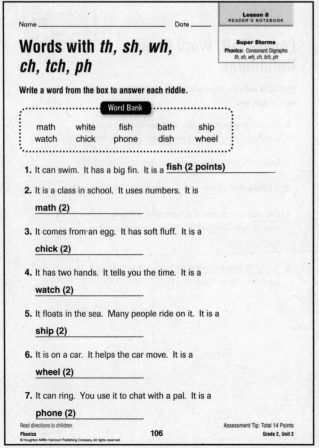

Name _____ Date _____

Lesson 8
READER'S NOTEBOOK

Super Storms
Phonics: Consonant Digraphs
th, sh, wh, ch, tch, ph

Words with *th, sh, wh, ch, tch, ph*

Write a word from the box to answer each riddle.

Word Bank

math	white	fish	bath	ship
watch	chick	phone	dish	wheel

1. It can swim. It has a big fin. It is a **fish (2 points)**

2. It is a class in school. It uses numbers. It is

   math (2)

3. It comes from an egg. It has soft fluff. It is a

   chick (2)

4. It has two hands. It tells you the time. It is a

   watch (2)

5. It floats in the sea. Many people ride on it. It is a

   ship (2)

6. It is on a car. It helps the car move. It is a

   wheel (2)

7. It can ring. You use it to chat with a pal. It is a

   phone (2)

Read directions to children.
Phonics
© Houghton Mifflin Harcourt Publishing Company. All rights reserved.
106
Assessment Tip: Total 14 Points
Grade 2, Unit 2

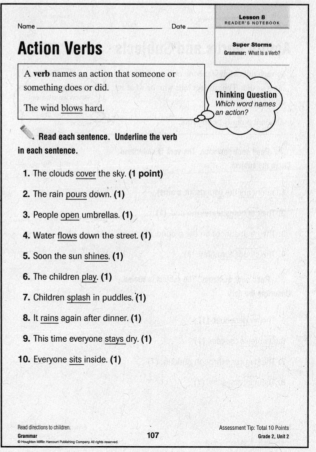

Action Verbs

A **verb** names an action that someone or something does or did.

The wind <u>blows</u> hard.

Thinking Question
Which word names an action?

Read each sentence. Underline the verb in each sentence.

1. The clouds <u>cover</u> the sky. **(1 point)**

2. The rain <u>pours</u> down. **(1)**

3. People <u>open</u> umbrellas. **(1)**

4. Water <u>flows</u> down the street. **(1)**

5. Soon the sun <u>shines</u>. **(1)**

6. The children <u>play</u>. **(1)**

7. Children <u>splash</u> in puddles. **(1)**

8. It <u>rains</u> again after dinner. **(1)**

9. This time everyone <u>stays</u> dry. **(1)**

10. Everyone <u>sits</u> inside. **(1)**

Read directions to children.
Grammar
© Houghton Mifflin Harcourt Publishing Company. All rights reserved.
107
Assessment Tip: Total 10 Points
Grade 2, Unit 2

Name _____ Date _____

Lesson 8
READER'S NOTEBOOK

Super Storms
Phonics: Consonant Digraphs
th, sh, wh, ch, tch, ph

Words with *th, sh, wh, ch, tch, ph*

Put these letters together to write words with *th, sh, wh, ch, tch,* or *ph*. Then read each word.

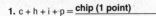

1. c + h + i + p = **chip (1 point)**

2. s + h + e + l + l = **shell (1)**

3. g + r + a + p + h = **graph (1)**

4. t + h + i + n = **thin (1)**

5. w + i + s + h = **wish (1)**

6. w + h + i + t + e = **white (1)**

7. m + a + t + c + h = **match (1)**

8. p + a + t + h = **path (1)**

Write a word you know that begins with each pair of letters. **Possible responses shown.**

9. ch **chick (1)**   11. sh **ship (1)**

10. th **think (1)**   12. ph **phone (1)**

Spelling Word Sort

Sort the Spelling Words under the headings below. If a word can sort into more than one place, choose one.

Spelling Words

th	*sh*	*wh*
than (1 point)	dish (1)	white (1)
thin (1)	push (1)	while (1)
these (1)	shine (1)	which (1)
then (1)	flash (1)	

ch
such (1)
chase (1)
chest (1)

Think about the letters *th, sh, wh,* and *ch*. Which Spelling Word could go under two of the headings above?

which **(1)**

Spelling Words

Basic Words
1. dish
2. than
3. chest
4. such
5. thin
6. push
7. shine
8. chase
9. white
10. while
11. these
12. flash

Review Words
13. whioh
14. then

Action Verbs and Subjects

A **verb** tells what someone or something does or did. The **subject** tells who or what is doing the action.

The hail <u>pounds</u> on the roof.

Thinking Questions
Which word names an action? Who does or did the action?

✏ Read each sentence. The verb is underlined. Circle the subject.

1. (Jan) hears the sounds. **(1 point)**

2. The (cat) hides under the bed. **(1)**

3. The (hail) bounces on the ground. **(1)**

4. The (clouds) turn gray. **(1)**

✏ Read each sentence. The subject is circled. Underline the verb.

5. The (air) gets cold. **(1)**

6. (Dan) feels the rain. **(1)**

7. The (dog) runs through puddles. **(1)**

8. The (mail) stays dry. **(1)**

Focus Trait: Word Choice
Definitions

Read each sentence. Draw a line under the definition of the word in dark type.

1. The rain shower became a **thunderstorm**, <u>a storm with heavy rain, thunder, and lightning.</u> **(1 point)**

2. They were in the **eye**, or <u>calm center,</u> of the storm. **(1)**

3. A **blizzard** is a <u>storm with fast winds and heavy snow.</u> **(1)**

4. The ship was caught in a **hurricane**, <u>a severe tropical storm with winds of more than seventy-five miles per hour.</u> **(1)**

5. <u>Scientists who follow the path of a storm to study it</u> are called **storm chasers**. **(1)**

Base Words and Endings -s, -ed, -ing

Read each word pair. Use the words to answer the clues.

1. prints   jumps

   Hops up and down   **jumps (1 point)**

   Writes words on paper   **prints (1)**

2. lifting   camping

   Pulling something up   **lifting (1)**

   Living outside and sleeping in a tent   **camping (1)**

3. packed   checked

   Looked at something again to be sure   **checked (1)**

   Put things in a box or a bag   **packed (1)**

4. passing   helping

   Doing part of the work   **helping (1)**

   Walking by a person or place   **passing (1)**

5. rested   hunted

   Took a nap   **rested (1)**

   Looked for something   **hunted (1)**

Reader's Guide

Super Storms

Write a Storm Poem

Let's look at types of storms. Read the text and study the illustrations. Find details to describe the storms. Then, use those details to write a poem.

Read page 271. Describe a thunderstorm in your own words.

Thunderstorms have lightning that shoots to the ground. You

can hear thunder booming.   (5 points)

Read page 273. Describe a tornado in your own words.

Tornadoes are funnel-shaped clouds that stretch to the ground.

They have winds that travel 300 miles per hour.   (5)

Read pages 276–278. Describe a hurricane in your own words.

Hurricanes stretch over wide distances. They have strong winds up

to 200 miles per hour. They cause big waves and heavy rain.   (5)

Read page 279. Describe a blizzard in your own words.

Blizzards are strong snowstorms. They have winds up to 35 miles per

per hour. A lot of snow falls very quickly. It is hard to see outside.   (5)

Use your notes to write a poem. Choose a storm that interests you. Answer the questions on the lines. Your answers will make a poem. When you are done, read your poem to a friend.

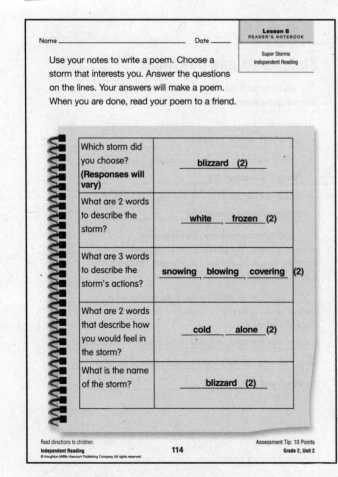

Which storm did you choose? **(Responses will vary)**	**blizzard (2)**
What are 2 words to describe the storm?	**white** , **frozen (2)**
What are 3 words to describe the storm's actions?	**snowing blowing covering (2)**
What are 2 words that describe how you would feel in the storm?	**cold** , **alone (2)**
What is the name of the storm?	**blizzard (2)**

Words with *th, sh, wh, ch, tch*

Write the Spelling Word that is the opposite of each word.

1. black **white (1 point)**   3. now **then (1)**

2. thick **thin (1)**   4. pull **push (1)**

Complete each Spelling Word with a consonant digraph.

7. di **s h** (1)   12. **w h** ile (1)

8. su **c h** (1)   13. **c h** ase (1)

9. **c h** est (1)   14. **t h** ese (1)

10. **t h** an (1)   15. **w h** i **c h** (1)

11. **f l** ash (1)   16. **s h** ine (1)

Spelling Words

Basic Words

1. dish
2. than
3. chest
4. such
5. thin
6. push
7. shine
8. chase
9. white
10. while
11. these
12. flash

Review Words

13. which
14. then

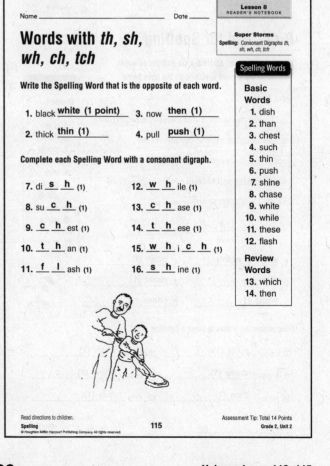

Action Verbs

Super Storms
Grammar: What Is a Verb?

✏️ **Read each sentence. Underline the verb.**

1. The wind ended. **(1 point)**

2. The thunder started. **(1)**

3. We cover our ears. **(1)**

4. We sit in the house **(1)**

✏️ **Read each sentence. The action verb is underlined.**
Circle the subject that is doing the action.

5. (Jerry) peeks out the window. **(1)**

6. The (rain) floods the street. **(1)**

7. The (water) flows down the hill. **(1)**

8. The (storm) stops the next day. **(1)**

Read directions to children.
Grammar
© Houghton Mifflin Harcourt Publishing Company. All rights reserved.
116
Assessment Tip: Total 8 Points
Grade 2, Unit 2

Compound Words

Super Storms
Vocabulary Strategies:
Compound Words

Choose the word from the box that completes the
compound word in each sentence. Write the word on
the line.

Word Bank

light	time	fly	house
writing	shine	book	print

1. We built a dog + **house (1 point)** for our new puppy
   to live in.

2. I have a flash + _____ **light (1)** _____ in case it gets dark.

3. Please use neat hand + _____ **writing (1)** _____ when you
   do your homework.

4. Dee saw an orange butter + _____ **fly (1)** _____ fluttering
   in the garden.

5. Mark read his favorite story + _____ **book (1)** _____ before bed.

6. Please don't touch the window with dirty hands.
   You'll leave a thumb + _____ **print (1)** _____

7. I can go out and play in the sun + _____ **shine (1)** _____

8. In the summer + _____ **time (1)** _____ we like to go to the
   pool.

Read directions to children.
Vocabulary Strategies
© Houghton Mifflin Harcourt Publishing Company. All rights reserved.
117
Assessment Tip: Total 8 Points
Grade 2, Unit 2

Proofread for Spelling

Super Storms
Spelling: Consonant Digraphs th,
sh, wh, ch, tch

Proofread the note. Circle the six misspelled words.
Then write the correct spellings on the lines below.

Dear Mom,

    I want you to know that I broke the (whitte) (dishe)
(Whil) I was trying to (pulsh) the door of the
(chast) closed, it slipped out of my hands. Spike was
covered in mud, and I was in a hurry to (chese) him
outside. I am sorry.

      Love,

      Matt

Spelling Words

Basic Words
1. dish
2. than
3. chest
4. such
5. thin
6. push
7. shine
8. chase
9. white
10. while
11. these
12. flash

1. **white (1 point)**   4. **push (1)**

2. **dish (1)**   5. **chest (1)**

3. **While (1)**   6. **chase (1)**

Unscramble the letters to make a Spelling Word.

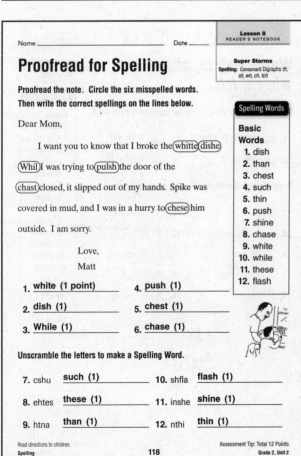

7. cshu   **such (1)**   10. shfla   **flash (1)**

8. ehtes   **these (1)**   11. inshe   **shine (1)**

9. htna   **than (1)**   12. nthi   **thin (1)**

Read directions to children.
Spelling
© Houghton Mifflin Harcourt Publishing Company. All rights reserved.
118
Assessment Tip: Total 12 Points
Grade 2, Unit 2

Statements and Questions

Super Storms
Grammar: Spiral Review

✏️ **Read each sentence. Circle the kind of sentence it is.**
Then rewrite the sentence correctly.

1. will it rain today   statement   (question)
   Will it rain today? (2 points)

2. i think it will snow   (statement)   question
   I think it will snow. (2)

3. did you see the clouds   statement   (question)
   Did you see the clouds? (2)

✏️ **Read the paragraph below. Then rewrite the**
paragraph correctly. Use question marks at the end of
questions. Use periods at the end of statements. Remember
to use capital letters.

    A storm hits our town we stay in the house. What
else can we do. mom gives us popcorn Dad reads to us
When will the storm end

A storm hits our town. We stay in the house. What else can

we do? Mom gives us popcorn. Dad reads to us. When will

the storm end? (6)

Read directions to children.
Grammar
© Houghton Mifflin Harcourt Publishing Company. All rights reserved.
119
Assessment Tip: Total 12 Points
Grade 2, Unit 2

Word Choice

Sentence without Exact Verbs	Sentence with Exact Verbs
The wind blew the door closed.	The wind slammed the door closed.

Sentence without Exact Verbs	Sentence with Exact Verbs
The storm goes through town.	The storm races through town.

Read the paragraph. Replace each underlined word with an exact word from the box. Write the exact words on the lines.

> pounded   stared   hid
> howled   swirled

The town was quiet. Then the wind blew loudly. Leaves went in circles. Rain fell on the streets. We put our bags under our coats. We stayed dry inside the bus stop. Then the rain stopped. We looked at a rainbow for a long time.

1. blew **howled (1 point)** _____
2. went **swirled (1)** _____
3. fell **pounded (1)** _____
4. put **hid (1)** _____
5. looked **stared (1)** _____

Base Words and Endings
-ed, -ing

Read the sentences. Draw a circle around each word that has the ending -ed or -ing.

1. Mom is (baking) a cake for dinner. **(1 point)**
2. Dad (closed) the window when it (started) to rain. **(2)**
3. The apple (tasted) cold and sweet. **(1)**
4. Jen (hoped) that her cat was (hiding) under the bed. **(2)**
5. The children went (hiking) last summer. **(1)**
6. Todd (raked) the leaves into piles. **(1)**

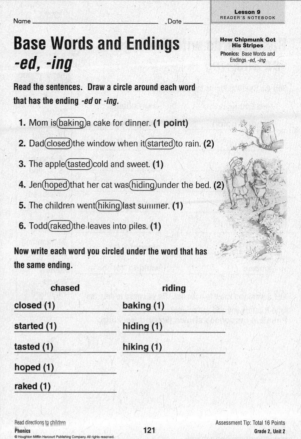

Now write each word you circled under the word that has the same ending.

chased	riding
closed **(1)**	baking **(1)**
started **(1)**	hiding **(1)**
tasted **(1)**	hiking **(1)**
hoped **(1)**	
raked **(1)**	

Adding -s to Verbs

A **verb** can name an action that is happening now. Add -s to this kind of verb when it tells about a noun that names one.

The chipmunk eats.
The chipmunks eat.

> **Thinking Question**
> Does the subject, or naming part, of the sentence name one or more than one?

Read each sentence. Then write it correctly.

1. The squirrels (see, sees) the chipmunk.
   The squirrels see the chipmunk. (1 point)

2. The chipmunk (share, shares) food.
   The chipmunk shares food. (1)

3. A squirrel (run, runs) down the tree.
   A squirrel runs down the tree. (1)

4. More chipmunks (help, helps) the squirrels.
   More chipmunks help the squirrels. (1)

5. The animals (eat, eats) together.
   The animals eat together. (1)

Base Words and Endings
-ed, -ing

Read each word. Then write the base word and ending on the lines. **(1 point each)**

1. hoped   **hope**   + **ed**
2. skating   **skate**   + **ing**
3. spilled   **spill**   + **ed**
4. chasing **chase**   + **ing**
5. saving   **save**   + **ing**

Now complete the sentences below with the words from above.

6. Ling **hoped (1)** _____ she would get a puppy.
7. Jack is **saving (1)** _____ his money to get a new mitt.
8. Maria **spilled (1)** _____ milk on her pink dress.
9. The boys like **skating (1)** _____ on the frozen lake.
10. My cat was **chasing (1)** _____ a mouse, but he didn't catch it.

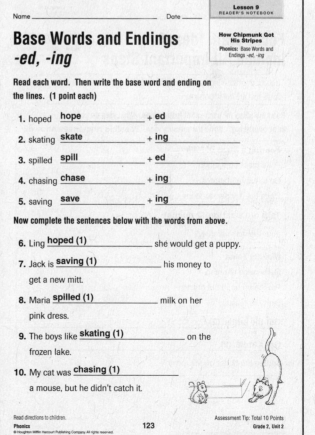

Lesson 9
READER'S NOTEBOOK

How Chipmunk Got
His Stripes
Spelling: Base Words with
Endings -ed and -ing

Base Words with Endings
-ed and -ing

Sort the Spelling Words by -ed and -ing endings.

-ed Endings	-ing Endings
liked (1 point)	using (1)
chased (1)	riding (1)
spilled (1)	making (1)
closed (1)	hoping (1)
baked (1)	hiding (1)
asked (1)	standing (1)
mixed (1)	sleeping (1)
walked (1)	walking (1)

Add a word you know to each list. Do you need to drop the final *e* before you add -ed or -ing?
Possible responses shown (walked, walking).

Spelling Words

Basic Words
1. liked
2. using
3. riding
4. chased
5. spilled
6. making
7. closed
8. hoping
9. baked
10. hiding
11. standing
12. asked

Review Words
13. mixed
14. sleeping

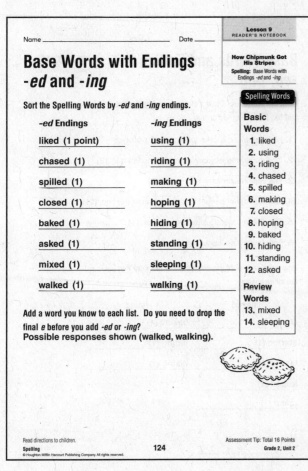

Read directions to children.
Spelling
© Houghton Mifflin Harcourt Publishing Company. All rights reserved.
124
Assessment Tip: Total 16 Points
Grade 2, Unit 2

Adding -*es* to Verbs

A **verb** can tell about an action that is happening now. Add -*es* to this kind of verb if it ends with *s, x, z, ch,* or *sh* and if it tells about a naming part that names one.

The <u>bear</u> messes the leaf pile.
The <u>bears</u> mess the leaf pile.

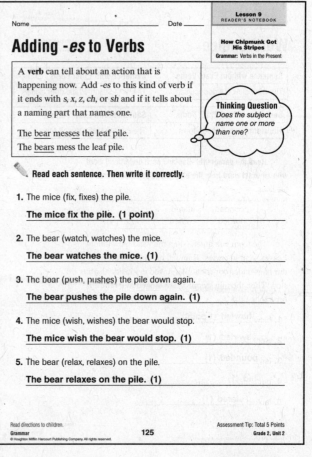

Thinking Question
Does the subject name one or more than one?

Read each sentence. Then write it correctly.

1. The mice (fix, fixes) the pile.

   The mice fix the pile. (1 point)

2. The bear (watch, watches) the mice.

   The bear watches the mice. (1)

3. The boar (push, pushes) the pile down again.

   The bear pushes the pile down again. (1)

4. The mice (wish, wishes) the bear would stop.

   The mice wish the bear would stop. (1)

5. The bear (relax, relaxes) on the pile.

   The bear relaxes on the pile. (1)

Read directions to children.
Grammar
© Houghton Mifflin Harcourt Publishing Company. All rights reserved.
125
Assessment Tip: Total 5 Points
Grade 2, Unit 2

Focus Trait: Ideas
Include All Important Steps

Good instructions include all the important steps. Writers leave out steps that are not important.

Read the steps for each set of instructions. What step do you think is missing? Write the missing step. Possible responses shown.

Pouring a Glass of Milk
Put a glass on a table.
Go to the refrigerator.
Open the refrigerator door.
Take out a carton. (2 points)
Pour the milk carefully.

Making Toast
Get a piece of bread.
Put the bread in the toaster.
Start the toaster.
Get the butter. (2)

Get a knife. (2)
Spread the butter on the toast.

Read directions to children.
Writing
© Houghton Mifflin Harcourt Publishing Company. All rights reserved.
126
Assessment Tip: Total 6 Points
Grade 2, Unit 2

CV Syllable Pattern

Read each word. Then write the word and draw a slash (/) between the two syllables.

1. pilot   pi / lot (1 point)
2. later   la / ter (1)
3. lemon   lem / on (1)
4. hotel   ho / tel (1)
5. tiger   ti / ger (1)

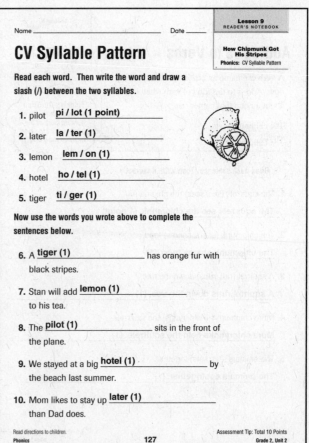

Now use the words you wrote above to complete the sentences below.

6. A tiger (1) _____ has orange fur with black stripes.

7. Stan will add lemon (1) _____ to his tea.

8. The pilot (1) _____ sits in the front of the plane.

9. We stayed at a big hotel (1) _____ by the beach last summer.

10. Mom likes to stay up later (1) _____ than Dad does.

Read directions to children.
Phonics
© Houghton Mifflin Harcourt Publishing Company. All rights reserved.
127
Assessment Tip: Total 10 Points
Grade 2, Unit 2

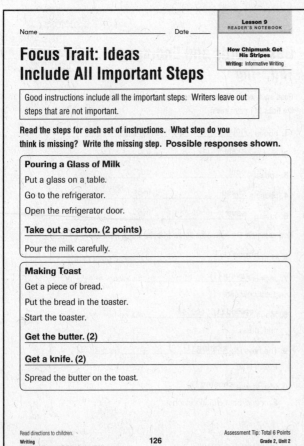

Name _____ Date _____

Lesson 9
READER'S NOTEBOOK

How Chipmunk Got
His Stripes
Independent Reading

Reader's Guide

How Chipmunk Got His Stripes

Write a Newspaper Article

Newspapers have many different parts. One part is the advice column. In this part, you can write a letter telling your problem. Other people write back telling you what they think you should do. Use examples from the text to help these kids solve their problems.

Read page 311. What would Grandmother tell the writer?

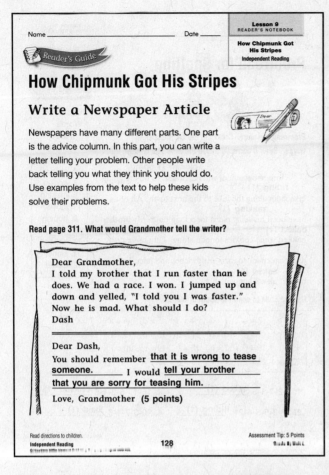

Dear Grandmother,
I told my brother that I run faster than he does. We had a race. I won. I jumped up and down and yelled, "I told you I was faster." Now he is mad. What should I do?
Dash

Dear Dash,
You should remember <u>that it is wrong to tease someone.</u> I would <u>tell your brother that you are sorry for teasing him.</u>

Love, Grandmother **(5 points)**

Read directions to children.
Independent Reading
© Houghton Mifflin Harcourt Publishing Company. All rights reserved.
128
Assessment Tip: 5 Points
Grade 2, Unit 2

Name _____ Date _____

Lesson 9
READER'S NOTEBOOK

How Chipmunk Got
His Stripes
Independent Reading

Read page 313. What would Bear tell the writer?

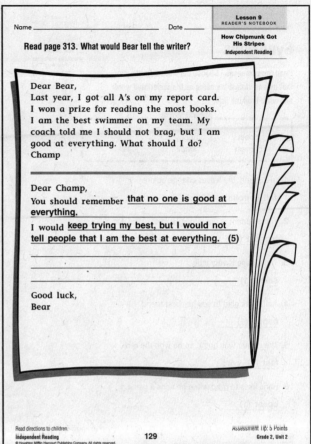

Dear Bear,
Last year, I got all A's on my report card. I won a prize for reading the most books. I am the best swimmer on my team. My coach told me I should not brag, but I am good at everything. What should I do?
Champ

Dear Champ,
You should remember <u>that no one is good at everything.</u>
I would <u>keep trying my best, but I would not tell people that I am the best at everything.</u> **(5)**

Good luck,
Bear

Read directions to children.
Independent Reading
© Houghton Mifflin Harcourt Publishing Company. All rights reserved.
129
Assessment Tip: 5 Points
Grade 2, Unit 2

Name _____ Date _____

Lesson 9
READER'S NOTEBOOK

How Chipmunk Got
His Stripes
Spelling: -ed and -ing Endings

-ed and -ing Endings

Use a Spelling Word to complete each sentence. (1 point each)

1. We <u>chased</u> the ball down the street.

2. You <u>liked</u> the play, didn't you?

3. We always keep that door <u>closed</u> .

4. Matt was <u>hoping</u> he could go to the game.

5. On the first day of school, Ms. Bell <u>asked</u> us our names.

6. The game is over, but Ivan is still <u>hiding</u> in the closet.

7. My dog enjoys <u>sleeping</u> near my bed at night.

Write the Spelling Word that best matches each set of clues.

8. bike, horse, bus <u>riding</u>

9. leak, drip, tip over <u>spilled</u>

10. bread, pie, muffins <u>baked</u>

11. sit, walk, dance <u>standing</u>

12. doze, nap, dream <u>sleeping</u>

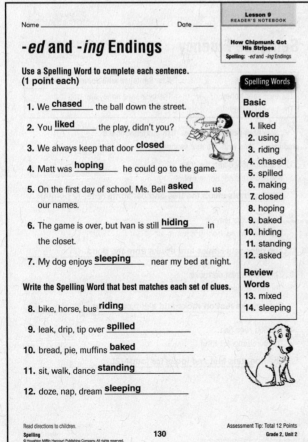

Spelling Words

Basic Words
1. liked
2. using
3. riding
4. chased
5. spilled
6. making
7. closed
8. hoping
9. baked
10. hiding
11. standing
12. asked

Review Words
13. mixed
14. sleeping

Read directions to children.
Spelling
© Houghton Mifflin Harcourt Publishing Company. All rights reserved.
130
Assessment Tip: Total 12 Points
Grade 2, Unit 2

Name _____ Date _____

Lesson 9
READER'S NOTEBOOK

How Chipmunk Got
His Stripes
Grammar: Verbs in the Present

Verbs with -s and -es

Draw a line under the verb that completes each sentence correctly.

1. The bear (walk, <u>walks</u>) through the woods. **(1 point)**

2. The snake (slide, <u>slides</u>) on the ground. **(1)**

3. The rabbit (hop, <u>hops</u>) though the grass. **(1)**

4. The mouse (run, <u>runs</u>) through the field. **(1)**

Write the verb correctly to go with the naming part of the sentence.

5. Chipmunk <u>mixes (1)</u> the stew. (mix)

6. Squirrel <u>reaches (1)</u> for a spoon. (reach)

7. Bear <u>rushes (1)</u> to eat. (rush)

8. Bear <u>wishes (1)</u> he had more. (wish)

Read directions to children.
Grammar
© Houghton Mifflin Harcourt Publishing Company. All rights reserved.
131
Assessment Tip: Total 8 Points
Grade 2, Unit 2

Synonyms

Name _____ Date _____

Lesson 9
READER'S NOTEBOOK

How Chipmunk Got
His Stripes
Vocabulary Strategies:
Synonyms

Read the sentences. Choose the word from the box that means almost the same as the underlined word and write it on the line.

Word Bank

boast	happy	fast
biggest	small	fall

1. In autumn, the leaves change colors.

   fall (1 point)

2. The elephant is the largest animal at the zoo.

   biggest (1)

3. The mouse is very little.

   small (1)

4. Anita was glad to see her best friend.

   happy (1)

5. The runner was quick, so he won the race.

   fast (1)

6. Hans likes to brag when he wins a game.

   boast (1)

Read directions to children.
Vocabulary Strategies
© Houghton Mifflin Harcourt Publishing Company. All rights reserved.
132
Assessment Tip: Total 6 Points
Grade 2, Unit 2

Proofread for Spelling

Name _____ Date _____

Lesson 9
READER'S NOTEBOOK

How Chipmunk Got
His Stripes
Spelling: -ed and -ing Endings

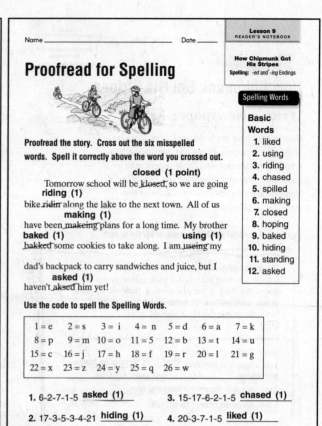

Proofread the story. Cross out the six misspelled words. Spell it correctly above the word you crossed out.

Spelling Words

Basic Words
1. liked
2. using
3. riding
4. chased
5. spilled
6. making
7. closed
8. hoping
9. baked
10. hiding
11. standing
12. asked

closed (1 point)
Tomorrow school will be klosed, so we are going
riding (1)
bike ridin along the lake to the next town. All of us
making (1)
have been makeing plans for a long time. My brother
baked (1)   **using (1)**
bakked some cookies to take along. I am useing my

dad's backpack to carry sandwiches and juice, but I
asked (1)
haven't aksed him yet!

Use the code to spell the Spelling Words.

1 = e	2 = s	3 = i	4 = n	5 = d	6 = a	7 = k
8 = p	9 = m	10 = o	11 = 5	12 = b	13 = t	14 = u
15 = c	16 = j	17 = h	18 = f	19 = r	20 = l	21 = g
22 = x	23 = z	24 = y	25 = q	26 = w		

1. 6-2-7-1-5 **asked (1)**   3. 15-17-6-2-1-5 **chased (1)**

2. 17-3-5-3-4-21 **hiding (1)**   4. 20-3-7-1-5 **liked (1)**

Read directions to children.
Spelling
© Houghton Mifflin Harcourt Publishing Company. All rights reserved.
133
Assessment Tip: Total 10 Points
Grade 2, Unit 2

Kinds of Nouns

Name _____ Date _____

Lesson 9
READER'S NOTEBOOK

How Chipmunk Got
His Stripes
Grammar: Spiral Review

Draw a line under the noun in each sentence. Write whether it names a person, place, thing, or animal.

1. The dog growls. **animal (2 points)**

2. The tree stands tall. **thing (2)**

3. Sally looks out. **person (2)**

4. The yard is busy. **place (2)**

Read the paragraph. Write a noun from the box in place of each underlined noun.

forest	mouse	owl	rock

The place is dark. An owl looks for food to eat. It sees a mouse near a big thing. The owl swoops down and lands on the rock. It wants to catch the animal. The mouse quickly scurries into a small space under the rock. It is safe! The animal flies back up to its nest.

5. place **forest (2)**   7. animal **mouse (2)**

6. thing **rock (2)**   8. animal **owl (2)**

Read directions to children.
Grammar
© Houghton Mifflin Harcourt Publishing Company. All rights reserved.
134
Assessment Tip: Total 16 Points
Grade 2, Unit 2

Sentence Fluency

Name _____ Date _____

Lesson 9
READER'S NOTEBOOK

How Chipmunk Got
His Stripes
Grammar: Connect to Writing

Short Sentences	New Sentence with Joined Predicates
The bear sees honey. The bear eats it all.	The bear sees honey and eats it all.

Join each pair of sentences. Use and between the predicates. Then write the new sentence.

1. The squirrels climb the tree.
   The squirrels eat some nuts.

   The squirrels climb the tree and eat some nuts. (2 points)

2. The deer eats leaves.
   The deer drinks from the pond.

   The deer eats leaves and drinks from the pond. (2)

3. Chipmunks rest on rocks.
   Chipmunks sleep on leaves.

   Chipmunks rest on rocks and sleep on leaves. (2)

4. The lion runs fast.
   The lion looks for food.

   The lion runs fast and looks for food. (2)

Read directions to children.
Grammar
© Houghton Mifflin Harcourt Publishing Company. All rights reserved.
135
Assessment Tip: Total 8 Points
Grade 2, Unit 2

Panel 1 (top-left)

Contractions

Put the words together to write contractions. Then read each contraction.

1. you + are = **you're (1 point)** _____
2. is + not = **isn't (1)** _____
3. we + will = **we'll (1)** _____
4. it + is = **it's (1)** _____
5. do + not = **don't (1)** _____
6. I + am = **I'm (1)** _____

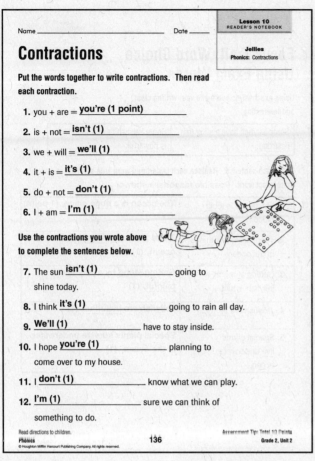

Use the contractions you wrote above to complete the sentences below.

7. The sun **isn't (1)** _____ going to shine today.
8. I think **it's (1)** _____ going to rain all day.
9. **We'll (1)** _____ have to stay inside.
10. I hope **you're (1)** _____ planning to come over to my house.
11. I **don't (1)** _____ know what we can play.
12. **I'm (1)** _____ sure we can think of something to do.

Read directions to children.
Phonics
© Houghton Mifflin Harcourt Publishing Company. All rights reserved.
136
Assessment Tip: Total 10 Points
Grade 2, Unit 2

Panel 2 (top-right)

Past Tense Verbs with -ed

Some **verbs** name actions that are happening now. Other **verbs** name actions that happened before now, or in the past. Add -ed to most verbs to show that the action happened in the past.

Yesterday the jellyfish (float, <u>floated</u>) in the water.

Thinking Question
When does or did the action happen?

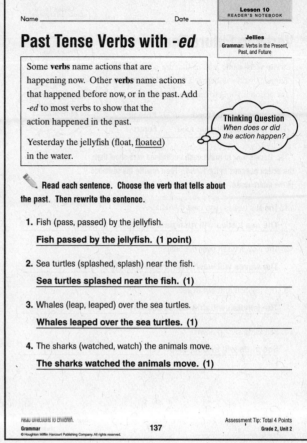

✎ Read each sentence. Choose the verb that tells about the past. Then rewrite the sentence.

1. Fish (pass, passed) by the jellyfish.
   Fish passed by the jellyfish. (1 point) _____

2. Sea turtles (splashed, splash) near the fish.
   Sea turtles splashed near the fish. (1) _____

3. Whales (leap, leaped) over the sea turtles.
   Whales leaped over the sea turtles. (1) _____

4. The sharks (watched, watch) the animals move.
   The sharks watched the animals move. (1) _____

Read directions to children.
Grammar
© Houghton Mifflin Harcourt Publishing Company. All rights reserved.
137
Assessment Tip: Total 4 Points
Grade 2, Unit 2

Panel 3 (bottom-left)

Contractions

Use the two words below the line to make a contraction. Write the contraction on the line. Then read each completed sentence.

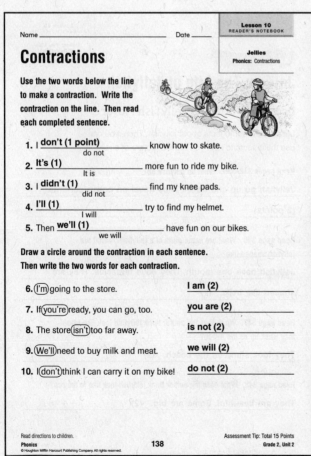

1. I **don't (1 point)** _____ know how to skate.
   do not

2. **It's (1)** _____ more fun to ride my bike.
   It is

3. I **didn't (1)** _____ find my knee pads.
   did not

4. **I'll (1)** _____ try to find my helmet.
   I will

5. Then **we'll (1)** _____ have fun on our bikes.
   we will

Draw a circle around the contraction in each sentence. Then write the two words for each contraction.

6. (I'm) going to the store.   **I am (2)** _____
7. If (you're) ready, you can go, too.   **you are (2)** _____
8. The store (isn't) too far away.   **is not (2)** _____
9. (We'll) need to buy milk and meat.   **we will (2)** _____
10. I (don't) think I can carry it on my bike!   **do not (2)** _____

Read directions to children.
Phonics
© Houghton Mifflin Harcourt Publishing Company. All rights reserved.
138
Assessment Tip: Total 15 Points
Grade 2, Unit 2

Panel 4 (bottom-right)

Contractions

Sort the Spelling Words by the word that is shortened to make each contraction. The first one is done for you.

with *not*	with *is*	with *have*
don't	**it's (1)**	**you've (1)**
isn't (1 point)	**that's (1)**	**I've (1)**
can't (1)		
didn't (1)		
wasn't (1)		

with *am*	with *will*	with *are*
I'm (1)	**we'll (1)**	**you're (1)**
	he'll (1)	**they're (1)**
		we're (1)

Spelling Words

Basic Words
1. I'm
2. don't
3. isn't
4. can't
5. we'll
6. it's
7. I've
8. didn't
9. you're
10. that's
11. wasn't
12. you've

Review Words
13. us
14. them

Then add three contractions that you know to any of the lists.
Possible responses shown: he'll, they're, we're

Read directions to children.
Spelling
© Houghton Mifflin Harcourt Publishing Company. All rights reserved.
139
Assessment Tip: Total 14 Points
Grade 2, Unit 2

Verbs in Future Tense

Some **verbs** name actions that are going to happen. Add *will* before a verb to show that the action is going to happen in the future.

The sea turtles <u>want</u> food.　**Present**
The sea turtles <u>will want</u> food.　**Future**

> **Thinking Question**
> How can I make the verb tell about a future action?

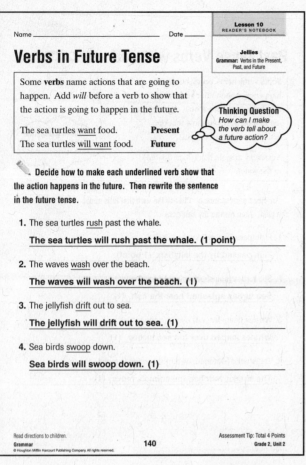

Decide how to make each underlined verb show that the action happens in the future. Then rewrite the sentence in the future tense.

1. The sea turtles <u>rush</u> past the whale.
   The sea turtles will rush past the whale. (1 point)

2. The waves <u>wash</u> over the beach.
   The waves will wash over the beach. (1)

3. The jellyfish <u>drift</u> out to sea.
   The jellyfish will drift out to sea. (1)

4. Sea birds <u>swoop</u> down.
   Sea birds will swoop down. (1)

Read directions to children.
Grammar
140
Assessment Tip: Total 4 Points
Grade 2, Unit 2
© Houghton Mifflin Harcourt Publishing Company. All rights reserved.

Focus Trait: Word Choice Using Exact Words

Using exact words can make your writing clear and interesting.

| Some jellyfish have a sting that is <u>strong</u>. | Some jellyfish have a sting that is <u>powerful</u>. |

Read each sentence. Replace each underlined word with a more exact word. Possible responses shown.

1. The ocean is a <u>big</u> place.	The ocean is a <u>huge</u> place. (1 point)
2. There are many <u>things</u> in the ocean.	There are many <u>animals</u> in the ocean. (1)
3. Getting stung by a jellyfish is <u>bad</u>.	Getting stung by a jellyfish is <u>painful</u>. (1)
4. Jellyfish are <u>pretty</u>.	Jellyfish are <u>beautiful</u>. (1)
5. Special plants <u>live</u> underwater in the ocean.	Special plants <u>survive</u> underwater in the ocean. (1)

Read directions to children.
Writing
141
Assessment Tip: Total 5 Points
Grade 2, Unit 2
© Houghton Mifflin Harcourt Publishing Company. All rights reserved.

Cumulative Review

Read each sentence. Choose the word from the box that completes each sentence and write the word on the line. Then read each completed sentence.

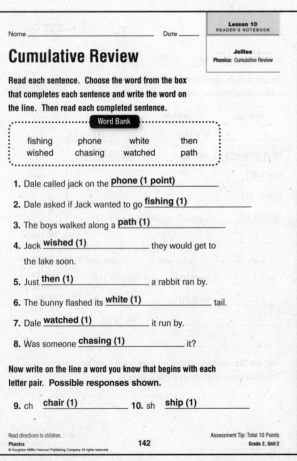

Word Bank

fishing	phone	white	then
wished	chasing	watched	path

1. Dale called Jack on the **phone (1 point)** _____
2. Dale asked if Jack wanted to go **fishing (1)**
3. The boys walked along a **path (1)** _____
4. Jack **wished (1)** _____ they would get to the lake soon.
5. Just **then (1)** _____, a rabbit ran by.
6. The bunny flashed its **white (1)** _____ tail.
7. Dale **watched (1)** _____ it run by.
8. Was someone **chasing (1)** _____ it?

Now write on the line a word you know that begins with each letter pair. Possible responses shown.

9. ch **chair (1)** _____　10. sh **ship (1)** _____

Read directions to children.
Phonics
142
Assessment Tip: Total 10 Points
Grade 2, Unit 2
© Houghton Mifflin Harcourt Publishing Company. All rights reserved.

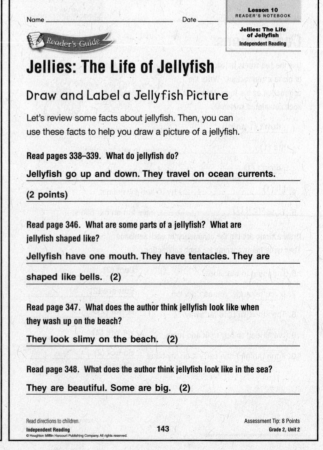 Reader's Guide

Jellies: The Life of Jellyfish

Draw and Label a Jellyfish Picture

Let's review some facts about jellyfish. Then, you can use these facts to help you draw a picture of a jellyfish.

Read pages 338–339. What do jellyfish do?
Jellyfish go up and down. They travel on ocean currents.

(2 points)

Read page 346. What are some parts of a jellyfish? What are jellyfish shaped like?
Jellyfish have one mouth. They have tentacles. They are

shaped like bells. (2)

Read page 347. What does the author think jellyfish look like when they wash up on the beach?
They look slimy on the beach. (2)

Read page 348. What does the author think jellyfish look like in the sea?
They are beautiful. Some are big. (2)

Read directions to children.
Independent Reading
143
Assessment Tip: 8 Points
Grade 2, Unit 2
© Houghton Mifflin Harcourt Publishing Company. All rights reserved.

Name _____ Date _____

Lesson 10
READER'S NOTEBOOK

Jellies: The Life
of Jellyfish
Independent Reading

Did you see a jellyfish that you thought was really interesting? Draw a picture of the jellyfish below. Make labels near parts of the jellyfish and tell how the jellyfish looks and acts.

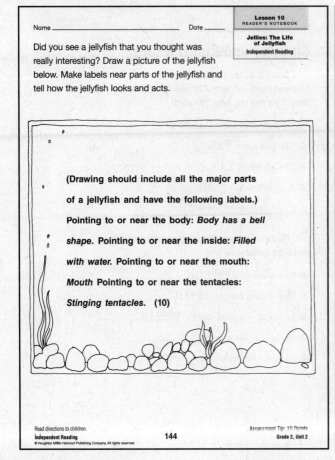

(Drawing should include all the major parts of a jellyfish and have the following labels.)
Pointing to or near the body: *Body has a bell shape.* Pointing to or near the inside: *Filled with water.* Pointing to or near the mouth: *Mouth* Pointing to or near the tentacles: *Stinging tentacles.* **(10)**

Contractions

Write the Spelling Word that has the same meaning.

1. you are **you're (1 point)**
2. cannot **can't (1)**
3. I am **I'm (1)**
4. is not **isn't (1)**
5. we will **we'll (1)**
6. you have **you've (1)**
7. it is **it's (1)**
8. I have **I've (1)**

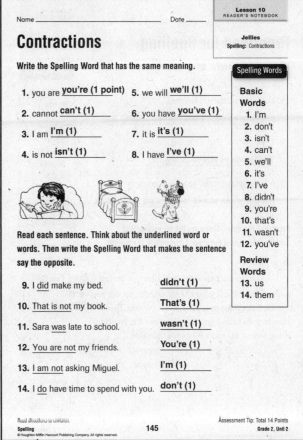

Read each sentence. Think about the underlined word or words. Then write the Spelling Word that makes the sentence say the opposite.

9. I <u>did</u> make my bed. **didn't (1)**
10. <u>That is</u> not my book. **That's (1)**
11. Sara <u>was</u> late to school. **wasn't (1)**
12. <u>You are</u> not my friends. **You're (1)**
13. <u>I am</u> not asking Miguel. **I'm (1)**
14. I <u>do</u> have time to spend with you. **don't (1)**

Spelling Words
Basic Words
1. I'm
2. don't
3. isn't
4. can't
5. we'll
6. it's
7. I've
8. didn't
9. you're
10. that's
11. wasn't
12. you've
Review Words
13. us
14. them

Name _____ Date _____

Lesson 10
READER'S NOTEBOOK

Jellies
Grammar: Verbs in the Present,
Past, and Future

Present, Past, and Future Tense

Rewrite each sentence. Change the verb so it is tense shown in parentheses.

1. The sea animals <u>want</u> food. (past tense)

   The sea animals wanted food. (1 point)

2. The crabs <u>searched</u> for small fish. (present tense)

   The crabs search for small fish. (1)

3. The jellyfish <u>look</u> under a big rock. (past tense)

   The jellyfish looked under a big rock. (1)

4. Waves <u>wash</u> away the sand castle. (future tense)

   Waves will wash away the sand castle. (1)

5. Max and Beth <u>play</u> in the water. (future tense)

   Max and Beth will play in the water. (1)

6. They <u>peek</u> inside a shell. (future tense)

   They will peek inside a shell. (1)

Name _____ Date _____

Lesson 10
READER'S NOTEBOOK

Jellies
Vocabulary Strategies:
Suffixes -er, -est

Suffixes -er, -est

Circle the comparing word that completes each sentence.

1. A mouse is (smaller) smallest than a cat. **(2 points)**
2. I am going to exercise so I can get (stronger) strongest. **(2)**
3. That is the bigger (biggest) spider I have ever seen! **(2)**
4. Being sick made me feel (weaker) weakest than I did before. **(2)**
5. Juan wants to be the smarter (smartest) student in the class. **(2)**
6. That side of the pool is (shallower) shallowest than this side. **(2)**
7. Chocolate is the sweeter (sweetest) kind of ice cream. **(2)**

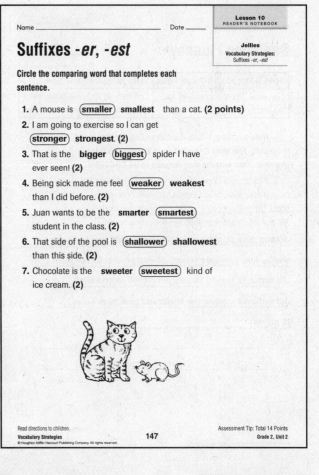

Proofread for Spelling

Rewrite each sentence. Use two contractions in each sentence.

1. I am sure he did not see me.

   I'm sure he didn't see me. (2 points)

2. That is where you are going.

   That's where you're going. (2)

3. It is our class picnic, so we will go early.

   It's our class picnic, so we'll go early. (2)

Proofread the note. Cross out the six misspelled contractions. Spell each word correctly in the margin.

Dear Pam,

I ~~kan't~~ **can't, I've (2)** go tomorrow because ~~I ave~~ got too much homework. I know ~~yo uve~~ **you've (1)** been counting on me. Maybe I can come over later in the evening. Then ~~wi'll~~ **we'll (1)** have time to talk. I hope ~~its~~ OK. I ~~am~~ **it's, I'm (2)** going to start my math problems right now.

Sincerely,

Carmen

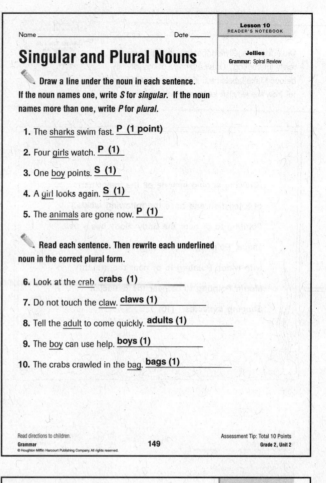

Read directions to children.
Spelling
© Houghton Mifflin Harcourt Publishing Company. All rights reserved.
148
Assessment Tip: Total 12 Points
Grade 2, Unit 2

Singular and Plural Nouns

Draw a line under the noun in each sentence. If the noun names one, write *S* for *singular*. If the noun names more than one, write *P* for *plural*.

1. The <u>sharks</u> swim fast. **P (1 point)**

2. Four <u>girls</u> watch. **P (1)**

3. One <u>boy</u> points. **S (1)**

4. A <u>girl</u> looks again. **S (1)**

5. The <u>animals</u> are gone now. **P (1)**

Read each sentence. Then rewrite each underlined noun in the correct plural form.

6. Look at the <u>crab</u>. **crabs (1)**

7. Do not touch the <u>claw</u>. **claws (1)**

8. Tell the <u>adult</u> to come quickly. **adults (1)**

9. The <u>boy</u> can use help. **boys (1)**

10. The crabs crawled in the <u>bag</u>. **bags (1)**

Read directions to children.
Grammar
© Houghton Mifflin Harcourt Publishing Company. All rights reserved.
149
Assessment Tip: Total 10 Points
Grade 2, Unit 2

Sentence Fluency

Verbs Telling About Different Times	Verbs Telling the Same Time
Last week Jill and Jake <u>walked</u> on the beach. They <u>play</u> in the water.	Last week Jill and Jake <u>walked</u> on the beach. They <u>played</u> in the water.

Read this story. It tells about something that happened in the past. Five verbs do not tell about the past. Fix these five verbs. Then write the story correctly on the lines below.

Jill and Jake skipped along the shore. Jake saw two large shells. Jake point to them. Jill rush over to see them. Jill and Jake look closely. Jill pick up one shell. Jill and Jake wash the shells and took them home.

Jill and Jake skipped along the shore. Jake saw two large

shells. Jake <u>pointed</u> to them. Jill <u>rushed</u> over to see them.

Jill and Jake <u>looked</u> closely. Jill <u>picked</u> up one shell.

Jill and Jake <u>washed</u> the shells and took them home.

(5 points)

_____

_____

Read directions to children.
Grammar
© Houghton Mifflin Harcourt Publishing Company. All rights reserved.
150
Assessment Tip: Total 5 Points
Grade 2, Unit 2

Name _____ Date _____

Unit 2
READER'S NOTEBOOK

Poppleton in Winter
Segment 1
Independent Reading

Reader's Guide

Poppleton in Winter

Interview with Patrick

Read pages 11–15. If news reporters interviewed Patrick about his day, what would he say? Read the questions below. Write the answers Patrick would give. Include details from the text and illustrations.

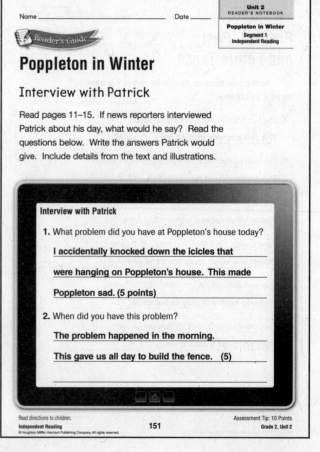

Interview with Patrick

1. What problem did you have at Poppleton's house today?

   I accidentally knocked down the icicles that

   were hanging on Poppleton's house. This made

   Poppleton sad. (5 points)

2. When did you have this problem?

   The problem happened in the morning.

   This gave us all day to build the fence. (5)

Read directions to children.
Independent Reading
© Houghton Mifflin Harcourt Publishing Company. All rights reserved.
151
Assessment Tip: 10 Points
Grade 2, Unit 2

Name _____ Date _____

Unit 2
READER'S NOTEBOOK

Poppleton in Winter
Segment 1
Independent Reading

Now answer questions about the events from Poppleton's point of view. Include details from the text and illustrations on pages 11–15.

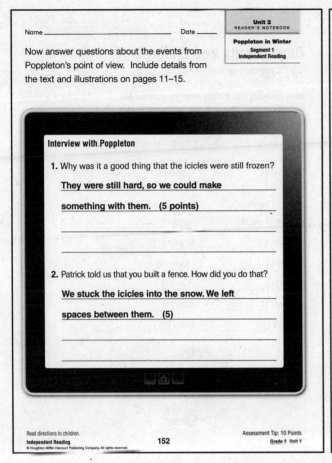

Interview with Poppleton

1. Why was it a good thing that the icicles were still frozen?

   They were still hard, so we could make

   something with them.   (5 points)

   _____

   _____

2. Patrick told us that you built a fence. How did you do that?

   We stuck the icicles into the snow. We left

   spaces between them.   (5)

   _____

Read directions to children.
Independent Reading
© Houghton Mifflin Harcourt Publishing Company. All rights reserved.
152
Assessment Tip: 10 Points
Grade 2, Unit 2

Name _____ Date _____

Unit 2
READER'S NOTEBOOK

Poppleton in Winter
Segment 2
Independent Reading

Reader's Guide

Poppleton in Winter

Letters to a Friend

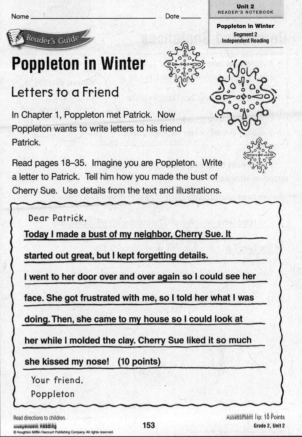

In Chapter 1, Poppleton met Patrick. Now Poppleton wants to write letters to his friend Patrick.

Read pages 18–35. Imagine you are Poppleton. Write a letter to Patrick. Tell him how you made the bust of Cherry Sue. Use details from the text and illustrations.

Dear Patrick,

Today I made a bust of my neighbor, Cherry Sue. It

started out great, but I kept forgetting details.

I went to her door over and over again so I could see her

face. She got frustrated with me, so I told her what I was

doing. Then, she came to my house so I could look at

her while I molded the clay. Cherry Sue liked it so much

she kissed my nose!   (10 points)

Your friend,
Poppleton

Read directions to children.
Independent Reading
© Houghton Mifflin Harcourt Publishing Company. All rights reserved.
153
Assessment Tip: 10 Points
Grade 2, Unit 2

Name _____ Date _____

Unit 2
READER'S NOTEBOOK

Poppleton in Winter
Segment 2
Independent Reading

Read pages 36–48. Write another letter from Poppleton. Tell Patrick about your birthday. Include details that tell how you felt at the beginning and at the end of the day.

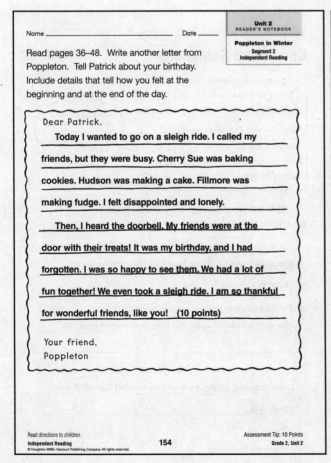

Dear Patrick,

   Today I wanted to go on a sleigh ride. I called my

friends, but they were busy. Cherry Sue was baking

cookies. Hudson was making a cake. Fillmore was

making fudge. I felt disappointed and lonely.

   Then, I heard the doorbell. My friends were at the

door with their treats! It was my birthday, and I had

forgotten. I was so happy to see them. We had a lot of

fun together! We even took a sleigh ride. I am so thankful

for wonderful friends, like you!   (10 points)

Your friend,
Poppleton

Read directions to children.
Independent Reading
© Houghton Mifflin Harcourt Publishing Company. All rights reserved.
154
Assessment Tip: 10 Points
Grade 2, Unit 2

Name _____ Date _____

Lesson 11
READER'S NOTEBOOK

Click, Clack, Moo:
Cows That Type
Phonics: Base Words and
Endings -s, -es

Base Words and Endings
-s, -es

Put the letters together to write a base word.
Then add the ending -s or -es.

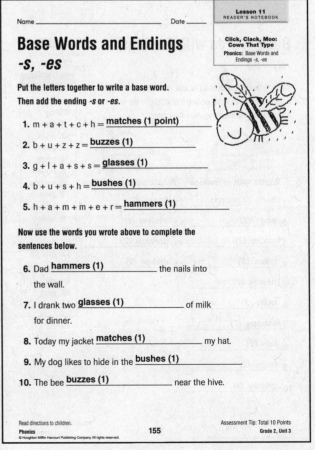

1. m + a + t + c + h = **matches (1 point)**

2. b + u + z + z = **buzzes (1)**

3. g + l + a + s + s = **glasses (1)**

4. b + u + s + h = **bushes (1)**

5. h + a + m + m + e + r = **hammers (1)**

Now use the words you wrote above to complete the sentences below.

6. Dad **hammers (1)** _____ the nails into the wall.

7. I drank two **glasses (1)** _____ of milk for dinner.

8. Today my jacket **matches (1)** _____ my hat.

9. My dog likes to hide in the **bushes (1)** _____

10. The bee **buzzes (1)** _____ near the hive.

Read directions to children.
Phonics
© Houghton Mifflin Harcourt Publishing Company. All rights reserved.
155
Assessment Tip: Total 10 Points
Grade 2, Unit 3

Name _____ Date _____

Lesson 11
READER'S NOTEBOOK

Click, Clack, Moo:
Cows That Type
Grammar: Compound Sentences

Compound Sentences

- A **compound sentence** is made up of two shorter sentences joined by and, but, or or.

The cows got blankets, but Duck kept the typewriter.

- A comma is used before the joining word.

> **Thinking Question**
> Is the sentence made up of two shorter sentences joined by and, but, or or?

✏ Draw a line under each shorter sentence in the compound sentences.

1. The cows wanted blankets, and Farmer Brown said, "No way."
   (2 points)

2. The cows went on strike, and Farmer Brown was upset. (2)

3. The hens had nests, but they were still cold. (2)

4. Farmer Brown needs milk and eggs, or he can't run his farm. (2)

5. Duck took the typewriter, and he decided to keep it. (2)

Read directions to children.
Grammar
156
Assessment Tip: Total 10 Points
Grade 2, Unit 3
© Houghton Mifflin Harcourt Publishing Company. All rights reserved.

Name _____ Date _____

Lesson 11
READER'S NOTEBOOK

Click, Clack, Moo:
Cows That Type
Phonics: Base Words and
Endings -s, -es

Base Words and Endings
-s, -es

Write the words from the box under the word that has the same ending. Then write two more words of your own in each column. Possible responses shown.

Word Bank

eggs	trucks	brushes	fixes
wishes	tigers	pinches	rafts

lunches	chicks
wishes (1 point)	eggs (1)
brushes (1)	trucks (1)
pinches (1)	tigers (1)
fixes (1)	rafts (1)
passes (1)	cats (1)
catches (1)	birds (1)

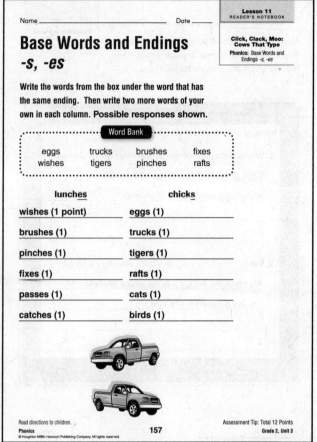

Read directions to children.
Phonics
157
Assessment Tip: Total 12 Points
Grade 2, Unit 3
© Houghton Mifflin Harcourt Publishing Company. All rights reserved.

Name _____ Date _____

Lesson 11
READER'S NOTEBOOK

Click, Clack, Moo:
Cows That Type
Spelling: Base Words with
Endings -s, -es

Base Words with Endings
-s, -es

Sort the Spelling Words by -s and -es endings. Then draw a line under each word ending that changed the word from meaning one to meaning more than one.

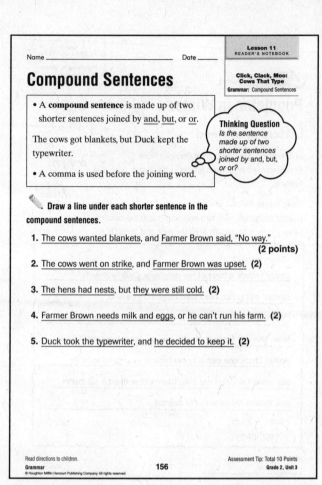

Words with -s Endings

1. hens (2 points)
2. eggs (2)
3. ducks (2)
4. bikes (2)
5. names (2)
6. bells (2)
7. stamps (2)
8. jets (2)
9. frogs (2)
10. grapes (2)

Words with -es Endings

11. boxes (2)
12. wishes (2)
13. dresses (2)
14. dishes (2)

Spelling Words

Basic Words
1. hens
2. eggs
3. ducks
4. bikes
5. boxes
6. wishes
7. dresses
8. names
9. bells
10. stamps
11. dishes
12. grapes

Review Words
13. jets
14. frogs

Read directions to children.
Spelling
158
Assessment Tip: Total 28 Points
Grade 2, Unit 3
© Houghton Mifflin Harcourt Publishing Company. All rights reserved.

Name _____ Date _____

Lesson 11
READER'S NOTEBOOK

Click, Clack, Moo:
Cows That Type
Grammar: Compound Sentences

Compound Sentences

- A **compound sentence** is made up of two shorter sentences joined by and, but, or or.
- A comma is used before the joining word.

The cows found an old typewriter.

The cows learned to type.

The cows found an old typewriter, and they learned to type.

> **Thinking Question**
> How can sentences be combined to make writing less choppy?

✏ Write each pair of sentences as a compound sentence.
Use a comma and a joining word.

1. The ducks need a diving board. The ducks will be bored.

   The ducks need a diving board, or they will be bored.

   (2 points)

2. The ducks liked to swim. The ducks preferred to dive.

   The ducks liked to swim, but they preferred to dive. (2)

3. Duck knocked on the door. Duck handed Farmer Brown a note.

   Duck knocked on the door, and he handed Farmer Brown

   a note. (2)

Read directions to children.
Grammar
159
Assessment Tip: Total 6 Points
Grade 2, Unit 3
© Houghton Mifflin Harcourt Publishing Company. All rights reserved.

Name _____ Date _____

Lesson 11
READER'S NOTEBOOK

Click, Clack, Moo:
Cows That Type
Writing: Opinion Writing

Focus Trait: Ideas
Stating a Clear Goal

Not a Clear Goal	Clear Goal
I would like you to <u>do something</u>.	I would like you to **take me to the park next weekend.**

A. Read each goal that is not clear. Fill in the blanks to state each goal more clearly. Possible responses shown.

Not a Clear Goal	Clear Goal
1. I would like you to buy <u>something</u> for our computer lab.	I would like you to buy **a computer** for our computer lab. **(2 points)**
2. I want you to send me <u>stuff</u> for a project.	I want you to send me **magazines** for a project. **(2)**

B. Read each goal that is not clear. Add a word or words to make the goal more clear. Write your new sentences.

Possible responses shown.

Not a Clear Goal	Clear Goal
3. We would like you to <u>do us a favor</u>.	**We would like you to take class photos for us. (2)**
4. I am writing to ask you to <u>do something</u> for the music room.	**I am writing to ask you to give us CDs for the music room. (2)**

Read directions to children.
Writing
© Houghton Mifflin Harcourt Publishing Company. All rights reserved.
160
Assessment Tip: Total 8 Points
Grade 2, Unit 3

Name _____ Date _____

Lesson 11
READER'S NOTEBOOK

Click, Clack, Moo:
Cows That Type
Phonics: Cumulative Review

Cumulative Review

Write the word that goes in each sentence.

> **Word Bank**
> cider   fever   later   virus

1. Jack has a <u>virus (1 point)</u> that makes him sick.

2. Mom says his <u>fever (1)</u> is very high.

3. "You can sit with Jack <u>later (1)</u> today," said Mom.

4. "I'll warm up some <u>cider (1)</u> for both of you," said Mom.

Write the words that make up each underlined contraction.

5. "I <u>won't</u> have lunch with Sam today," said Jack.

   <u>will not (2)</u>

6. "<u>I'll</u> tell Sam you miss him, Jack," I said.

   <u>I will (2)</u>

7. "<u>You're</u> a good sister," said Jack.

   <u>you are (2)</u>

Read directions to children
Phonics
© Houghton Mifflin Harcourt Publishing Company. All rights reserved.
161
Assessment Tip: Total 10 Points
Grade 2, Unit 3

Name _____ Date _____

Lesson 11
READER'S NOTEBOOK

Click, Clack, Moo:
Cows That Type
Independent Reading

Reader's Guide

Click, Clack, Moo:
Cows That Type

Make a Cartoon

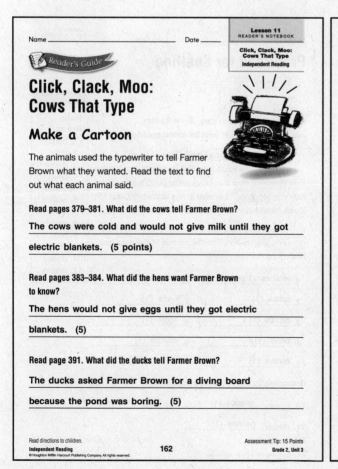

The animals used the typewriter to tell Farmer Brown what they wanted. Read the text to find out what each animal said.

Read pages 379–381. What did the cows tell Farmer Brown?

The cows were cold and would not give milk until they got

electric blankets. (5 points)

Read pages 383–384. What did the hens want Farmer Brown to know?

The hens would not give eggs until they got electric

blankets. (5)

Read page 391. What did the ducks tell Farmer Brown?

The ducks asked Farmer Brown for a diving board

because the pond was boring. (5)

Read directions to children.
Independent Reading
© Houghton Mifflin Harcourt Publishing Company. All rights reserved.
162
Assessment Tip: 15 Points
Grade 2, Unit 3

Name _____ Date _____

Lesson 11
READER'S NOTEBOOK

Click, Clack, Moo:
Cows That Type
Independent Reading

Which was your favorite animal? What if Farmer Brown and that animal could talk to each other? What would they say? Use the examples from the text and illustrations you found to make a cartoon. Use speech bubbles to show what Farmer Brown and the animal might say.

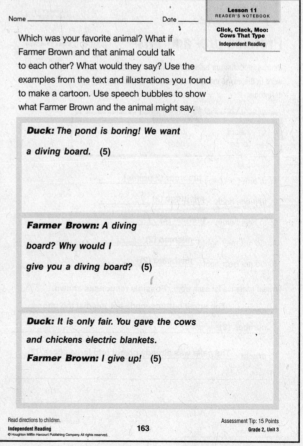

Duck: The pond is boring! We want a diving board. (5)

Farmer Brown: A diving board? Why would I give you a diving board? (5)

Duck: It is only fair. You gave the cows and chickens electric blankets.
Farmer Brown: I give up! (5)

Read directions to children.
Independent Reading
© Houghton Mifflin Harcourt Publishing Company. All rights reserved.
163
Assessment Tip: 15 Points
Grade 2, Unit 3

Name _____ Date _____

Lesson 11
READER'S NOTEBOOK

Click, Clack, Moo:
Cows That Type
Spelling: Base Words with
Endings -s, -es

Base Words with Endings -s, -es

Write the Spelling Word or Spelling Words that match each clue.

1. These are animals. hens (1 point)
   ducks (1)   frogs (1)

2. You can eat these. eggs (1)
   grapes (1)

3. Put things inside these. boxes (1)

4. Put food on these. dishes (1)

5. Ride on these. bikes (1)

6. These ring. bells (1)

7. These are airplanes. jets (1)

8. You hope these come true. wishes (1)

9. Girls sometimes wear these. dresses (1)

10. Put these on letters. stamps (1)

11. We give pets these. names (1)

Read directions to children.
Spelling
© Houghton Mifflin Harcourt Publishing Company. All rights reserved.
164
Assessment Tip: Total 14 Points
Grade 2, Unit 3

Name _____ Date _____

Lesson 11
READER'S NOTEBOOK

Click, Clack, Moo:
Cows That Type
Grammar: Compound Sentences

Compound Sentences

- A **compound sentence** is made up of two shorter sentences.
- The two shorter sentences are joined by and, but, or or.
- A comma is used before the joining word.

Farmer Brown was angry. Farmer Brown finally made a deal with the cows.

Farmer Brown was angry, but he finally made a deal with the cows.

Write each pair of sentences as a compound sentence.

1. The animals tried to listen. The animals couldn't understand Moo.

   The animals tried to listen, but they couldn't understand

   Moo. (2 points)

2. The cows had a meeting. The cows decided what to do.

   The cows had a meeting, and they decided what to do. (2)

3. The cows needed to be happy. The cows wouldn't give milk.

   The cows needed to be happy, or they wouldn't give

   milk. (2)

Read directions to children.
Grammar
© Houghton Mifflin Harcourt Publishing Company. All rights reserved.
165
Assessment Tip: Total 6 Points
Grade 2, Unit 3

Name _____ Date _____

Lesson 11
READER'S NOTEBOOK

Click, Clack, Moo:
Cows That Type
Vocabulary Strategies: Prefixes
pre- and mis-

Prefixes pre- and mis-

Read each definition below. Add mis- or pre- to a word in the box to make a new word that matches each definition.

Word Bank

| heard | judge | read |
| order | heat | |

1. to order before preorder (2 points)

2. to judge badly misjudge (2)

3. to heat before preheat (2)

4. did not read right misread (2)

5. did not hear right misheard (2)

Write a sentence for each word. Possible responses shown.

6. misdial The small buttons made her misdial the phone
   number. (2)

7. precut The cake was already precut into large slices. (2)

Read directions to children.
Vocabulary Strategies
© Houghton Mifflin Harcourt Publishing Company. All rights reserved.
166
Assessment Tip: Total 14 Points
Grade 2, Unit 3

Name _____ Date _____

Lesson 11
READER'S NOTEBOOK

Click, Clack, Moo:
Cows That Type
Spelling: Base Words with
Endings -s, -es

Proofread for Spelling

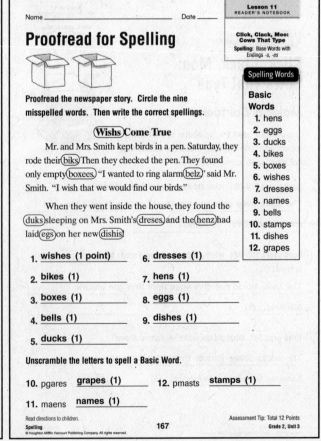

Proofread the newspaper story. Circle the nine misspelled words. Then write the correct spellings.

Wishs Come True

    Mr. and Mrs. Smith kept birds in a pen. Saturday, they rode their biks. Then they checked the pen. They found only empty boxees. "I wanted to ring alarm belz," said Mr. Smith. "I wish that we would find our birds."

    When they went inside the house, they found the duks sleeping on Mrs. Smith's dreses and the henz had laid egs on her new dishis.

1. wishes (1 point)   6. dresses (1)

2. bikes (1)   7. hens (1)

3. boxes (1)   8. eggs (1)

4. bells (1)   9. dishes (1)

5. ducks (1)

Unscramble the letters to spell a Basic Word.

10. pgares grapes (1)   12. pmasts stamps (1)

11. maens names (1)

Read directions to children.
Spelling
© Houghton Mifflin Harcourt Publishing Company. All rights reserved.
167
Assessment Tip: Total 12 Points
Grade 2, Unit 3

More Plural Nouns

Circle the noun that correctly shows more than one.

1. We eat (sandwichs, (sandwiches)) in the barn. **(1 point)**

2. Our (dresss, (dresses)) get dirty. **(1)**

3. The (mouses, (mice)) play in the hay. **(1)**

4. The (horse, (horses)) stomp their feet. **(1)**

5. The (cow, (cows)) stand still. **(1)**

Read each sentence. Then rewrite each sentence to use the correct plural form of the underlined noun.

6. Two <u>fox</u> visit the farm.

   Two foxes visit the farm. (1)

7. Many <u>man</u> help plant seeds.

   Many men help plant seeds. (1)

8. How many <u>child</u> are in your school?

   How many children are in your school? (1)

Read directions to children.
Grammar
© Houghton Mifflin Harcourt Publishing Company. All rights reserved.
160
Assessment Tip: Total 8 Points
Grade 2, Unit 3

Compound Sentences

Short, Choppy Sentences	Compound Sentence
Cows give us milk. Hens lay eggs.	Cows give us milk, and hens lay eggs.

Write each pair of sentences as a compound sentence.
Use a comma and a joining word.

1. The cows can type. The cows can't dance.

   The cows can type, but they can't dance. (2 points)

2. The cows want electric blankets. The ducks want a diving board.

   The cows want electric blankets, and the ducks want a diving

   board. (2)

3. The cows will get blankets. The cows will stay cold.

   The cows will get blankets, or they will stay cold. (2)

4. The ducks can dive. The ducks need a board.

   The ducks can dive, but they need a board. (2)

Read directions to children
Grammar
© Houghton Mifflin Harcourt Publishing Company. All rights reserved.
169
Assessment Tip: Total 8 Points
Grade 2, Unit 3

Words with *ai, ay*

Write a word from the box to complete each sentence.

Word Bank

pail	maybe	say
tail	play	wait

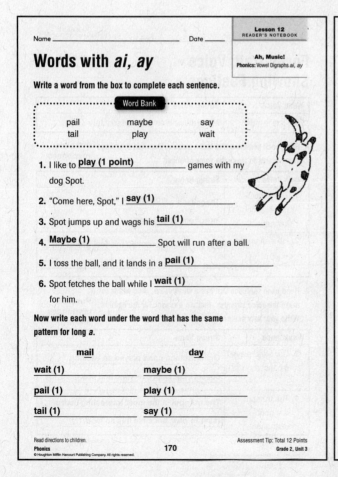

1. I like to **play (1 point)** _____ games with my dog Spot.

2. "Come here, Spot," I **say (1)**

3. Spot jumps up and wags his **tail (1)** _____

4. **Maybe (1)** _____ Spot will run after a ball.

5. I toss the ball, and it lands in a **pail (1)** _____

6. Spot fetches the ball while I **wait (1)** _____ for him.

Now write each word under the word that has the same pattern for long *a*.

m<u>ai</u>l	d<u>ay</u>
wait (1)	maybe (1)
pail (1)	play (1)
tail (1)	say (1)

Read directions to children.
Phonics
© Houghton Mifflin Harcourt Publishing Company. All rights reserved.
170
Assessment Tip: Total 12 Points
Grade 2, Unit 3

Compound Sentences

- A **compound sentence** is two simpler sentences joined by a comma and the word <u>and</u>, <u>but</u>, or <u>or</u>.
- Moving words around and adding details in a compound sentence can make the sentence more interesting.

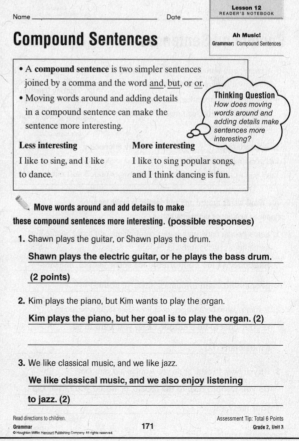

Thinking Question
How does moving words around and adding details make sentences more interesting?

Less interesting	More interesting
I like to sing, and I like to dance.	I like to sing popular songs, and I think dancing is fun.

Move words around and add details to make these compound sentences more interesting. (possible responses)

1. Shawn plays the guitar, or Shawn plays the drum.

   Shawn plays the electric guitar, or he plays the bass drum.

   (2 points)

2. Kim plays the piano, but Kim wants to play the organ.

   Kim plays the piano, but her goal is to play the organ. (2)

3. We like classical music, and we like jazz.

   We like classical music, and we also enjoy listening

   to jazz. (2)

Read directions to children.
Grammar
© Houghton Mifflin Harcourt Publishing Company. All rights reserved.
171
Assessment Tip: Total 6 Points
Grade 2, Unit 3

Page 1 (top left)

Words with *ai, ay*

Read the letter. Draw a circle around the words with
ai and *ay*. Then write two sentences to finish the
letter. Choose two words from the box to use in your
sentences. Possible responses shown.

Word Bank

rain	hail	day	may
gray	mail	pay	trail

Dear (Jay.) **(1 point)**

(Today) my class went on a trip. I could not (wait!) **(2)**
We saw people make crafts. A man made pots out of
(clay.) One woman wove a (braid) for a rug. The people **(2)**
sell their crafts and then they get (paid.) **(1)** _____

It started to rain on the way home. (1) _____

I hope we can go back another day. (1) _____

Your friend,

_____

Page 2 (top right)

Words with *ai, ay*

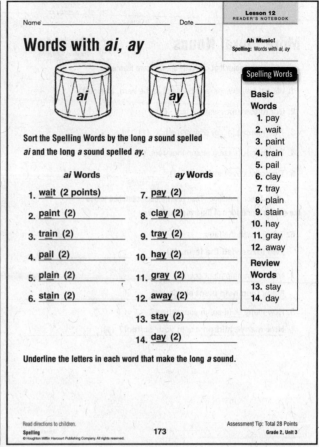

Sort the Spelling Words by the long *a* sound spelled
ai and the long *a* sound spelled *ay*.

Spelling Words

**Basic
Words**
1. pay
2. wait
3. paint
4. train
5. pail
6. clay
7. tray
8. plain
9. stain
10. hay
11. gray
12. away

**Review
Words**
13. stay
14. day

ai Words	*ay* Words
1. wait (2 points)	7. pay (2)
2. paint (2)	8. clay (2)
3. train (2)	9. tray (2)
4. pail (2)	10. hay (2)
5. plain (2)	11. gray (2)
6. stain (2)	12. away (2)
	13. stay (2)
	14. day (2)

Underline the letters in each word that make the long *a* sound.

Page 3 (bottom left)

Compound Sentences

- A **compound sentence** is two simple sentences
  joined by a comma and the word and, but, or or.
- Moving words around and adding details in a
  compound sentence can make the sentence
  more interesting.

Thinking Question
*How does moving
words around and
adding details make
sentences more
interesting?*

Less interesting	More interesting
Lin prefers loud music, but Lin's sister prefers soft music.	Loud music is Lin's favorite, but her sister prefers soft music.

Move words around and add details to make these
compound sentences more interesting.

1. Some people find headphones comfortable, but some people find
   headphones uncomfortable.

   Headphones are comfortable for some people, but other

   people find them uncomfortable. (2 points)

2. Is your goal to be a singer, or is your goal to be a musician?

   Is your goal to be a singer, or do you want to be

   a musician? (2)

3. Do you want to clap, or do you want to tap your feet?

   Do you want to clap to the music, or would you rather tap

   your feet? (2)

Page 4 (bottom right)

Focus Trait: Voice
Showing Feelings

Weak Voice	Strong Voice
I like movie music.	Movie music is so great to listen to!

A. Read each sentence that has a weak voice. Add or change
some words to make the voice stronger.

Possible
responses
shown.

Weak Voice	Strong Voice
1. The guitar is a musical instrument.	The guitar is a **wonderful** _____ musical instrument. **(2 points)**
2. I like all music.	Any kind of music **makes me feel great! (2)**

B. Read each sentence that has a weak voice. Add words to
make the voice stronger. Include a reason for the opinion.
Write your new sentences.

Possible
responses
shown.

Weak Voice	Strong Voice
3. Our band played a concert.	**Our marching band played an exciting concert, because everyone had practiced. (2)**
4. The trumpet is a good instrument.	**The trumpet is the most interesting instrument to play, because it is so loud. (2)**

Cumulative Review

Write the word that goes in each sentence.

Word Bank

snails   boxes   glasses   bikes

1. "I can't lift these big **boxes (1 point)** of books," said Meg.

2. "We'll ride our **bikes (1)** to school," Rick said.

3. "I've filled three **glasses (1)** with milk," said Max.

4. "You're moving at the speed of **snails (1)** this morning," Mom said.

Now write each word from the Word Bank under the word that has the same ending.

paints	patches
bikes (1)	boxes (1)
snails (1)	glasses (1)

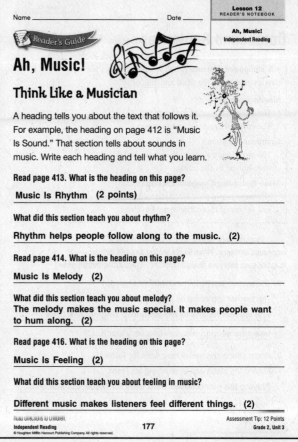

Reader's Guide

Ah, Music!

Think Like a Musician

A heading tells you about the text that follows it. For example, the heading on page 412 is "Music Is Sound." That section tells about sounds in music. Write each heading and tell what you learn.

Read page 413. What is the heading on this page?
Music Is Rhythm   (2 points)

What did this section teach you about rhythm?
Rhythm helps people follow along to the music.   (2)

Read page 414. What is the heading on this page?
Music Is Melody   (2)

What did this section teach you about melody?
The melody makes the music special. It makes people want to hum along.   (2)

Read page 416. What is the heading on this page?
Music Is Feeling   (2)

What did this section teach you about feeling in music?
Different music makes listeners feel different things.   (2)

Now teach others. Based on details from the text, think like a musician. Pretend a friend is going to a performance. Give your friend advice about rhythm, melody, and feeling in music. Remember you can find information in the book by using headings.

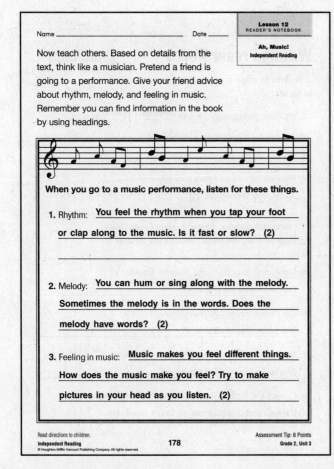

When you go to a music performance, listen for these things.

1. Rhythm: **You feel the rhythm when you tap your foot or clap along to the music. Is it fast or slow?**   (2)

2. Melody: **You can hum or sing along with the melody. Sometimes the melody is in the words. Does the melody have words?**   (2)

3. Feeling in music: **Music makes you feel different things. How does the music make you feel? Try to make pictures in your head as you listen.**   (2)

Words with *ai, ay*

Spelling Words

Basic Words
1. pay
2. wait
3. paint
4. train
5. pail
6. clay
7. tray
8. plain
9. stain
10. hay
11. gray
12. away

Review Words
13. stay
14. day

Read each word aloud. Then write the Spelling Word or Spelling Words that rhyme with the word.

1. main   train (1 point)   plain (1)
     stain (1)

2. faint   paint (1)

3. play   pay (1)   clay (1)
     tray (1)   hay (1)
     gray (1)   away (1)
     stay (1)   day (1)

Compound Sentences

- A **compound sentence** is two simple sentences joined by a comma and the word and, but, or or.

Simple Sentences
The crowd sang along to the music.
The crowd was moved by the music.

Compound Sentence
The crowd sang along to the music, and they were moved by the music.

More Interesting Compound Sentence
The large crowd sang along to the joyful music, and the music moved the crowd to cheer.

Combine each pair of simple sentences into a compound sentence. Move words around and add details to make each sentence more interesting. **(possible responses)**

1. The teacher listens to the children's singing.
   The teacher is pleased by the children's singing.

   The teacher listens to the children's singing, and their

   beautiful singing pleases him very much. (3)

2. Playing the piano well is hard work for Tasha.
   Playing the piano well is satisfying for Tasha.

   Playing the piano well is hard work for Tasha, but she also

   finds it satisfying. (3)

Read directions to children.
Grammar   180   Assessment Tip: Total 6 Points
© Houghton Mifflin Harcourt Publishing Company. All rights reserved.   Grade 2, Unit 3

Idioms

Read the sentence. Choose the idiom from the box that could replace the underlined words. Write the idiom.

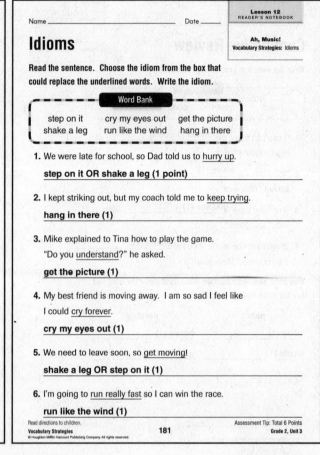

```
Word Bank

step on it      cry my eyes out    get the picture
shake a leg     run like the wind  hang in there
```

1. We were late for school, so Dad told us to hurry up.
   step on it OR shake a leg (1 point)

2. I kept striking out, but my coach told me to keep trying.
   hang in there (1)

3. Mike explained to Tina how to play the game.
   "Do you understand?" he asked.
   got the picture (1)

4. My best friend is moving away. I am so sad I feel like
   I could cry forever.
   cry my eyes out (1)

5. We need to leave soon, so get moving!
   shake a leg OR step on it (1)

6. I'm going to run really fast so I can win the race.
   run like the wind (1)

Read directions to children.
Vocabulary Strategies   181   Assessment Tip: Total 6 Points
© Houghton Mifflin Harcourt Publishing Company. All rights reserved.   Grade 2, Unit 3

Proofread for Spelling

Proofread the journal entry. Circle the ten misspelled words. Then write the correct spellings on the lines below.

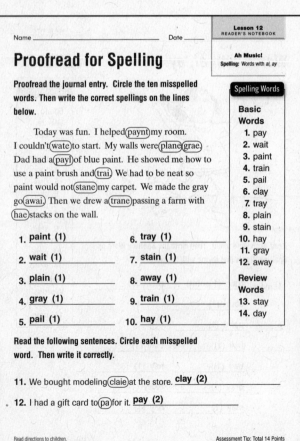

Today was fun. I helped (paynt) my room. I couldn't (wate) to start. My walls were (plane)(grae). Dad had a (payl) of blue paint. He showed me how to use a paint brush and (trai.) We had to be neat so paint would not (stane) my carpet. We made the gray go (awai.) Then we drew a (trane) passing a farm with (hae) stacks on the wall.

Spelling Words

Basic Words
1. pay
2. wait
3. paint
4. train
5. pail
6. clay
7. tray
8. plain
9. stain
10. hay
11. gray
12. away

Review Words
13. stay
14. day

1. **paint (1)**   6. **tray (1)**
2. **wait (1)**   7. **stain (1)**
3. **plain (1)**   8. **away (1)**
4. **gray (1)**   9. **train (1)**
5. **pail (1)**   10. **hay (1)**

Read the following sentences. Circle each misspelled word. Then write it correctly.

11. We bought modeling (claie) at the store. **clay (2)**

12. I had a gift card to (pa) for it. **pay (2)**

Read directions to children.
Spelling   182   Assessment Tip: Total 14 Points
© Houghton Mifflin Harcourt Publishing Company. All rights reserved.   Grade 2, Unit 3

Writing Proper Nouns

Write the proper noun in each sentence correctly on the line.

1. My friend jessica plays the flute. **Jessica (1 point)**

2. The concert is in chicago. **Chicago (1)**

3. She will bring her dog willy. **Willy (1)**

4. After the concert we'll have juicy jelly smoothies.

   Juicy Jelly Smoothies (1)

Read each sentence. Choose the correct proper noun to replace the underlined words. Write the new sentence on the line.

5. The woman loves the piano. (Carmen, Canada)
   Carmen loves the piano. (1)

6. She plays it for her fish. (New Mexico, Bubbles)
   She plays it for Bubbles. (1)

7. She feeds her fish its food. (Fin Flakes, Main Street)
   She feeds her fish Fin Flakes. (1)

8. Carmen and Bubbles live on drake road. (Florida, Drake Road)
   Carmen and Bubbles live on Drake Road. (1)

Read directions to children.
Grammar   183   Assessment Tip: Total 8 Points
© Houghton Mifflin Harcourt Publishing Company. All rights reserved.   Grade 2, Unit 3

Compound Sentences

Moving words around and adding details in a compound sentence can make the sentence more interesting.

Less Interesting	**More Interesting**
Do you like vocals, or do you like instrumentals?	So you like vocals, or are instrumentals your favorite?
My brother only listens to pop, and my sister only listens to country.	My brother only listens to popular music, and country music is all my sister wants to hear.

✎ **Move words around and add details to each sentence.**

1. Mom plays the guitar, and Mom is teaching Manny.

Mom plays the guitar very well, and Manny is learning

from her. (2 points)

2. Shawn is a singer, but Shawn is not a dancer.

Shawn is a great singer, but he is not a very good dancer. (2)

3. Do you enjoy concerts, or do you find concerts too loud?

Do you enjoy live concerts, or are they too loud for you? (2)

Name _____ Date _____

Lesson 13
READER'S NOTEBOOK

Schools Around
the World
Phonics: Words with ee, ea

Words with *ee, ea*

Write a word for each clue.

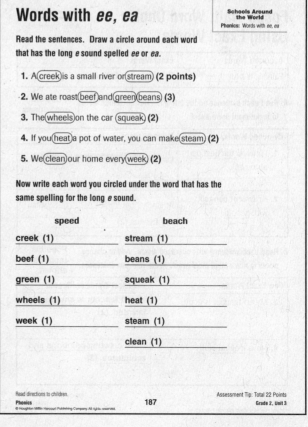

1. It rhymes with *see*.

It begins like *bat*. __bee (1 point)__

2. It rhymes with *beaches*.

It begins like *pig*. __peaches (1)__

3. It rhymes with *sweet*.

It begins like *mail*. __meet or meat (1)__

4. It rhymes with *sheep*.

It begins like *kitten*. __keep (1)__

5. It rhymes with *beast*.

It begins like *fox*. __feast (1)__

6. It rhymes with *clean*.

It begins like *bay*. __bean (1)__

Use two of the words you wrote above in sentences of your own. Possible responses shown.

7. __I picked a bean. (1)__

8. __We had a big feast. (1)__

Name _____ Date _____

Lesson 13
READER'S NOTEBOOK

Schools Around
the World
Grammar: Quotation Marks

Using Quotation Marks

When you write, show what someone says by putting **quotation marks (" ")** at the beginning and end of the speaker's exact words.

Luis said, "I play the drums."

Kim said, "I play the guitar."

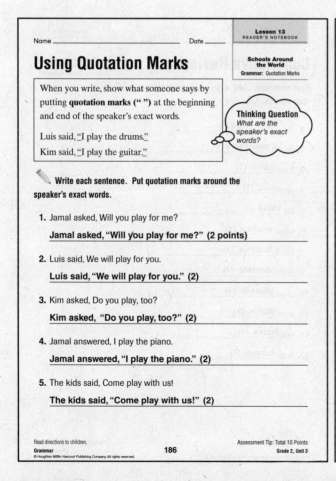

Thinking Question
What are the speaker's exact words?

✎ **Write each sentence. Put quotation marks around the speaker's exact words.**

1. Jamal asked, Will you play for me?

Jamal asked, "Will you play for me?" (2 points)

2. Luis said, We will play for you.

Luis said, "We will play for you." (2)

3. Kim asked, Do you play, too?

Kim asked, "Do you play, too?" (2)

4. Jamal answered, I play the piano.

Jamal answered, "I play the piano." (2)

5. The kids said, Come play with us!

The kids said, "Come play with us!" (2)

Name _____ Date _____

Lesson 13
READER'S NOTEBOOK

Schools Around
the World
Phonics: Words with ee, ea

Words with *ee, ea*

Read the sentences. Draw a circle around each word that has the long *e* sound spelled *ee* or *ea*.

1. A creek is a small river or stream (2 points)

2. We ate roast beef and green beans (3)

3. The wheels on the car squeak (2)

4. If you heat a pot of water, you can make steam (2)

5. We clean our home every week (2)

Now write each word you circled under the word that has the same spelling for the long *e* sound.

speed	**beach**
creek (1)	stream (1)
beef (1)	beans (1)
green (1)	squeak (1)
wheels (1)	heat (1)
week (1)	steam (1)
	clean (1)

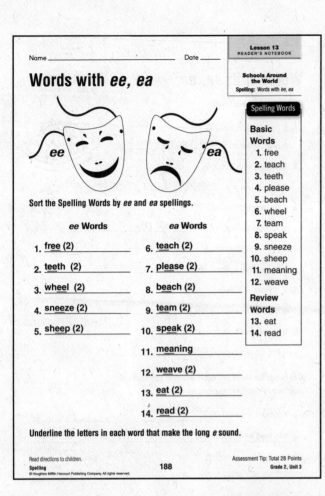

Words with *ee, ea*

ee   ea

Sort the Spelling Words by *ee* and *ea* spellings.

ee Words	ea Words
1. free (2)	6. teach (2)
2. teeth (2)	7. please (2)
3. wheel (2)	8. beach (2)
4. sneeze (2)	9. team (2)
5. sheep (2)	10. speak (2)
	11. meaning
	12. weave (2)
	13. eat (2)
	14. read (2)

Underline the letters in each word that make the long *e* sound.

Spelling Words

Basic Words
1. free
2. teach
3. teeth
4. please
5. beach
6. wheel
7. team
8. speak
9. sneeze
10. sheep
11. meaning
12. weave

Review Words
13. eat
14. read

Read directions to children.
Spelling
© Houghton Mifflin Harcourt Publishing Company. All rights reserved.
188
Assessment Tip: Total 28 Points
Grade 2, Unit 3

Quotation Marks

Follow these rules when you use quotation marks.

1. Put a **comma** after words such as *said* and *asked.*
2. Begin the first word inside the quotation marks with a **capital letter.**
3. Put the **end mark** inside the quotation marks.

Example: Jenna said, "I wrote a poem."

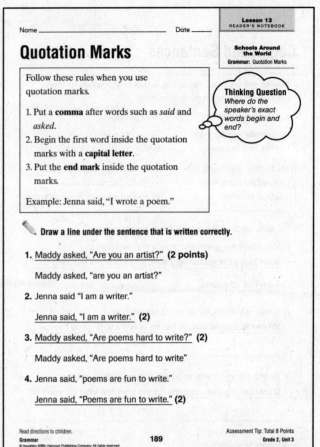

Thinking Question
Where do the speaker's exact words begin and end?

Draw a line under the sentence that is written correctly.

1. Maddy asked, "Are you an artist?" **(2 points)**

   Maddy asked, "are you an artist?"

2. Jenna said "I am a writer."

   Jenna said, "I am a writer." **(2)**

3. Maddy asked, "Are poems hard to write?" **(2)**

   Maddy asked, "Are poems hard to write"

4. Jenna said, "poems are fun to write."

   Jenna said, "Poems are fun to write." **(2)**

Read directions to children.
Grammar
© Houghton Mifflin Harcourt Publishing Company. All rights reserved.
189
Assessment Tip: Total 8 Points
Grade 2, Unit 3

Focus Trait: Word Choice Using Exact Words

Overused Words	Exact Words
Painting is a <u>fun thing</u>.	Painting is an **artistic hobby**.

A. Read each sentence on the left side. Add or change words to make them more exact.

Possible responses shown.

Overused Words	Exact Words
1. Lunch is <u>the best part</u> of the day.	Lunch is **my favorite time (2 points)** of the day.
2. At lunch, I can <u>talk</u> with <u>people</u>.	At lunch, I can **laugh** with **my friends (2)**.

B. Read each sentence with overused words. Add or change words to make them more exact. Write your new sentences.

Possible responses shown.

Few Exact Words	Add Exact Words or Phrases
3. My art teacher is <u>good</u>.	My art teacher is **smart and talented. (2)**
4. I love <u>making stuff</u>.	I love **creating paintings and sculptures. (2)**

Read directions to children.
Writing
© Houghton Mifflin Harcourt Publishing Company. All rights reserved.
190
Assessment Tip: Total 8 Points
Grade 2, Unit 3

Cumulative Review

Read each word. Add *-s* or *-es* to each base word. Then write the new word.

1. rain   rains (1 point)
2. peach peaches (1)
3. train trains (1)
4. pail   pails (1)
5. fox   foxes (1)
6. wash   washes (1)
7. teach teaches (1)
8. catch catches (1)
9. glass glasses (1)
10. stain stains (1)
11. box   boxes (1)
12. buzz   buzzes (1)

Read directions to children.
Phonics
© Houghton Mifflin Harcourt Publishing Company. All rights reserved.
191
Assessment Tip: Total 12 Points
Grade 2, Unit 3

Lesson 13
READER'S NOTEBOOK

Schools Around the World
Spelling: Words with *ee, ea*

Lesson 13
READER'S NOTEBOOK

Schools Around the World
Grammar: Quotation Marks

Lesson 13
READER'S NOTEBOOK

Schools Around the World
Writing: Opinion Writing

Lesson 13
READER'S NOTEBOOK

Schools Around the World
Phonics: Cumulative Review

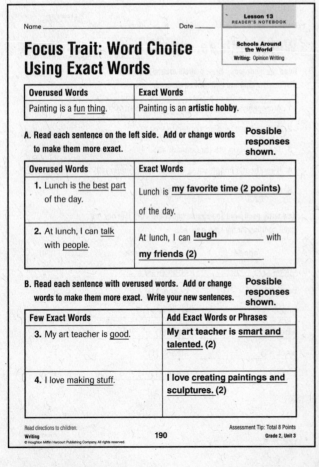

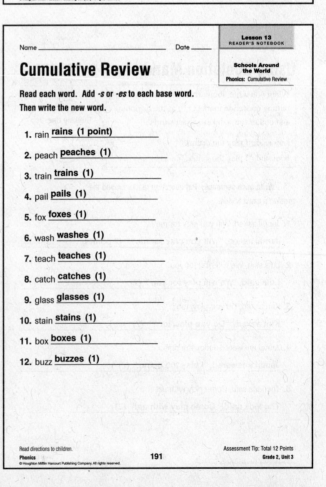

Name _____ Date _____

Lesson 13
READER'S NOTEBOOK

Schools Around
the World
Independent Reading

Schools Around the World

Create Your Own School

There were many different schools in the story.
Some were like your school, and some were different.

Read page 441. How are all schools the same?

All schools are where children go to learn.   (2 points)

Read page 442. How are school buildings different?

School buildings are made of different materials.   (2)

Read page 443. What are some ways students get to school?

Children can walk, or they can ride in a car or on a bike.   (2)

Read page 444. How do children dress at school?

Some students wear uniforms. Others do not.   (2)

Read pages 445–447. What are some things children do at school?

Children learn reading, writing, and math.   (2)

Name _____ Date _____

Lesson 13
READER'S NOTEBOOK

Schools Around
the World
Independent Reading

You are going to open your own school!
Write an announcement telling people what
makes your school special so they will want to
come to your school. Think about the school
building, what children will wear, what children
will learn, and what children will do.

A new school will open soon in our town!

The name of the school is   (Responses will vary.)

Example: Science Stars Academy   (2)

This school is different from other schools in these
three ways:

1. At this school, every student will have a
   computer.   (2)

2. Students will learn about science all day long, even
   in history and math class!   (2)

3. Students wear lab coats as uniforms. They will look
   and feel like real scientists.   (2)

$\frac{2}{3}$ a b c + 5 × $\frac{1}{2}$

Assessment Tip: 8 Points

Name _____ Date _____

Lesson 13
READER'S NOTEBOOK

Schools Around
the World
Spelling: Words with ee, ea

Words with *ee, ea*

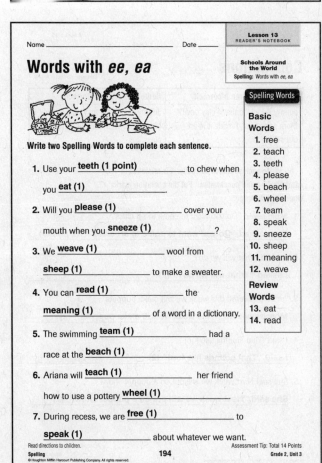

Write two Spelling Words to complete each sentence.

1. Use your **teeth (1 point)** _____ to chew when
   you **eat (1)** _____

2. Will you **please (1)** _____ cover your
   mouth when you **sneeze (1)** _____?

3. We **weave (1)** _____ wool from
   sheep (1) _____ to make a sweater.

4. You can **read (1)** _____ the
   meaning (1) _____ of a word in a dictionary.

5. The swimming **team (1)** _____ had a
   race at the **beach (1)** _____

6. Ariana will **teach (1)** _____ her friend
   how to use a pottery **wheel (1)** _____

7. During recess, we are **free (1)** _____ to
   speak (1) _____ about whatever we want.

> **Spelling Words**
>
> **Basic Words**
> 1. free
> 2. teach
> 3. teeth
> 4. please
> 5. beach
> 6. wheel
> 7. team
> 8. speak
> 9. sneeze
> 10. sheep
> 11. meaning
> 12. weave
>
> **Review Words**
> 13. eat
> 14. read

Read directions to children.
Spelling
© Houghton Mifflin Harcourt Publishing Company. All rights reserved.
194
Assessment Tip: Total 14 Points
Grade 2, Unit 3

Name _____ Date _____

Lesson 13
READER'S NOTEBOOK

Schools Around
the World
Grammar: Quotation Marks

Quotation Marks

Write each sentence correctly.

1. Mrs. Smith said, Artists mix colors.
   Mrs. Smith said, "Artists mix colors." (2 points)

2. Greg said, I will mix blue and yellow.
   Greg said, "I will mix blue and yellow." (2)

3. Annie said, You will make green!
   Annie said, "You will make green!" (2)

Draw a line under the sentence that is written correctly.

4. Jamie said "I made a basket."
   Jamie said, "I made a basket." (2)

5. Robin asked, "how did you do it"?
   Robin asked, "How did you do it?" (2)

6. Jamie answered, "I made it out of straw." (2)
   Jamie answered ",I made it out of straw."

Read directions to children.
Grammar
© Houghton Mifflin Harcourt Publishing Company. All rights reserved.
195
Assessment Tip: Total 12 Points
Grade 2, Unit 3

Lesson 13
READER'S NOTEBOOK

Schools Around
the World
Vocabulary Strategies:
Using a Dictionary

Using a Dictionary

Read the names for parts of a dictionary entry. Then read the dictionary entry. Write in the boxes the labels for the parts of the dictionary entry. (1 point each)

example sentence   part of speech   pronunciation

word meaning   entry word

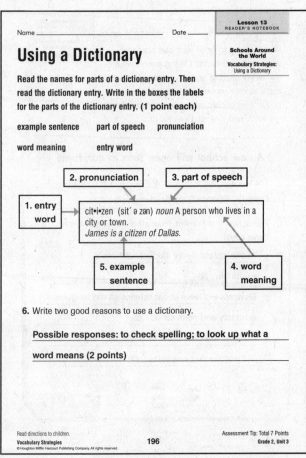

6. Write two good reasons to use a dictionary.

Possible responses: to check spelling; to look up what a

word means (2 points)

Read directions to children.
Vocabulary Strategies
© Houghton Mifflin Harcourt Publishing Company. All rights reserved.
196
Assessment Tip: Total 7 Points
Grade 2, Unit 3

Proofread for Spelling

Proofread the letter. Circle the twelve misspelled words. Then write the correct spellings on the lines below.

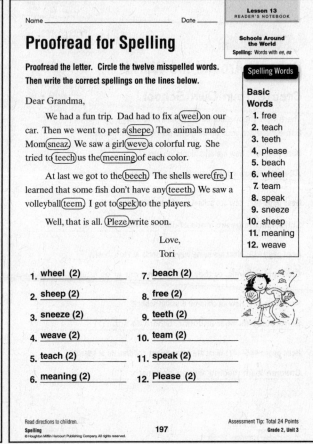

Dear Grandma,

We had a fun trip. Dad had to fix a (weel) on our car. Then we went to pet a (shepe.) The animals made Mom (sneaz.) We saw a girl (weve) a colorful rug. She tried to (teech) us the (meening) of each color.

At last we got to the (beech.) The shells were (fre.) I learned that some fish don't have any (teeeth.) We saw a volleyball (teem.) I got to (spek) to the players.

Well, that is all. (Pleze) write soon.

Love,
Tori

Spelling Words

Basic Words
1. free
2. teach
3. teeth
4. please
5. beach
6. wheel
7. team
8. speak
9. sneeze
10. sheep
11. meaning
12. weave

1. **wheel (2)** _____
2. **sheep (2)** _____
3. **sneeze (2)** _____
4. **weave (2)** _____
5. **teach (2)** _____
6. **meaning (2)** _____
7. **beach (2)** _____
8. **free (2)** _____
9. **teeth (2)** _____
10. **team (2)** _____
11. **speak (2)** _____
12. **Please (2)** _____

Read directions to children.
Spelling
© Houghton Mifflin Harcourt Publishing Company. All rights reserved.
197
Assessment Tip: Total 24 Points
Grade 2, Unit 3

Action Verbs

Circle the verb. Underline the subject that is doing the action.

1. Bobby (jumps) to his feet. **(2 points)**
2. He (dances) to the music. **(2)**
3. Sasha (sings) out loud. **(2)**
4. They (cheer) for the band. **(2)**

Underline the verb in the sentence. Circle the verb that makes the action more exact. Then write the new sentence.

5. The class made a picture. ((painted), watered)

The class painted a picture. (2)

6. They used the brushes. (jumped, (shared))

They shared the brushes. (2)

7. Carla put the pictures on the wall. ((hung) walked)

Carla hung the pictures on the wall. (2)

8. Children liked the artwork. (saved, (loved))

Children loved the artwork. (2)

Read directions to children.
Grammar
© Houghton Mifflin Harcourt Publishing Company. All rights reserved.
198
Assessment Tip: Total 16 Points
Grade 2, Unit 3

Conventions

Sentences Written Incorrectly	Sentences Written Correctly
Jimmy asked "Is that a clay bowl?" Mom said. "yes, I made it in art class."	Jimmy asked, "Is that a clay bowl?" Mom said, "Yes, I made it in art class."

Write each sentence correctly. Fix mistakes in capitalization and punctuation. Put the quotation marks where they belong.

1. Mom asked "Do you want to come to art class?

Mom asked, "Do you want to come to art class?" (2 points)

2. I asked, what will we do?"

I asked, "What will we do?" (2)

3. "mom answered this week we will make puppets"

Mom answered, "This week we will make puppets." (2)

4. I said "That sounds like fun!

I said, "That sounds like fun!" (2)

5. She said Next week we will put on a puppet show!"

She said, "Next week we will put on a puppet show!" (2)

Read directions to children.
Grammar
© Houghton Mifflin Harcourt Publishing Company. All rights reserved.
199
Assessment Tip: Total 10 Points
Grade 2, Unit 3

Long *o (o, oa, ow)*

Write a word for each clue.

> **Word Bank**
>
> | zero | clover | coast |
> |------|--------|-------|
> | groan | gold | glow |

1. It rhymes with **toast.**

   It begins like **cap.** **coast (1 point)**

2. It rhymes with **loan.**

   It begins like **grapes.** **groan (1)**

3. It rhymes with **fold.**

   It begins like **gap.** **gold (1)**

4. It rhymes with **show.**

   It begins like **glad.** **glow (1)**

5. It rhymes with **hero.**

   It begins like **zip.** **zero (1)**

6. It rhymes with **over.**

   It begins like **clip.** **clover (1)**

Read directions to children.
Phonics
© Houghton Harcourt Publishing Company. All rights reserved.
200
Assessment Tip: Total 6 Points
Grade 2, Unit 3

Days of the Week

> • There are seven days in a week.
> • The names of the days of the week begin with **capital letters.**
>
> | Monday | Thursday | Saturday |
> |--------|----------|----------|
> | Tuesday | Friday | Sunday |
> | Wednesday | | |
>
> Bonnie teaches sign language on <u>Tuesday</u>.

Thinking Question
Which word names a day of the week?

Write each sentence correctly.

1. Bonnie teaches Jessica on wednesday.

   Bonnie teaches Jessica on Wednesday. (1 point)

2. Jessica has a piano lesson on Tuesday.

   Jessica has a piano lesson on Tuesday. (1)

3. Jessica mails Bonnie a card on Friday.

   Jessica mails Bonnie a card on Friday. (1)

4. On monday Bonnie gets the card in the mail.

   On Monday Bonnie gets the card in the mail. (1)

5. On saturday Bonnie sends Jessica a card.

   On Saturday Bonnie sends Jessica a card. (1)

Read directions to children.
Grammar
© Houghton Mifflin Harcourt Publishing Company. All rights reserved.
201
Assessment Tip: Total 5 Points
Grade 2, Unit 3

Long *o (o, oa, ow)*

Read the sentences. Draw a circle around each word that has the long *o* sound spelled *o, oa,* or *ow.*

1. A (crow) sat on the branch of the (old) (oak) tree. **(3 points)**

2. (Snow) began to fall on a (cold) winter day. **(2)**

3. (Throw) a stick in the water and see if it (floats) **(2)**

4. You can (fold) your (own) paper and put it away. **(2)**

5. I (know) that the (coach) has a (gold) ring. **(3)**

Now write each word you circled under the word that has the same spelling for long *o.*

told	loan	blow
old (1)	oak (1)	crow (1)
cold (1)	floats (1)	snow (1)
fold (1)	coach (1)	throw (1)
gold (1)		own (1)
		know (1)

Read directions to children.
Phonics
Copyright © Houghton Mifflin Company All rights reserved.
202
Assessment Tip: Total 24 Points
Grade 2, Unit 3

Long *o (o, oa, ow)*

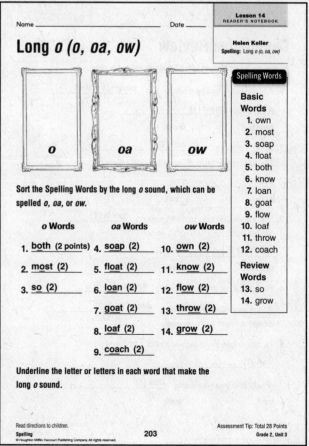

o   *oa*   *ow*

Sort the Spelling Words by the long *o* sound, which can be spelled *o, oa,* or *ow.*

o Words	*oa* Words	*ow* Words
1. both (2 points)	4. soap (2)	10. own (2)
2. most (2)	5. float (2)	11. know (2)
3. so (2)	6. loan (2)	12. flow (2)
	7. goat (2)	13. throw (2)
	8. loaf (2)	14. grow (2)
	9. coach (2)	

Underline the letter or letters in each word that make the long *o* sound.

Spelling Words

Basic Words
1. own
2. most
3. soap
4. float
5. both
6. know
7. loan
8. goat
9. flow
10. loaf
11. throw
12. coach

Review Words
13. so
14. grow

Read directions to children.
Spelling
© Houghton Mifflin Harcourt Publishing Company. All rights reserved.
203
Assessment Tip: Total 28 Points
Grade 2, Unit 3

Months of the Year and Holidays

The names of months and holidays begin with **capital letters**.

January	February	March	April
May	June	July	August
September	October	November	December

Thanksgiving   Labor Day   Arbor Day

In July, we celebrate Independence Day.

> **Thinking Question**
> Which word names a month or a holiday?

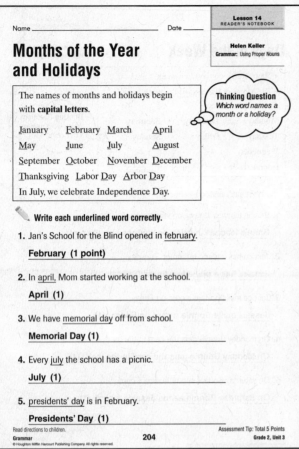 Write each underlined word correctly.

1. Jan's School for the Blind opened in <u>february</u>.

   February (1 point)

2. In <u>april</u>, Mom started working at the school.

   April (1)

3. We have <u>memorial day</u> off from school.

   Memorial Day (1)

4. Every <u>july</u> the school has a picnic.

   July (1)

5. <u>presidents' day</u> is in February.

   Presidents' Day (1)

Read directions to children.
Grammar
© Houghton Mifflin Harcourt Publishing Company. All rights reserved.
204
Assessment Tip: Total 5 Points
Grade 2, Unit 3

Focus Trait: Ideas Facts and Opinions

A **fact** can be proved. An **opinion** cannot be proved. An opinion tells what someone thinks or feels. Words such as <u>I think</u>, <u>I like</u>, or <u>I believe</u> are used to show opinions.

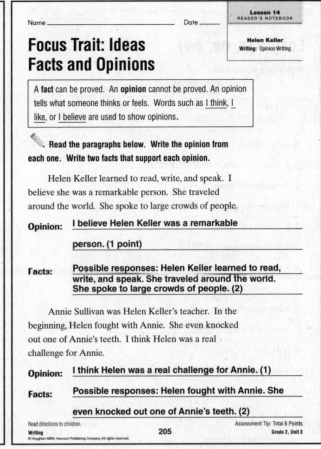 Read the paragraphs below. Write the opinion from each one. Write two facts that support each opinion.

Helen Keller learned to read, write, and speak. I believe she was a remarkable person. She traveled around the world. She spoke to large crowds of people.

Opinion: I believe Helen Keller was a remarkable person. (1 point)

Facts: Possible responses: Helen Keller learned to read, write, and speak. She traveled around the world. She spoke to large crowds of people. (2)

Annie Sullivan was Helen Keller's teacher. In the beginning, Helen fought with Annie. She even knocked out one of Annie's teeth. I think Helen was a real challenge for Annie.

Opinion: I think Helen was a real challenge for Annie. (1)

Facts: Possible responses: Helen fought with Annie. She even knocked out one of Annie's teeth. (2)

Read directions to children.
Writing
© Houghton Mifflin Harcourt Publishing Company. All rights reserved.
205
Assessment Tip: Total 6 Points
Grade 2, Unit 3

Cumulative Review

Answer each pair of clues using the words below the clues.

1. A place with sand by a lake or sea   **beach (1 point)**

   A big meal   **feast (1)**

   beach   **feast**

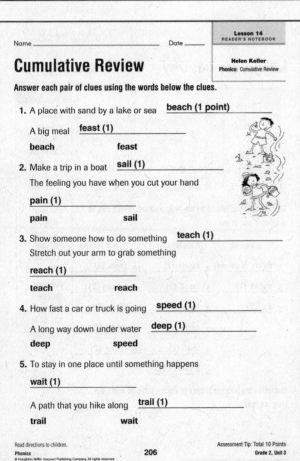

2. Make a trip in a boat   **sail (1)**

   The feeling you have when you cut your hand

   pain (1)

   pain   **sail**

3. Show someone how to do something   **teach (1)**

   Stretch out your arm to grab something

   reach (1)

   teach   **reach**

4. How fast a car or truck is going   **speed (1)**

   A long way down under water   **deep (1)**

   deep   **speed**

5. To stay in one place until something happens

   wait (1)

   A path that you hike along   **trail (1)**

   trail   **wait**

Read directions to children.
Phonics
© Houghton Mifflin Harcourt Publishing Company. All rights reserved.
206
Assessment Tip: Total 10 Points
Grade 2, Unit 3

> **Reader's Guide**

Helen Keller

Make a Speech

When Helen Keller grew up, she gave speeches. Now you will write a speech about Helen Keller's life.

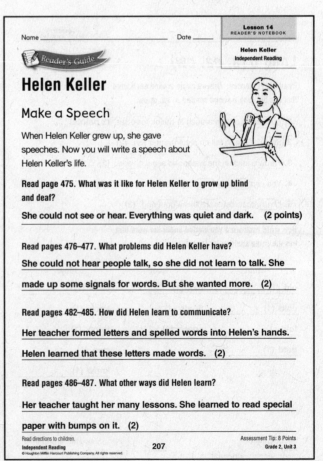

Read page 475. What was it like for Helen Keller to grow up blind and deaf?

She could not see or hear. Everything was quiet and dark.   (2 points)

Read pages 476–477. What problems did Helen Keller have?

She could not hear people talk, so she did not learn to talk. She made up some signals for words. But she wanted more.   (2)

Read pages 482–485. How did Helen learn to communicate?

Her teacher formed letters and spelled words into Helen's hands. Helen learned that these letters made words.   (2)

Read pages 486–487. What other ways did Helen learn?

Her teacher taught her many lessons. She learned to read special paper with bumps on it.   (2)

Read directions to children.
Independent Reading
© Houghton Mifflin Harcourt Publishing Company. All rights reserved.
207
Assessment Tip: 8 Points
Grade 2, Unit 3

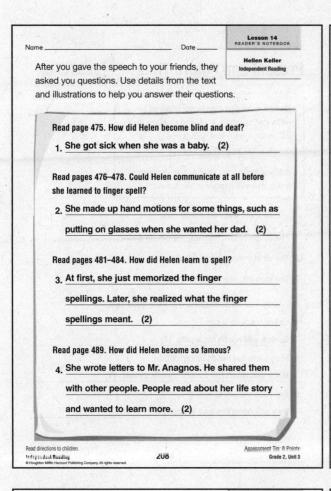

After you gave the speech to your friends, they asked you questions. Use details from the text and illustrations to help you answer their questions.

Read page 475. How did Helen become blind and deaf?

1. She got sick when she was a baby.   (2)

Read pages 476–478. Could Helen communicate at all before she learned to finger spell?

2. She made up hand motions for some things, such as putting on glasses when she wanted her dad.   (2)

Read pages 481–484. How did Helen learn to spell?

3. At first, she just memorized the finger spellings. Later, she realized what the finger spellings meant.   (2)

Read page 489. How did Helen become so famous?

4. She wrote letters to Mr. Anagnos. He shared them with other people. People read about her life story and wanted to learn more.   (2)

Read directions to children.
Independent Reading
208
Assessment Tip: 8 Points
Grade 2, Unit 3
© Houghton Mifflin Harcourt Publishing Company. All rights reserved.

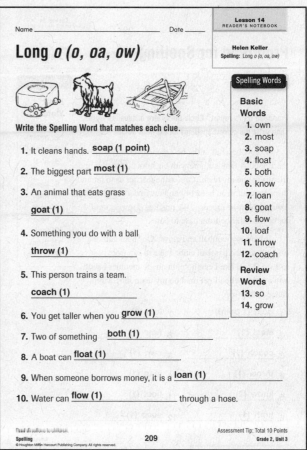

Long *o* (*o, oa, ow*)

Write the Spelling Word that matches each clue.

Spelling Words

Basic Words
1. own
2. most
3. soap
4. float
5. both
6. know
7. loan
8. goat
9. flow
10. loaf
11. throw
12. coach

Review Words
13. so
14. grow

1. It cleans hands. soap (1 point)

2. The biggest part most (1)

3. An animal that eats grass goat (1)

4. Something you do with a ball throw (1)

5. This person trains a team. coach (1)

6. You get taller when you grow (1)

7. Two of something both (1)

8. A boat can float (1)

9. When someone borrows money, it is a loan (1)

10. Water can flow (1) through a hose.

Read directions to children.
Spelling
209
Assessment Tip: Total 10 Points
Grade 2, Unit 3
© Houghton Mifflin Harcourt Publishing Company. All rights reserved.

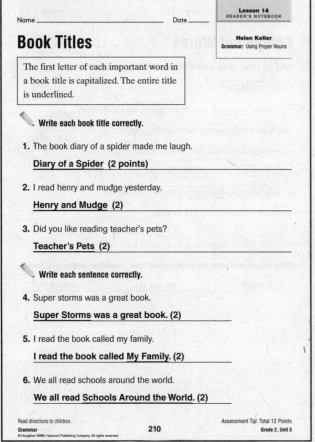

Book Titles

The first letter of each important word in a book title is capitalized. The entire title is underlined.

✏ **Write each book title correctly.**

1. The book diary of a spider made me laugh.
   Diary of a Spider (2 points)

2. I read henry and mudge yesterday.
   Henry and Mudge (2)

3. Did you like reading teacher's pets?
   Teacher's Pets (2)

✏ **Write each sentence correctly.**

4. Super storms was a great book.
   Super Storms was a great book. (2)

5. I read the book called my family.
   I read the book called My Family. (2)

6. We all read schools around the world.
   We all read Schools Around the World. (2)

Read directions to children.
Grammar
210
Assessment Tip: Total 12 Points
Grade 2, Unit 3
© Houghton Mifflin Harcourt Publishing Company. All rights reserved.

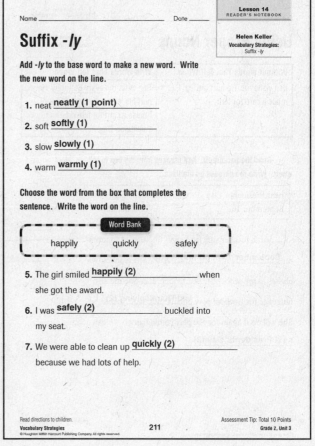

Name _____ Date _____

Lesson 14
READER'S NOTEBOOK

Helen Keller
Vocabulary Strategies:
Suffix -ly

Suffix -*ly*

Add -*ly* to the base word to make a new word. Write the new word on the line.

1. neat neatly (1 point)

2. soft softly (1)

3. slow slowly (1)

4. warm warmly (1)

Choose the word from the box that completes the sentence. Write the word on the line.

Word Bank

happily   quickly   safely

5. The girl smiled happily (2) when she got the award.

6. I was safely (2) buckled into my seat.

7. We were able to clean up quickly (2) because we had lots of help.

Read directions to children.
Vocabulary Strategies
211
Assessment Tip: Total 10 Points
Grade 2, Unit 3
© Houghton Mifflin Harcourt Publishing Company. All rights reserved.

Proofread for Spelling

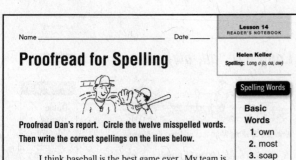

Proofread Dan's report. Circle the twelve misspelled words. Then write the correct spellings on the lines below.

Spelling Words

Basic Words
1. own
2. most
3. soap
4. float
5. both
6. know
7. loan
8. goat
9. flow
10. loaf
11. throw
12. coach

I think baseball is the best game ever. My team is the Rams. A ram is a (gote) with big horns. (Moast) of my friends are on my team. Our (coche) teaches us to hit and (throa) the ball. You need to (kno) how to do (bothe) to play. You can't (lofe) at practice. We practice throwing until we make the ball (floe) from base to base.

I have my (oan) ball and glove. Our hard hats are on (lon) from the baseball club. I like to run from base to base. I feel like I can (flote) on air. Sometimes I slide into a base. When I get mud on my team shirt, Mom cleans it with (sop).

1. goat (1 point)   7. loaf (1)
2. Most (1)   8. flow (1)
3. coach (1)   9. own (1)
4. throw (1)   10. loan (1)
5. know (1)   11. float (1)
6. both (1)   12. soap (1)

Read directions to children.
Spelling
© Houghton Mifflin Harcourt Publishing Company. All rights reserved.
212
Assessment Tip: Total 12 Points
Grade 2, Unit 3

Present and Future Time

• Add -s to the end of the verb when it tells about a noun that names one. Add -es to verbs ending with s, x, ch, and sh when they tell about a noun that names one.
Examples: The boy jumps. The egg hatches.

• Add will before the verb to tell about an action that will happen in the future.

Draw a line under the correct verb.

1. The coach (teach, teaches) the girl. **(1 point)**

2. The child (read, reads) in Braille. **(1)**

3. The man (fix, fixes) their answers. **(1)**

Write each sentence correctly to show future time.

4. Carlos reach for a pen.
Carlos will reach for a pen. (1)

5. Mary wash her hands before dinner.
Mary will wash her hands before dinner. (1)

6. Ben pass the ball to me.
Ben will pass the ball to me. (1)

Read directions to children.
Grammar
© Houghton Mifflin Harcourt Publishing Company. All rights reserved.
213
Assessment Tip: Total 6 Points
Grade 2, Unit 3

Using Proper Nouns

Without Words That Tell When	With Words That Tell When
Ben visits me. He hurt his leg. I made a card for him.	Ben visits me every Saturday. He hurt his leg on June 12, 2012. I made a card for him on Valentine's Day.

Read the paragraph. Add phrases from the box to tell when. Write the phrases on the lines.

next Presidents' Day	last Thanksgiving
September 16	every Thursday

Sarah teaches sign language. She started to teach on **September 16 (2 points)**, 2012. She teaches two classes at my school **every Thursday**. She did sign language for a school play **last Thanksgiving (2)**.

She will do it again for the play coming up **next Presidents' Day (2)**.

Read directions to children.
Grammar
© Houghton Mifflin Harcourt Publishing Company. All rights reserved.
214
Assessment Tip: Total 6 Points
Grade 2, Unit 3

Compound Words

Read the letter. Draw a circle around each compound word.

Dear (Grandfather,)

This (afternoon) I went to the (playground) with some kids from my (classroom.) We played (baseball) until (sunset.) It was so much fun! Then I went (inside) to do my (homework.) I went (upstairs) and saw the photo of us at the (seashore) in the (summertime.) I still have the (seashell) we found there! **(12 points)**

Love,
Julia

Write a compound word you know on each line. **Possible answers shown.**

haircut (1)   airport (1)   backpack (1)

Read directions to children.
Phonics
© Houghton Mifflin Harcourt Publishing Company. All rights reserved.
215
Assessment Tip: Total 15 Points
Grade 2, Unit 3

Titles for People

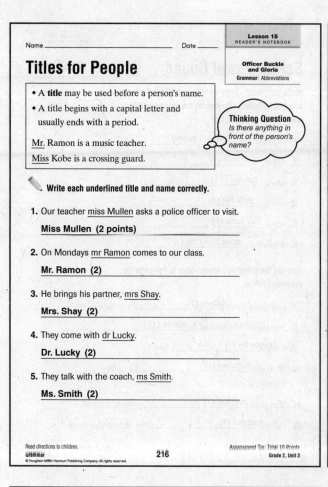

- A **title** may be used before a person's name.
- A title begins with a capital letter and usually ends with a period.

Mr. Ramon is a music teacher.

Miss Kobe is a crossing guard.

Thinking Question
Is there anything in front of the person's name?

✎ Write each underlined title and name correctly.

1. Our teacher miss Mullen asks a police officer to visit.

   Miss Mullen (2 points)

2. On Mondays mr Ramon comes to our class.

   Mr. Ramon (2)

3. He brings his partner, mrs Shay.

   Mrs. Shay (2)

4. They come with dr Lucky.

   Dr. Lucky (2)

5. They talk with the coach, ms Smith.

   Ms. Smith (2)

Name _____ Date _____

Lesson 15
READER'S NOTEBOOK

Officer Buckle
and Gloria
Phonics: Compound Words

Compound Words

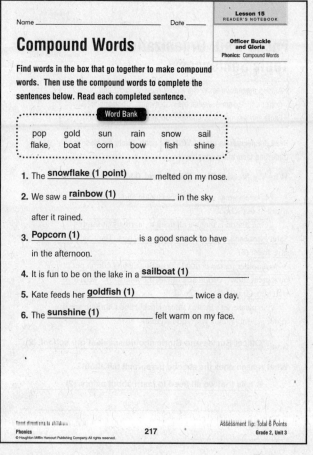

Find words in the box that go together to make compound words. Then use the compound words to complete the sentences below. Read each completed sentence.

Word Bank

pop	gold	sun	rain	snow	sail
flake	boat	corn	bow	fish	shine

1. The **snowflake (1 point)** _____ melted on my nose.

2. We saw a **rainbow (1)** _____ in the sky after it rained.

3. **Popcorn (1)** _____ is a good snack to have in the afternoon.

4. It is fun to be on the lake in a **sailboat (1)** _____

5. Kate feeds her **goldfish (1)** _____ twice a day.

6. The **sunshine (1)** _____ felt warm on my face.

Name _____ Date _____

Lesson 15
READER'S NOTEBOOK

Officer Buckle
and Gloria
Spelling: Compound Words

Compound Words

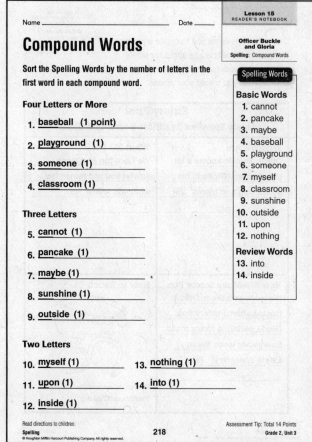

Sort the Spelling Words by the number of letters in the first word in each compound word.

Four Letters or More

1. **baseball (1 point)**
2. **playground (1)**
3. **someone (1)**
4. **classroom (1)**

Three Letters

5. **cannot (1)**
6. **pancake (1)**
7. **maybe (1)**
8. **sunshine (1)**
9. **outside (1)**

Two Letters

10. **myself (1)**
11. **upon (1)**
12. **inside (1)**
13. **nothing (1)**
14. **into (1)**

Spelling Words

Basic Words
1. cannot
2. pancake
3. maybe
4. baseball
5. playground
6. someone
7. myself
8. classroom
9. sunshine
10. outside
11. upon
12. nothing

Review Words
13. into
14. inside

Name _____ Date _____

Lesson 15
READER'S NOTEBOOK

Officer Buckle
and Gloria
Grammar: Abbreviations

Abbreviations for Days and Months

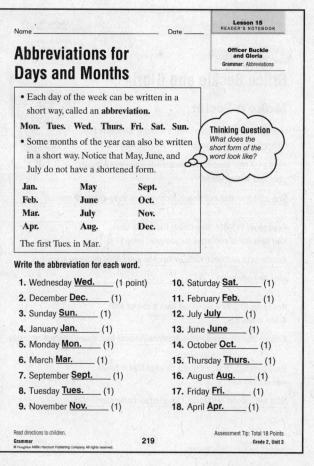

- Each day of the week can be written in a short way, called an **abbreviation**.

  Mon. Tues. Wed. Thurs. Fri. Sat. Sun.

- Some months of the year can also be written in a short way. Notice that May, June, and July do not have a shortened form.

Thinking Question
What does the short form of the word look like?

Jan.	May	Sept.
Feb.	June	Oct.
Mar.	July	Nov.
Apr.	Aug.	Dec.

The first Tues. in Mar.

Write the abbreviation for each word.

1. Wednesday **Wed.** (1 point)
2. December **Dec.** (1)
3. Sunday **Sun.** (1)
4. January **Jan.** (1)
5. Monday **Mon.** (1)
6. March **Mar.** (1)
7. September **Sept.** (1)
8. Tuesday **Tues.** (1)
9. November **Nov.** (1)
10. Saturday **Sat.** (1)
11. February **Feb.** (1)
12. July **July** (1)
13. June **June** (1)
14. October **Oct.** (1)
15. Thursday **Thurs.** (1)
16. August **Aug.** (1)
17. Friday **Fri.** (1)
18. April **Apr.** (1)

Name _____ Date _____

Lesson 15
READER'S NOTEBOOK

Officer Buckle
and Gloria
Writing: Opinion Writing

Focus Trait: Organization
Topic Sentences

A good persuasive essay has a goal, reasons, facts, and examples. The **goal** is what the writer wants. **Reasons** tell why. **Facts** and **examples** give more information about the reason.

Read the persuasive essay. Write the goal. Circle the reasons. Underline facts and examples.

Why We Need Officer Buckle and Gloria

I have a great idea! Officer Buckle and Gloria should speak at our school. (One reason is that we all need to learn about safety.) Safety tips can keep us from hurting ourselves. They can even save lives! (6)
(Another reason is that Officer Buckle and Gloria put on a great show!) Gloria acts out all the safety tips. Kids love watching Gloria! (6)
So please, let's invite Officer Buckle and Gloria to speak at our school. I think it would be great!

Goal: Officer Buckle and Gloria should speak at our school. (2)

What reason does the second paragraph tell about?

It tells that we all need to learn about safety. (2)

Read directions to children.
Writing
© Houghton Mifflin Harcourt Publishing Company. All rights reserved.
220
Assessment Tip: Total 16 Points
Grade 2, Unit 3

Name _____ Date _____

Lesson 15
READER'S NOTEBOOK

Officer Buckle
and Gloria
Phonics: Schwa Vowel Sound

Schwa Vowel Sound

Write each word. Draw a slash (/) to divide the word between syllables. Then circle the quieter syllable with the schwa sound.

1. happen   hap / (pen) (1 point) _____
2. about   (a) / bout (1) _____
3. talent   tal / (ent) (1) _____
4. nickel   nick / (el) (1) _____
5. alone   (a) / lone (1) _____
6. dragonfly   drag / (on) / fly (1) _____

Now use the words you wrote above to complete the sentences below.

7. Luis has a lot of **talent (1)** _____ for singing.
8. Sometimes Mia likes to be **alone (1)** _____
9. A **dragonfly (1)** _____ flew by.
10. What will **happen (1)** _____ if it rains during the game?
11. Stan paid a **nickel (1)** _____ for a gumball.
12. Tell me **about (1)** _____ the picture you made.

Read directions to children.
Phonics
© Houghton Mifflin Harcourt Publishing Company. All rights reserved.
221
Assessment Tip: Total 12 Points
Grade 2, Unit 3

Name _____ Date _____

Lesson 15
READER'S NOTEBOOK

Officer Buckle
and Gloria
Independent Reading

Reader's Guide

Office Buckle and Gloria

Make a Poster

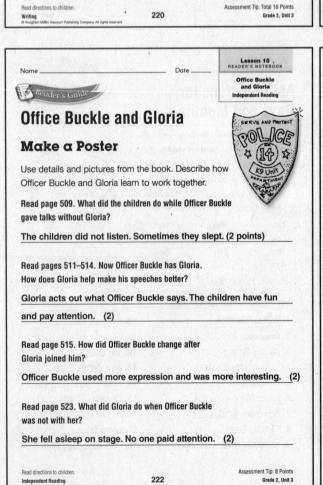

Use details and pictures from the book. Describe how Officer Buckle and Gloria learn to work together.

Read page 509. What did the children do while Officer Buckle gave talks without Gloria?

The children did not listen. Sometimes they slept. (2 points)

Read pages 511–514. Now Officer Buckle has Gloria. How does Gloria help make his speeches better?

Gloria acts out what Officer Buckle says. The children have fun and pay attention. (2)

Read page 515. How did Officer Buckle change after Gloria joined him?

Officer Buckle used more expression and was more interesting. (2)

Read page 523. What did Gloria do when Officer Buckle was not with her?

She fell asleep on stage. No one paid attention. (2)

Read directions to children.
Independent Reading
© Houghton Mifflin Harcourt Publishing Company. All rights reserved.
222
Assessment Tip: 8 Points
Grade 2, Unit 3

Name _____ Date _____

Lesson 15
READER'S NOTEBOOK

Officer Buckle
and Gloria
Independent Reading

Officer Buckle wants you to create a poster. The poster will tell people about his safety speeches. Use details and pictures from the book to help you create your poster.

Safety First	
Safety Speeches by Officer Buckle and Gloria	
Who We Are Officer Buckle knows a lot about safety. Gloria is his police dog and friend. (5)	**What We Do** We have fun and teach safety! You will remember what you learn! (5)
How We Make Safety Fun We work as a team. Officer Buckle shares safety tips. Gloria performs funny tricks. Everybody loves these safety speeches! (5)	**How to Reach Us** 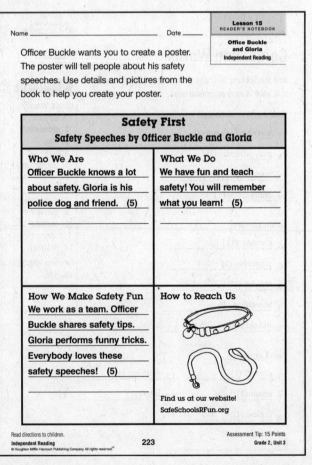 Find us at our website! SafeSchoolsRFun.org

Read directions to children.
Independent Reading
© Houghton Mifflin Harcourt Publishing Company. All rights reserved.
223
Assessment Tip: 15 Points
Grade 2, Unit 3

Name _____ Date _____

Compound Words

Draw lines to match the words that form the Spelling Words. Then write the Spelling Words.

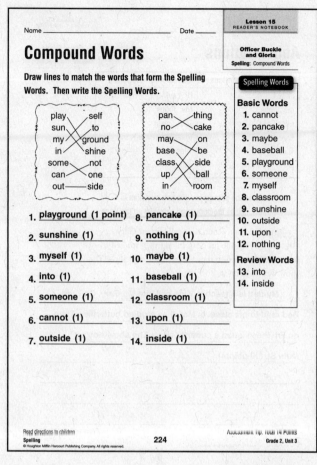

play — self
sun — to
my — ground
in — shine
some — not
can — one
out — side

pan — thing
no — cake
may — on
base — be
class — side
up — ball
in — room

Spelling Words

Basic Words
1. cannot
2. pancake
3. maybe
4. baseball
5. playground
6. someone
7. myself
8. classroom
9. sunshine
10. outside
11. upon
12. nothing

Review Words
13. into
14. inside

1. **playground** (1 point)
2. **sunshine** (1)
3. **myself** (1)
4. **into** (1)
5. **someone** (1)
6. **cannot** (1)
7. **outside** (1)
8. **pancake** (1)
9. **nothing** (1)
10. **maybe** (1)
11. **baseball** (1)
12. **classroom** (1)
13. **upon** (1)
14. **inside** (1)

Name _____ Date _____

Abbreviations for Places

✏ Write each underlined place correctly. Use abbreviations.

1. I live on Robin Road.

   Robin Rd. (2 points)

2. The pool is on Shore drive.

   Shore Dr. (2)

3. Where is Third avenue?

   Third Ave. (2)

✏ Write the name of the underlined words correctly. Write each abbreviation in its long form.

4. Max lives on North St.

   North Street (2)

5. Gloria visited a school on Elm Ave.

   Elm Avenue (2)

6. Rose Rd. is only two blocks long.

   Rose Road (2)

Name _____ Date _____

Root Words

Lesson 15
READER'S NOTEBOOK

Officer Buckle
and Gloria
Vocabulary Strategies:
Root Words

Underline the root word in each word. Use what you know about the root word to figure out the word's meaning. Complete each sentence by writing the word whose meaning fits the best.

Vocabulary

timer   unwrap   deepest   retake
restacked   freezer   reddish   fielder
(8 points)

1. Joe didn't pass the math test. He will **retake** the test next week. **(1 point)**

2. I put the meat in the **freezer** because it must stay cold. **(1)**

3. Sarah used a **timer** to see how long she swam. **(1)**

4. After he ran, his face was a **reddish** color. **(1)**

5. You can't **unwrap** your presents until your birthday. **(1)**

6. Scientists want to learn what lives in the **deepest** part of the ocean. **(1)**

7. Maria **restacked** the books on her desk. **(1)**

8. Roger was a good **fielder**, so he played in the outfield. **(1)**

Name _____ Date _____

Proofread for Spelling

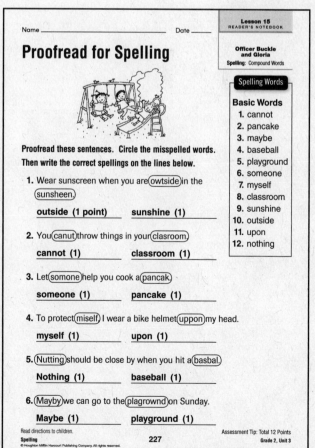

Proofread these sentences. Circle the misspelled words. Then write the correct spellings on the lines below.

Spelling Words

Basic Words
1. cannot
2. pancake
3. maybe
4. baseball
5. playground
6. someone
7. myself
8. classroom
9. sunshine
10. outside
11. upon
12. nothing

1. Wear sunscreen when you are (owtside) in the (sunsheen).

   outside (1 point)   **sunshine (1)**

2. You (canut) throw things in your (clasroom).

   cannot (1)   **classroom (1)**

3. Let (somone) help you cook a (pancak).

   someone (1)   **pancake (1)**

4. To protect (miself), I wear a bike helmet (uppon) my head.

   myself (1)   **upon (1)**

5. (Nutting) should be close by when you hit a (basbal).

   Nothing (1)   **baseball (1)**

6. (Mayby) we can go to the (plagrownd) on Sunday.

   Maybe (1)   **playground (1)**

Name _____ Date _____

Lesson 15
READER'S NOTEBOOK

Officer Buckle
and Gloria
Grammar: Spiral Review

Past and Future Time

✎ Rewrite each sentence to change when the action happened. Use the word in ( ).

1. The police officers talk about safety. (past)

   The police officers talked about safety. (1 point)

2. The children listen to them. (future)

   The children will listen to them. (1)

3. They follow the rules. (future)

   They will follow the rules. (1)

✎ Read the story. Find five verbs that do not tell about the past, and fix them. Write the story correctly on the lines.

The policeman and his dog walked to the school. They wait at the front door. Then the dog bark. The principal open the door. The policeman talk with the children about safety. The children thank him.

The policeman and his dog walked to the school. They

waited at the front door. Then the dog barked. The principal

opened the door. The policeman talked with the children

about safety. The children thanked him. (5)

Read directions to children.
Grammar
© Houghton Mifflin Harcourt Publishing Company. All rights reserved.
228
Assessment Tip: Total 8 Points
Grade 2, Unit 3

Name _____ Date _____

Lesson 15
READER'S NOTEBOOK

Officer Buckle
and Gloria
Grammar: Connect to Writing

Abbreviations

Incorrect Abbreviations	Correct Abbreviations
dr levi	Dr. Levi
ms Jones	Ms. Jones
miss Oaks	Miss Oaks
River st	River St.
Tues	Tues.
jan.	Jan.

✎ Proofread the paragraph. Fix any mistakes in abbreviations. Write the paragraph correctly on the lines.

My dad is a teacher. Kids call him mr Gary. On tues Dad read to his class. In mar they studied butterflies. Then on fri they visited a butterfly show. The show was on Main st.

My dad is a teacher. Kids call him Mr. Gary. On Tues.

Dad read to his class. In Mar. they studied butterflies. Then

on Fri. they visited a butterfly show. The show was on

Main St. (10 points)

Read directions to children.
Grammar
© Houghton Mifflin Harcourt Publishing Company. All rights reserved.
229
Assessment Tip: Total 10 Points
Grade 2, Unit 3

Contents

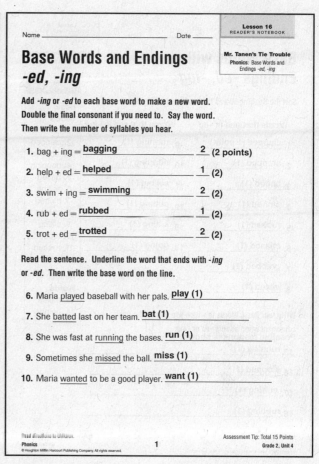

Name _____ Date _____

Base Words and Endings -ed, -ing

Add -ing or -ed to each base word to make a new word.
Double the final consonant if you need to. Say the word.
Then write the number of syllables you hear.

1. bag + ing = **bagging** _____ **2** (2 points)

2. help + ed = **helped** _____ **1** (2)

3. swim + ing = **swimming** _____ **2** (2)

4. rub + ed = **rubbed** _____ **1** (2)

5. trot + ed = **trotted** _____ **2** (2)

Read the sentence. Underline the word that ends with -ing
or -ed. Then write the base word on the line.

6. Maria played baseball with her pals. **play (1)** _____

7. She batted last on her team. **bat (1)** _____

8. She was fast at running the bases. **run (1)** _____

9. Sometimes she missed the ball. **miss (1)** _____

10. Maria wanted to be a good player. **want (1)** _____

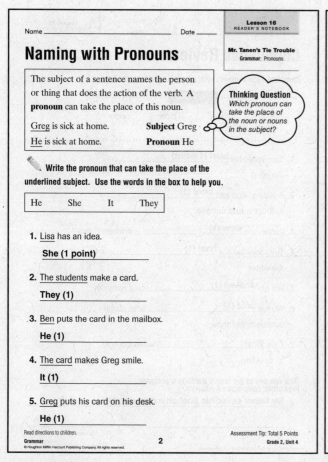

Name _____ Date _____

Naming with Pronouns

The subject of a sentence names the person
or thing that does the action of the verb. A
pronoun can take the place of this noun.

Greg is sick at home. **Subject** Greg

He is sick at home. **Pronoun** He

Thinking Question
Which pronoun can
take the place of
the noun or nouns
in the subject?

Write the pronoun that can take the place of the
underlined subject. Use the words in the box to help you.

| He | She | It | They |

1. Lisa has an idea.

    She (1 point)

2. The students make a card.

    They (1)

3. Ben puts the card in the mailbox.

    He (1)

4. The card makes Greg smile.

    It (1)

5. Greg puts his card on his desk.

    He (1)

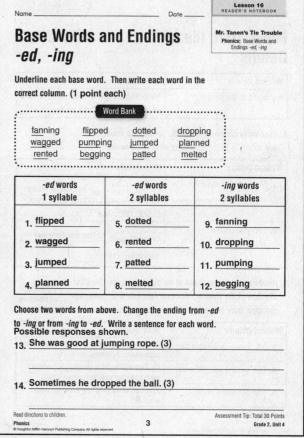

Name _____ Date _____

Base Words and Endings -ed, -ing

Underline each base word. Then write each word in the
correct column. (1 point each)

Word Bank

fanning	flipped	dotted	dropping
wagged	pumping	jumped	planned
rented	begging	patted	melted

-ed words 1 syllable	-ed words 2 syllables	-ing words 2 syllables
1. flipped	5. dotted	9. fanning
2. wagged	6. rented	10. dropping
3. jumped	7. patted	11. pumping
4. planned	8. melted	12. begging

Choose two words from above. Change the ending from -ed
to -ing or from -ing to -ed. Write a sentence for each word.
Possible responses shown.

13. **She was good at jumping rope. (3)** _____

_____

14. **Sometimes he dropped the ball. (3)** _____

Base Words with Endings -ed, -ing

Sort the Spelling Words that end in -ed and -ing.

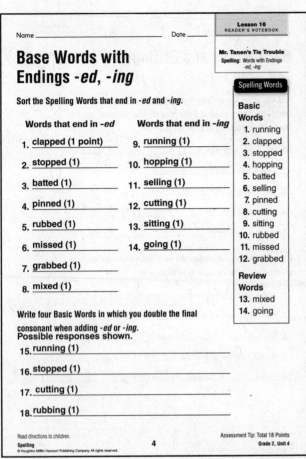

Words that end in -ed	Words that end in -ing
1. clapped (1 point)	9. running (1)
2. stopped (1)	10. hopping (1)
3. batted (1)	11. selling (1)
4. pinned (1)	12. cutting (1)
5. rubbed (1)	13. sitting (1)
6. missed (1)	14. going (1)
7. grabbed (1)	
8. mixed (1)	

Spelling Words

Basic Words
1. running
2. clapped
3. stopped
4. hopping
5. batted
6. selling
7. pinned
8. cutting
9. sitting
10. rubbed
11. missed
12. grabbed

Review Words
13. mixed
14. going

Write four Basic Words in which you double the final consonant when adding -ed or -ing.
Possible responses shown.

15. running (1)
16. stopped (1)
17. cutting (1)
18. rubbing (1)

Using Pronouns

- Use a **pronoun** to replace a noun that comes after a verb.
- Use these pronouns: *me, him, her, it, us,* and *them.*

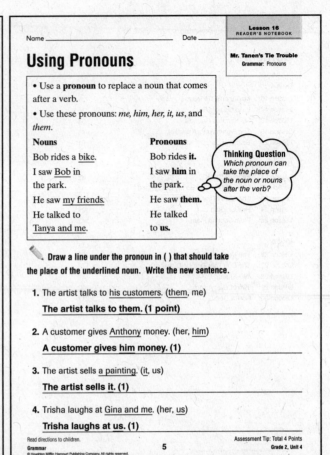

Nouns	Pronouns
Bob rides a <u>bike</u>.	Bob rides **it**.
I saw <u>Bob</u> in the park.	I saw **him** in the park.
He saw <u>my friends</u>.	He saw **them**.
He talked to <u>Tanya and me</u>.	He talked to **us**.

Thinking Question
Which pronoun can take the place of the noun or nouns after the verb?

✏ Draw a line under the pronoun in ( ) that should take the place of the underlined noun. Write the new sentence.

1. The artist talks to <u>his customers</u>. (<u>them</u>, me)
   The artist talks to them. (1 point)

2. A customer gives <u>Anthony</u> money. (her, <u>him</u>)
   A customer gives him money. (1)

3. The artist sells <u>a painting</u>. (<u>it</u>, us)
   The artist sells it. (1)

4. Trisha laughs at <u>Gina and me</u>. (her, <u>us</u>)
   Trisha laughs at us. (1)

Focus Trait: Ideas Details

Without Details	With Details
He looked at the people.	He looked **out the window** at the **crowd of people shouting and waving.**

A. Read these sentences about *Mr. Tanen's Tie Trouble.*
   Add details to help readers see what is happening.

Without Details	With Details
1. Mr. Tanen was upset.	Mr. Tanen was upset **because there wasn't enough money for a new playground. (1 point)**
2. Everyone came.	Everyone came **to the auction on Saturday. (1)**

B. Read each sentence. Look at the picture on pages 24–25 of *Mr. Tanen's Tie Trouble.* Add your own details to make each sentence more interesting. Write your new sentences.

Possible responses shown.

Without Details	With Details
3. Mr. Tanen held up a tie.	Mr. Tanen held up a green tie that had pictures of hotdogs on it. (1)
4. The dentist bought a tie.	Dr. Demi bought a purple tie covered with colorful toothbrushes. (1)
5. The ties were nice.	The ties were brightly colored and wild. (1)

Cumulative Review

Complete each sentence with a long *o* word from the box.

Word Bank

float	boat	blow	slow
cold	go	soaked	

1. Sam sailed his **boat (1 point)** on the pond.

2. A strong wind can **blow (1)** a sailboat across the lake.

3. Turtles are **slow (1)** animals.

4. The rocks did not **float (1)** in the water.

5. We got **soaked (1)** on a rainy day.

6. We felt **cold (1)** after playing outside in the snow.

7. Cars **go (1)** when the light turns green.

Now use one of the long *o* words in a sentence.
Possible responses shown.

8. **My father sailed his boat on a cold day. (3)**

Reader's Guide

Mr. Tanen's Tie Trouble

Draw a Tie

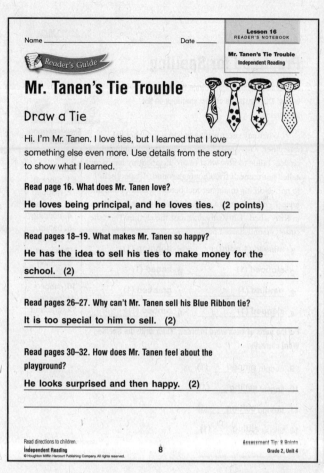

Hi. I'm Mr. Tanen. I love ties, but I learned that I love something else even more. Use details from the story to show what I learned.

Read page 16. What does Mr. Tanen love?

He loves being principal, and he loves ties. (2 points)

Read pages 18–19. What makes Mr. Tanen so happy?

He has the idea to sell his ties to make money for the

school. (2)

Read pages 26–27. Why can't Mr. Tanen sell his Blue Ribbon tie?

It is too special to him to sell. (2)

Read pages 30–32. How does Mr. Tanen feel about the

playground?

He looks surprised and then happy. (2)

Mr. Tanen wants to have a tie made to remember the special day when the playground opened. Use details from the story to create the tie. Write a sentence to tell about the tie you made for Mr. Tanen.

(Drawings might include a heart with a slide in it or a swing with a bow of ties around it.) (5)

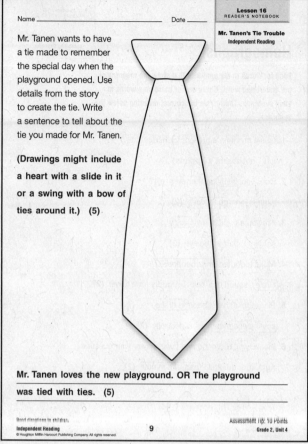

Mr. Tanen loves the new playground. OR The playground

was tied with ties. (5)

Name _____ Date _____

Lesson 16
READER'S NOTEBOOK

Mr. Tanen's Tie Trouble
Spelling: Base Words with
Endings -ed, -ing

Base Words with Endings -ed, -ing

Write the base word of each Spelling Word.

1. pinned **pin (1 point)**   4. batted **bat (1)**

2. rubbed **rub (1)**   5. mixed **mix (1)**

3. missed **miss (1)**   6. going **go (1)**

Write the Basic Word that belongs with each pair of words.

7. jogging, skipping **running (1)**

8. buying, paying **selling (1)**

9. took, pulled **grabbed (1)**

10. cheered, applauded **clapped (1)**

11. ripping, trimming **cutting (1)**

12. jumping, leaping **hopping (1)**

13. halted, ended **stopped (1)**

14. resting, sleeping **sitting (1)**

Spelling Words
Basic Words
1. running
2. clapped
3. stopped
4. hopping
5. batted
6. selling
7. pinned
8. cutting
9. sitting
10. rubbed
11. missed
12. grabbed
Review Words
13. mixed
14. going

Naming Yourself Last

Rewrite each sentence correctly.

1. I and Ann had a picnic by myself.

Ann and I had a picnic by ourselves. (1 point)

2. When do she and i need to come in?

When do she and I need to come in? (1)

3. Yesterday, i played at home by ourselves.

Yesterday, I played at home by myself. (1)

Underline the pronoun that can take the place of the underlined noun or nouns. Then write the new sentence.

4. The team captain picked Caitlin and Eric. (them, we)

The team captain picked them. (1)

5. The coach helped Molly. (she, her)

The coach helped her. (1)

6. The tall kid hit the ball. (them, it)

The tall kid hit it. (1)

Homographs

Look for words in the sentence that show the meaning of
the underlined word. Circle one or more clue words in
each sentence. Then circle the correct meaning below the
sentence.

1. I gave my mom a present for her birthday.

   gift   not absent   (2 points)

2. Does your baby brother ever rest?

   what is left   go to sleep   (2)

3. Are you a pupil in my class?

   student   part of the eye   (2)

4. Make a ring around your answer.

   circle   sound of a bell   jewelry for a finger   (2)

5. Please take this slip to the office.

   small piece of paper   slide easily   (2)

6. Please wait a second and I will answer your question.

   right after the first   part of a minute   (2)

Proofread for Spelling

Proofread the paragraph. Circle the eight misspelled
words. Then write the correct spellings on the
lines below.

When my sister went away to school, her cat
mised her. Kitty stoped eating. She started runing in
circles. I didn't know what to do. I claped my hands and
called her name. I tried hoping around. I bated balls
to her. Nothing made her feel better! Finally, I had an
idea. I grabed some of my sister's clothes and put them
in Kitty's bed. Kitty rubed against the clothes. Then she
curled up and started purring!

1. missed (1 point)	5. hopping (1)
2. stopped (1)	6. batted (1)
3. running (1)	7. grabbed (1)
4. clapped (1)	8. rubbed (1)

Spelling Words

Basic Words
1. running
2. clapped
3. stopped
4. hopping
5. batted
6. selling
7. pinned
8. cutting
9. sitting
10. rubbed
11. missed
12. grabbed

Put the parts of each word in order. Then write the Spelling
Word correctly.

9. nedpin   pinned   (1)

10. lingsel   selling   (1)

11. ttuingc   cutting   (1)

12. tingsit   sitting   (1)

Kinds of Sentences

Write whether the sentence is a statement, command,
or question. Write the sentence correctly on the line.

1. where is the bake sale   question

   Where is the bake sale? (1 point)

2. hang this sign   command

   Hang this sign. (1)

3. the money helps the school   statement

   The money helps the school. (1)

4. do you like cookies   question

   Do you like cookies? (1)

5. share with your sister   command

   Share with your sister. (1)

6. I like cookies with green icing   statement

   I like cookies with green icing. (1)

Sentence Fluency

Sentences with Repeated Subjects	Better Sentences
Tony walks to the store. Tony buys milk and eggs.	Tony walks to the store. **He** buys milk and eggs.

Sentences with Repeated Subjects	Better Sentences
Mr. Shay and Mrs. Shay need help shopping. Mr. Shay and Mrs. Shay cannot go to the store.	Mr. Shay and Mrs. Shay need help shopping. **They** cannot go the store.

Use a pronoun to replace the subject in the underlined
sentence. Write the new sentence.

1. Tony likes to help the Shays. Tony goes to their
   house each day.

   He goes to their house each day. (1 point)

2. Mrs. Shay likes Tony. Mrs. Shay makes lunch for
   Tony.

   She makes lunch for him. (1)

3. Tony and Mr. Shay sit on the porch. Tony and
   Mr. Shay play chess.

   They play chess. (1)

4. Tony goes to the store. The store sells good food.

   It sells good food. (1)

Long *i* (*i, igh, ie, y*)

Write a word from the box to complete each sentence.

Word Bank

might	pie	kind
find	night	My

1. Do you like **pie (1 point)** _____ made with fruit?

2. What **kind (1)** _____ of pie do you like best?

3. **My (1)** _____ mom will go to the store to get fresh peaches.

4. I **might (1)** _____ go with her.

5. We will **find (1)** _____ the best peaches together.

6. At **night (1)** _____ we will eat peach pie.

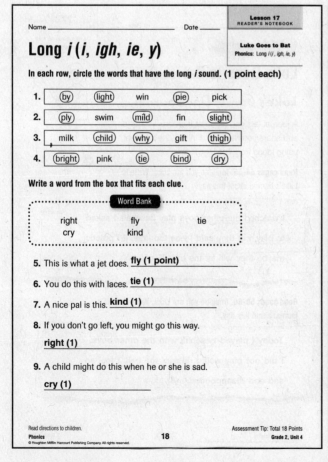

Subjects and Verbs

- In a sentence that tells about now, singular subjects use a verb that ends in -*s*. The teacher (sits) in the bleachers.

- In a sentence that tells about now, plural subjects use a verb without the -*s*. The teachers (sit) in the bleachers.

Thinking Question
When should I add -s to the end of a verb that tells about now?

✎ Circle the correct verb to go with the subject. Then rewrite the sentence.

1. The coaches (ride, rides) the bus to the game.
   The coaches ride the bus to the game. (1 point)

2. My friend (hand, hands) the man a ticket.
   My friend hands the man a ticket. (1)

3. Mom and Dad (cheer, cheers) at the game.
   Mom and Dad cheer at the game. (1)

4. The players (look, looks) at the goalie.
   The players look at the goalie. (1)

5. The kicker (kick, kicks) the ball.
   The kicker kicks the ball. (1)

Long *i* (*i, igh, ie, y*)

In each row, circle the words that have the long *i* sound. (1 point each)

1. (by) (light) win (pie) pick
2. (ply) swim (mild) fin (slight)
3. milk (child) (why) gift (thigh)
4. (bright) pink (tie) (bind) (dry)

Write a word from the box that fits each clue.

Word Bank

right	fly	tie
cry	kind	

5. This is what a jet does. **fly (1 point)** _____

6. You do this with laces. **tie (1)** _____

7. A nice pal is this. **kind (1)** _____

8. If you don't go left, you might go this way.
   right (1) _____

9. A child might do this when he or she is sad.
   cry (1) _____

Long *i* (*i, igh, y*)

Sort the Spelling Words. Put words with the long *i* sound spelled *i*, *igh*, and *y* under the correct baseball glove.

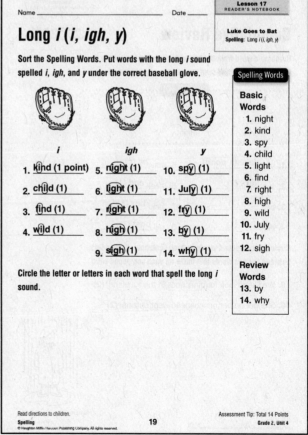

Spelling Words

Basic Words
1. night
2. kind
3. spy
4. child
5. light
6. find
7. right
8. high
9. wild
10. July
11. fry
12. sigh

Review Words
13. by
14. why

i	*igh*	*y*
1. kind (1 point)	5. night (1)	10. spy (1)
2. child (1)	6. light (1)	11. July (1)
3. find (1)	7. right (1)	12. fry (1)
4. wild (1)	8. high (1)	13. by (1)
	9. sigh (1)	14. why (1)

Circle the letter or letters in each word that spell the long *i* sound.

Subjects and More Verbs

In a sentence that tells about now, add *-es* to a verb that ends in *s, sh, ch, tch, z,* or *x* to match a singular subject.

Thinking Question
When should I add -es to the end of a verb that tells about now?

The trains pass the rink.   The train passes the rink.

The girls watch the skaters.   The girl watches the skaters.

The chefs mix hot soup.   The chef mixes hot soup.

The boys reach for a ball.   The boy reaches for a ball.

✎ **Draw a line under each correct sentence.**

1. The coach fix the skates.
   The coach fixes the skates. **(1 point)**

2. The kids dash around the rink. **(1)**
   The kids dashes around the rink.

3. The teacher teaches them a trick. **(1)**
   The teacher teach them a trick.

4. Dad misses a turn. **(1)**
   Dad miss a turn.

5. Mom watch from the stands.
   Mom watches from the stands. **(1)**

Focus Trait: Voice
Using Dialogue

Without Dialogue	With Dialogue
Dani wanted to go to the baseball game.	Dani begged, "Mom, please let me go to the baseball game. Please!"

A. Rewrite each sentence. Use dialogue. Possible responses shown.

Without Dialogue	With Dialogue
1. Dani asked Mom about the score.	"What's the score _____?" Dani asked Mom. **(1 point)**
2. Mom told her it was tied.	"The score is tied _____," Mom said. **(1)**

B. Rewrite each sentence. Use dialogue.   Possible responses shown.

Sentence	Dialogue
3. Tad told Dani she couldn't play.	"You can't play with us," said Tad. **(1)**
4. Dani wanted to know why.	"Why can't I play?" asked Dani. **(1)**
5. Tad said she was too young.	"You're too young to play on our team," Tad said. **(1)**

Cumulative Review

Combine a word from the box with a word below. Write the word on the line, and read the whole compound word.

Word Bank

be	box	hive
cake	boat	ball
end	light	

1. pan **cake (1 point)**   5. may **be (1)**

2. sun **light (1)**   6. week **end (1)**

3. bee **hive (1)**   7. sand **box (1)**

4. base **ball (1)**   8. sail **boat (1)**

Circle two compound words in each sentence. Draw a line between the two words that make up each compound word.

9. We like to look for pine|cones in the sun|shine. **(2)**

10. She put on her rain|coat and went out|side. **(2)**

Reader's Guide

Luke Goes to Bat

Luke's Game-Day Journal

A journal lets you tell what happens in your day and share your feelings. Finish Luke's journal, using ideas from the text.

Read pages 54–55. Imagine you are Luke. Write in Luke's journal about this day.

> I watched the other boys play baseball. I asked to play, but they said I was too little. If I practice, maybe they will let me try.   **(5 points)**

Read pages 58–60. Imagine you are Luke. Write in Luke's journal about this day.

> Today I played baseball with the other boys. I did not play well. I missed the ball. I feel so sad and disappointed.   **(5)**

Read pages 63–65. What is important about this day?
Write two or three sentences in Luke's journal.

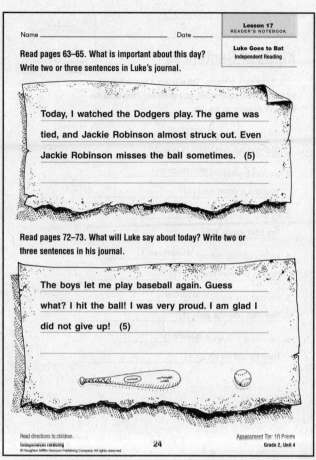

Today, I watched the Dodgers play. The game was
tied, and Jackie Robinson almost struck out. Even
Jackie Robinson misses the ball sometimes. (5)

Read pages 72–73. What will Luke say about today? Write two or
three sentences in his journal.

The boys let me play baseball again. Guess
what? I hit the ball! I was very proud. I am glad I
did not give up! (5)

Long *i* (*i, igh, y*)

Write a Spelling Word for each clue.

			Spelling Words
1. This is a month of the year.	July (1 point)		**Basic Words**
2. You can cook food this way.	fry (1)		1. night
3. This also means *correct*.	right (1)		2. kind
4. The opposite of *tame*	wild (1)		3. spy
5. A young person	child (1)		4. child
6. A word that asks a question	why (1)		5. light
7. When the sky is dark	night (1)		6. find
8. A word that can mean *next to*	by (1)		7. right

Add and subtract letters from the words below to write
Spelling Words.

Spelling Words

Basic Words
1. night
2. kind
3. spy
4. child
5. light
6. find
7. right
8. high
9. wild
10. July
11. fry
12. sigh

Review
13. by
14. why

9. (spray – ra) = __spy (1)__

10. (bright – br) + l = __light (1)__

11. (signal – nal) + h = __sigh (1)__

12. (fight – ght) + nd = __find (1)__

Pronouns and Verbs

- If the pronoun *he, she,* or *it* is the subject of
  a sentence that tells about now, add –*s* or –*es*
  to the verb.
  He (throws) the ball. She (catches) the ball.

- If the pronoun *I, you, we,* or *they* is the
  subject of a sentence that tells about now, do
  not add –*s* or –*es* to the verb.
  They (watch) the game. We (cheer) very loudly.

Circle the correct verb to match the subject. Then write
the sentence.

1. We (climb, climbs) to our seats.

   We climb to our seats. (1 point)

2. She (hand, hands) programs to people.

   She hands programs to people. (1)

3. I (reach, reaches) for one.

   I reach for one. (1)

4. You (look, looks) cold.

   You look cold. (1)

5. He (fix, fixes) a snack.

   He fixes a snack. (1)

Antonyms

Draw a line from each word on the left to its antonym
on the right.

find	whispered (1 point)
below	above (1)
yelled	lose (1)
final	beginning (1)

Read each sentence. Think of a word that has the opposite
meaning of the underlined word and write it on the line.

1. Emily had to find her library book.

   lose (1)

2. After the game, the final score was six to three.

   beginning (1)

3. We yelled when the parade came down the street.

   whispered (1)

4. You can't ride if your head is below the line.

   above (1)

Proofread for Spelling

Proofread the journal entry. Circle the misspelled words.
Then write the correct spellings on the lines below.

Last (knight) I was so afraid. I heard a (wilde)
scream from somewhere outside. I tried to turn on
the (lite), but it was up too (hi). It was so cold. It seemed
more like January than (Jully). I didn't know what to do.
I let out a (sye) and went to sleep. **(1 point each)**

Spelling Words

Basic Words
1. night
2. kind
3. spy
4. child
5. light
6. find
7. right
8. high
9. wild
10. July
11. fry
12. sigh

1. __night (1 point)__   4. __high (1)__

2. __wild (1)__   5. __July (1)__

3. __light (1)__   6. __sigh (1)__

Find and circle six Spelling Words with long *i*. The words
can read across or down. **(1 point each)**

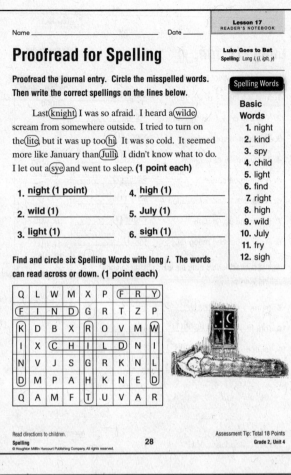

Q	L	W	M	X	P	F	R	Y
F	I	N	D	G	R	T	Z	P
K	D	B	X	R	O	V	M	W
I	X	C	H	I	L	D	N	I
N	V	J	S	G	R	K	N	L
D	M	P	A	H	K	N	E	D
Q	A	M	F	T	U	V	A	R

Kinds of Sentences

Read each sentence. Tell whether it is a statement,
an exclamation, a command, or a question. Then write the
sentence correctly on the line.

1. did you hit that ball __question__

   Did you hit that ball? (1 point)

2. you did a great job __exclamation__

   You did a great job! (1)

3. try that again __command__

   Try that again. (1)

4. Hanna pitches the ball __statement__

   Hanna pitches the ball. (1)

5. her dad hits the ball __statement__

   Her dad hits the ball. (1)

6. how far did he hit it __question__

   How far did he hit it? (1)

Subjects and Verbs

Subject and Verb Don't Match	Subject and Verb Match
Jared pitch the ball.	Jared pitches the ball.
She swing the bat.	She swings the bat.

Proofread the paragraphs. Find five places where the
subject and verb do not match. Write the corrected sentences
on the lines below.

Mike play baseball with me. He pitches the ball.
I hit the ball. It get dark out. Mom call me. She yells,
"Dinner!"

I wave at Mike. He wave back. He rush home, too.

1. __Mike plays baseball with me. (1 point)__

2. __It gets dark out. (1)__

3. __Mom calls me. (1)__

4. __He waves back. (1)__

5. __He rushes home, too. (1)__

Long *e* Sound for *y*

Circle the word that tells about each picture. Then use
the words to complete the sentences below.

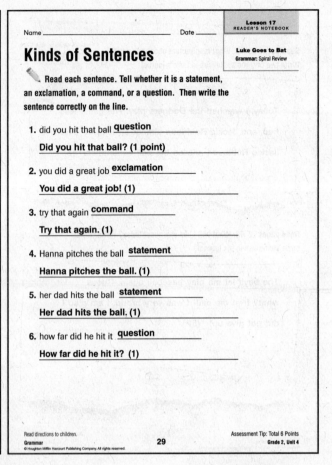

1. bath (baby) brick **(1 point)**   2. furry (funny) find **(1)**

3. (pretty) pretzel kitty **(1)**   4. pond penny (pony) **(1)**

5. (slippery) slope sloppy **(1)**   6. (penny) pencil painted **(1)**

7. We slid on the __slippery (1)__ sidewalk.

8. I gave my mom a __pretty (1)__ rose.

9. The __funny (1)__ story made me smile.

10. The __pony (1)__ lives at the farm.

Using *am*, *is*, and *are*

The verb *be* takes different forms. *Is*, *are*, and *am* tell about something happening now. Make sure the form of *be* agrees with the subject.

Use **is** with one.	**The day is** starting.
Use **are** with more than one.	**The farmers are** in the fields.
Use **am** with I.	**I am** there.

Thinking Question
Does the subject tell about one or more than one, or is the subject I?

Underline the correct sentence.

1. The sun is out. **(1 point)**
   The sun am out.

2. The corn plants is high.
   The corn plants are high. **(1)**

3. The workers is cutting them down.
   The workers are cutting them down. **(1)**

4. I is watching them.
   I am watching them. **(1)**

Long *e* Sound for *y*

Choose a word from the box to complete each sentence. Write it on the line.

Word Bank

funny	tiny	lady	many
sunny	muddy	puppy	happy

1. Today is a hot, __sunny (1 point)__ day.

2. My baby sister is __tiny (1)__

3. Wipe your __muddy (1)__ feet before you come in.

4. Do you want to hear a __funny (1)__ joke?

5. A __lady (1)__ in the store helped me find a gift for Mom.

6. How __many (1)__ children are in our class?

7. I always feel __happy (1)__ when I sing.

8. My __puppy (1)__ likes to bark at the moon.

Long *e* Spelled *y*

Write the Basic Words with double consonants in one list. Write the words with single consonants in another list.

Double Consonants	Single Consonants
1. happy (1 point)	8. baby (1)
2. pretty (1)	9. very (1)
3. puppy (1)	10. lucky (1)
4. funny (1)	11. only (1)
5. carry (1)	12. city (1)
6. sunny (1)	
7. penny (1)	

Spelling Words

Basic Words
1. happy
2. pretty
3. baby
4. very
5. puppy
6. funny
7. carry
8. lucky
9. only
10. sunny
11. penny
12. city

Review Words
13. tiny
14. many

Using *was* and *were*

The verb *be* takes different forms. **Was** and **were** tell about something that happened in the past. Make sure the form of **be** agrees with the subject.

Use **was** with one.	The **market was** busy.
Use **were** with more than one.	**Papa and Emelina were** shopping.

Thinking Question
Does the subject tell about one or more than one, or is the subject I?

Write each sentence correctly.

1. Mama (was, were) cooking.
   Mama was cooking. (1 point)

2. The beans (was, were) boiling.
   The beans were boiling. (1)

3. The rice (was, were) done.
   The rice was done. (1)

4. We (was, were) hungry.
   We were hungry. (1)

Focus Trait: Word Choice
Using Sense Words

Without Sense Words	With Sense Words
I took off my glove and touched the snow.	I took off my glove and touched the cold, white snow.

Read each description. Use sense words to fill in the blanks.
Possible responses shown.

Without Sense Words	With Sense Words
1. I drank some juice.	I drank some juice that tasted like **sour grapes** _____ **(1 point)**
2. The barn was filled with pigs.	The barn was filled with **little pink** _____ pigs. (1)

Pair/Share Work with a partner to add sense words.
Possible responses shown.

Without Sense Words	With Sense Words
3. I saw a field.	I saw a field of soft green clover. (1)
4. She laughed.	I could hear her soft giggle. (1)
5. I ate a pickle.	I tasted a sour pickle. (1)

Changing *y* to *i*

Read the word. Then change *y* to *i* and add *es* to make
the word mean more than one. Write the new word.

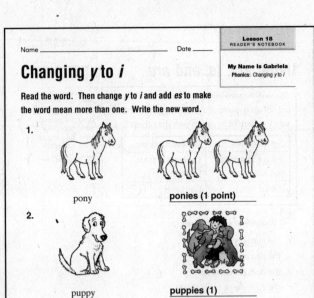

1. pony ___ **ponies (1 point)**

2. puppy ___ **puppies (1)**

3. baby ___ **babies (1)**

Write two sentences with the words that you wrote.
Possible responses shown.

4. **There are two babies on the rug. (1)**

5. **I saw two ponies at the farm. (1)**

Reader's Guide

My Name Is Gabriela

Make an Invitation

Garbriela Mistral is a famous writer who won an award
for her writing. Gather some details about her life.

**Read pages 92–95. Does Gabriela Mistral have a good
imagination? How can you tell?**

Yes. She thinks about polka-dot zebras. She thinks about

rainbow-colored flowers. She thinks about angels reading

books. (5 points)

**Read pages 100–101. Gabriela Mistral liked to play school.
Do you think she was a good pretend teacher? How can you tell?**

Yes. She made Pedro write his ABCs until he learned them

all. She sang songs with her pretend pupils. (5)

**Read pages 103 and 107. Did Gabriela Mistral still have a
good imagination after she grew up? How can you tell?**

Yes. She wrote poems about all kinds of things. She wrote

happy and sad stories. She wrote about fisherfolk who slept

in the sand and dreamed of the sea. (5)

Imagine you are having a party for Gabriela
Mistral. Use what you learned about Gabriela's
life to finish the invitation. Make an illustration
showing something from Gabriela's imagination.

Who: Gabriela Mistral

What: A Celebration of Gabriela's Nobel Prize

Where: Gabriela's family home in Elqui Valley

When: Saturday at 2:00

**Read pages 104–106. Say what you think Gabriela will tell her
friends about her life.**

Gabriela will give a short talk. She will tell us about

her travels to Europe and the United States. She will also tell

about how children everywhere want to learn. (5)

**Think about what you learned about Gabriela Mistral. What would
she want for the schools?**

Instead of a gift for Gabriela, please bring a gift for
the local school. Bring: **books about animals and learning**

and travel (OR paintings that show imagination). (5)

**Draw a picture from Gabriela's
imagination. (Possible drawing:
polka-dot zebra) (5)**

Long *e* Spelled *y*

Write a Basic Word that has the same or almost the same meaning for each word.

Spelling Words

Basic
Words
1. happy
2. pretty
3. baby
4. very
5. puppy
6. funny
7. carry
8. lucky
9. only
10. sunny
11. penny
12. city

Review
Words
13. tiny
14. many

1. beautiful   **pretty (1 point)**

2. dog 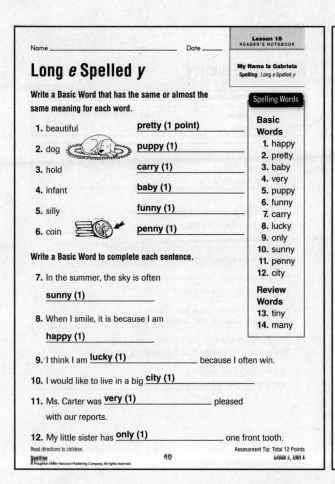   **puppy (1)**

3. hold   **carry (1)**

4. infant   **baby (1)**

5. silly   **funny (1)**

6. coin   **penny (1)**

Write a Basic Word to complete each sentence.

7. In the summer, the sky is often

   sunny (1)

8. When I smile, it is because I am

   happy (1)

9. I think I am **lucky (1)** because I often win.

10. I would like to live in a big **city (1)**.

11. Ms. Carter was **very (1)** pleased
    with our reports.

12. My little sister has **only (1)** one front tooth.

Using *Being* Verbs

Underline the correct sentence.

1. The rodeo is here. **(1 point)**
   The rodeo are here.
   The rodeo am here.

2. The crowds is clapping.
   The crowds are clapping. **(1)**
   The crowds am clapping.

Write each sentence correctly.

3. Gabriela (was, were) a teacher.
   Gabriela was a teacher. (1)

4. She (was, were) speaking.
   She was speaking. (1)

5. Her students (was, were) listening.
   Her students were listening. (1)

6. They (was, were) learning a lot.
   They were learning a lot. (1)

Name _____ Date _____

Lesson 18
READER'S NOTEBOOK

My Name Is Gabriela
Vocabulary Strategies:
Suffixes -y and -ful

Suffixes *-y* and *-ful*

Read each sentence. Add the suffix *-y* or *-ful* to
complete the underlined word.

1. The garden smells <u>flower</u> + **y (1 point)**

2. Joel's smile showed he was <u>joy</u> + **ful (1)**

3. The <u>play</u> + **ful (1)** kitten
   knocked over a vase.

Circle the word that correctly completes each sentence.

4. I always look both ways before crossing the street.
   I am very _____
   (careful)   carefully (1)

5. The weather was bad today.
   It was very _____
   rainful   (rainy) (1)

6. My lemonade was _____ after
   the ice in it melted.
   (watery)   waterful (1)

Proofread for Spelling

Proofread Tony's letter. Circle six misspelled words.
Then write each misspelled word correctly.

Spelling Words

Basic
Words
1. happy
2. pretty
3. baby
4. very
5. puppy
6. funny
7. carry
8. lucky
9. only
10. sunny
11. penny
12. city

Dear Grandma and Grandpa,

Last Friday, I got a new (puppe). I was (veray)
surprised! Dad and Mom let me (carey) her home. She
was the (onlee) one I really liked. I'm going to name her
(Peny). Don't you think that's a (prettie) name?

Love,
Tony

1. **puppy (1 point)**   4. **only (1)**

2. **very (1)**   5. **Penny (1)**

3. **carry (1)**   6. **pretty (1)**

Write the Basic Word that answers each question.

7. I am very young. What am I? **baby (1)**

8. When I feel like this, I laugh. How do I feel? **happy (1)**

9. It is warm outside. How is the weather? **sunny (1)**

10. Where do you see big buildings? **city (1)**

Name _____ Date _____

Writing Quotations

My Name Is Gabriela
Grammar: Spiral Review

✏️ **Underline the correct sentence.**

1. <u>Dad said, "It snowed." **(1 point)**</u>
   Dad said "it snowed."

2. I asked, may I play outside?
   <u>I asked, "May I play outside?" **(1)**</u>

3. Mom said "have fun!"
   <u>Mom said, "Have fun!" **(1)**</u>

✏️ **Read each paragraph. Then write each paragraph correctly. Fix five mistakes in capitalization and punctuation.**

The cook said "i will make corn. He put corn in the bag.

Mama said "I will cook rice. She put rice in the bag.

The cook said, "I will make corn." He put

corn in the bag.

Mama said, "I will cook rice." She put rice

in the bag. (5)

Name _____ Date _____

Sentence Fluency

My Name Is Gabriela
Grammar: Connect to Writing

Sentences with Repeated Subjects	Sentences with Combined Subjects
The weather is rainy. The weather is cool.	The weather is rainy and cool.

Sentences with Repeated Subjects	Sentences with Combined Subjects
The students are reading. The students are learning.	The students are reading and learning.

✏️ **Combine the sentences with repeating subjects. Write the new sentence on the line.**

1. The animals are eating. The animals are sleeping.
   The animals are eating and sleeping. (1 point)

2. They were running. They were playing.
   They were running and playing. (1)

3. Sasha was reading. Sasha was writing.
   Sasha was reading and writing. (1)

4. The country is growing. The country is changing.
   The country is growing and changing. (1)

5. I am chatting. I am laughing.
   I am chatting and laughing. (1)

Name _____ Date _____

Words with *ar*

The Signmaker's Assistant
Phonics: Words with *ar*

Circle the word that completes each sentence. Then write the word on the line.

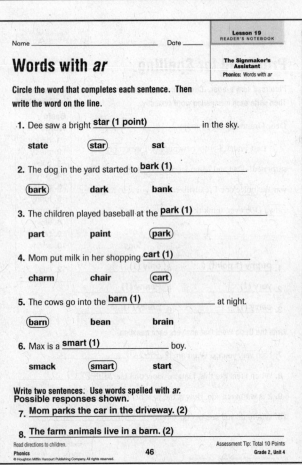

1. Dee saw a bright <u>star **(1 point)**</u> in the sky.
   state   (star)   sat

2. The dog in the yard started to <u>bark **(1)**</u>
   (bark)   dark   bank

3. The children played baseball at the <u>park **(1)**</u>
   part   paint   (park)

4. Mom put milk in her shopping <u>cart **(1)**</u>
   charm   chair   (cart)

5. The cows go into the <u>barn **(1)**</u> at night.
   (barn)   bean   brain

6. Max is a <u>smart **(1)**</u> boy.
   smack   (smart)   start

Write two sentences. Use words spelled with *ar*.
Possible responses shown.

7. **Mom parks the car in the driveway. (2)**

8. **The farm animals live in a barn. (2)**

Name _____ Date _____

Commas in Dates

The Signmaker's Assistant
Grammar: Commas in Dates and Places

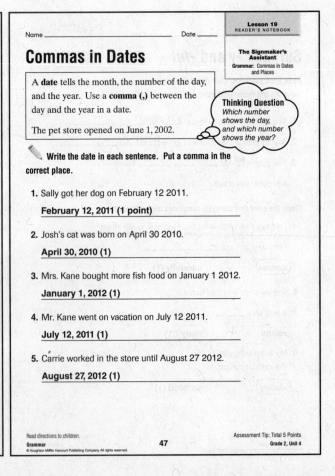

A **date** tells the month, the number of the day, and the year. Use a **comma (,)** between the day and the year in a date.

The pet store opened on June 1, 2002.

Thinking Question
Which number shows the day, and which number shows the year?

✏️ **Write the date in each sentence. Put a comma in the correct place.**

1. Sally got her dog on February 12 2011.
   February 12, 2011 (1 point)

2. Josh's cat was born on April 30 2010.
   April 30, 2010 (1)

3. Mrs. Kane bought more fish food on January 1 2012.
   January 1, 2012 (1)

4. Mr. Kane went on vacation on July 12 2011.
   July 12, 2011 (1)

5. Carrie worked in the store until August 27 2012.
   August 27, 2012 (1)

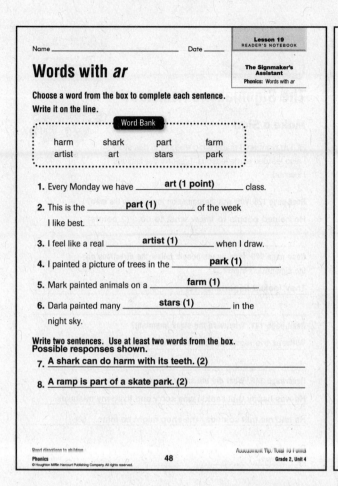

Words with *ar*

Choose a word from the box to complete each sentence.
Write it on the line.

Word Bank

| harm | shark | part | farm |
| artist | art | stars | park |

1. Every Monday we have ____ art (1 point) ____ class.

2. This is the ____ part (1) ____ of the week
I like best.

3. I feel like a real ____ artist (1) ____ when I draw.

4. I painted a picture of trees in the ____ park (1) ____

5. Mark painted animals on a ____ farm (1) ____

6. Darla painted many ____ stars (1) ____ in the
night sky.

Write two sentences. Use at least two words from the box.
Possible responses shown.

7. A shark can do harm with its teeth. (2)

8. A ramp is part of a skate park. (2)

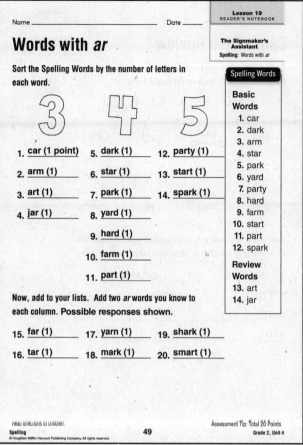

Words with *ar*

Sort the Spelling Words by the number of letters in
each word.

3 4 5

1. car (1 point)   5. dark (1)   12. party (1)
2. arm (1)   6. star (1)   13. start (1)
3. art (1)   7. park (1)   14. spark (1)
4. jar (1)   8. yard (1)
9. hard (1)
10. farm (1)
11. part (1)

Now, add to your lists. Add two *ar* words you know to
each column. Possible responses shown.

15. far (1)   17. yarn (1)   19. shark (1)
16. tar (1)   18. mark (1)   20. smart (1)

Spelling Words

**Basic
Words**
1. car
2. dark
3. arm
4. star
5. park
6. yard
7. party
8. hard
9. farm
10. start
11. part
12. spark

**Review
Words**
13. art
14. jar

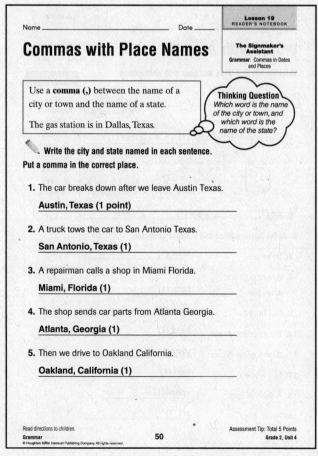

Name _____ Date _____

Lesson 19
READER'S NOTEBOOK

The Signmaker's Assistant
Grammar: Commas in Dates
and Places

Commas with Place Names

Use a **comma (,)** between the name of a
city or town and the name of a state.

The gas station is in Dallas, Texas.

Thinking Question
Which word is the name
of the city or town, and
which word is the
name of the state?

Write the city and state named in each sentence.
Put a comma in the correct place.

1. The car breaks down after we leave Austin Texas.

   Austin, Texas (1 point)

2. A truck tows the car to San Antonio Texas.

   San Antonio, Texas (1)

3. A repairman calls a shop in Miami Florida.

   Miami, Florida (1)

4. The shop sends car parts from Atlanta Georgia.

   Atlanta, Georgia (1)

5. Then we drive to Oakland California.

   Oakland, California (1)

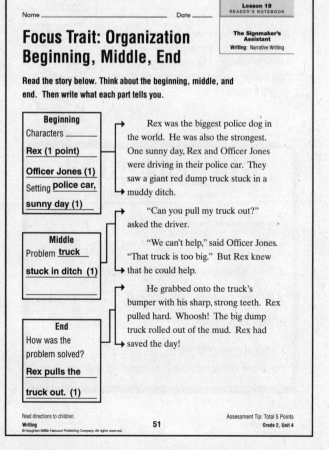

Focus Trait: Organization
Beginning, Middle, End

Read the story below. Think about the beginning, middle, and
end. Then write what each part tells you.

Beginning
Characters _____
Rex (1 point)
Officer Jones (1)
Setting **police car,**
sunny day (1)

Rex was the biggest police dog in
the world. He was also the strongest.
One sunny day, Rex and Officer Jones
were driving in their police car. They
saw a giant red dump truck stuck in a
muddy ditch.

"Can you pull my truck out?"
asked the driver.

Middle
Problem **truck**
stuck in ditch (1)

"We can't help," said Officer Jones.
"That truck is too big." But Rex knew
that he could help.

End
How was the
problem solved?
Rex pulls the
truck out. (1)

He grabbed onto the truck's
bumper with his sharp, strong teeth. Rex
pulled hard. Whoosh! The big dump
truck rolled out of the mud. Rex had
saved the day!

Cumulative Review

Lesson 19
READER'S NOTEBOOK

The Signmaker's Assistant
Phonics: Cumulative Review

Circle the word that goes with each picture. Underline the letters that spell the long *i* or long *e* sound.

1.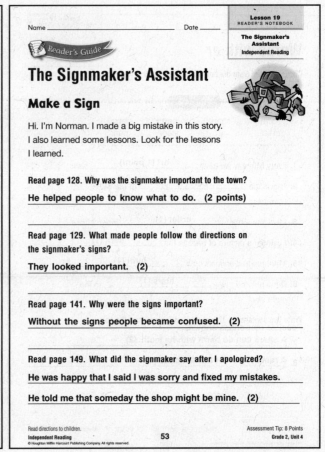
(light)   late
(1 point)

2. (pie)   pig (1)

3. (shine)   shy (1)

4. part   (party) (1)

Write words you know with long *i* spelled *y*. Write words you know with long *e* spelled *y*. Possible responses shown.

Long *i*	Long *e*
why (1)	messy (1)
my (1)	city (1)
try (1)	really (1)

Read directions to children.
Phonics
© Houghton Mifflin Harcourt Publishing Company. All rights reserved.
52
Assessment Tip: Total 10 Points
Grade 2, Unit 4

Lesson 19
READER'S NOTEBOOK

The Signmaker's Assistant
Independent Reading

📓 **Reader's Guide**

The Signmaker's Assistant

Make a Sign

Hi. I'm Norman. I made a big mistake in this story. I also learned some lessons. Look for the lessons I learned.

Read page 128. Why was the signmaker important to the town?

He helped people to know what to do. (2 points)

Read page 129. What made people follow the directions on the signmaker's signs?

They looked important. (2)

Read page 141. Why were the signs important?

Without the signs people became confused. (2)

Read page 149. What did the signmaker say after I apologized?

He was happy that I said I was sorry and fixed my mistakes.

He told me that someday the shop might be mine. (2)

Read directions to children.
Independent Reading
© Houghton Mifflin Harcourt Publishing Company. All rights reserved.
53
Assessment Tip: 8 Points
Grade 2, Unit 4

Lesson 19
READER'S NOTEBOOK

The Signmaker's Assistant
Independent Reading

Now the sign shop is mine, and I need an assistant. Think about the work I did when I was the assistant. Use details and pictures from the story to see what a good signmaker assistant does.

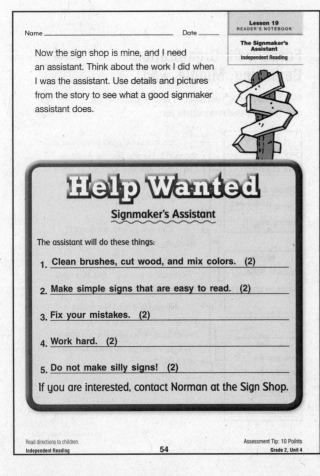

Help Wanted

Signmaker's Assistant

The assistant will do these things:

1. Clean brushes, cut wood, and mix colors. (2)

2. Make simple signs that are easy to read. (2)

3. Fix your mistakes. (2)

4. Work hard. (2)

5. Do not make silly signs! (2)

If you are interested, contact Norman at the Sign Shop.

Read directions to children.
Independent Reading
54
Assessment Tip: 10 Points
Grade 2, Unit 4

Lesson 19
READER'S NOTEBOOK

The Signmaker's Assistant
Spelling: Words with ar

Words with *ar*

Write the Spelling Word that goes with each picture.

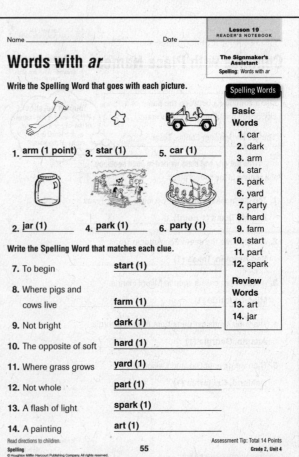

1. arm (1 point)   3. star (1)   5. car (1)

2. jar (1)   4. park (1)   6. party (1)

Write the Spelling Word that matches each clue.

7. To begin	start (1)
8. Where pigs and cows live	farm (1)
9. Not bright	dark (1)
10. The opposite of soft	hard (1)
11. Where grass grows	yard (1)
12. Not whole	part (1)
13. A flash of light	spark (1)
14. A painting	art (1)

Spelling Words

Basic Words
1. car
2. dark
3. arm
4. star
5. park
6. yard
7. party
8. hard
9. farm
10. start
11. part
12. spark

Review Words
13. art
14. jar

Read directions to children.
Spelling
© Houghton Mifflin Harcourt Publishing Company. All rights reserved.
55
Assessment Tip: Total 14 Points
Grade 2, Unit 4

Commas in Parts of Letters

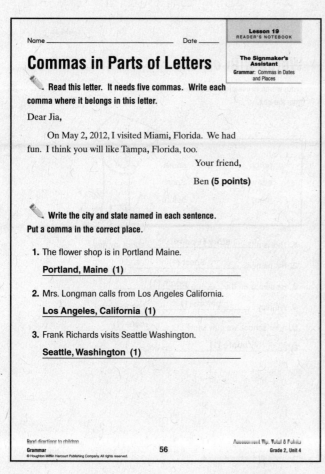 Read this letter. It needs five commas. Write each comma where it belongs in this letter.

Dear Jia,

On May 2, 2012, I visited Miami, Florida. We had fun. I think you will like Tampa, Florida, too.

Your friend,

Ben **(5 points)**

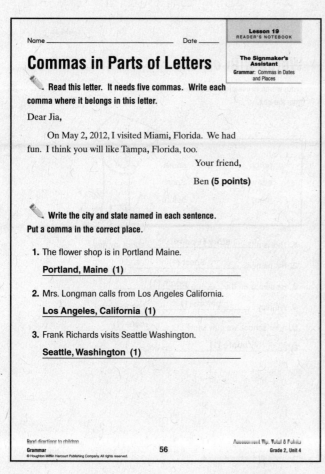 Write the city and state named in each sentence. Put a comma in the correct place.

1. The flower shop is in Portland Maine.

Portland, Maine (1)

2. Mrs. Longman calls from Los Angeles California.

Los Angeles, California (1)

3. Frank Richards visits Seattle Washington.

Seattle, Washington (1)

Shades of Meaning

Choose the best word from the Word Bank to complete each sentence. Use every word.

Word Bank

tumble	slide	slip

1. The wall of mud began to ____ **slide** ____ slowly down the hill. **(1 point)**

2. Be careful not to ____ **slip** ____ on the slimy seaweed! **(1)**

3. Turning over and over, the child began to ____ **tumble** ____ down the grassy hill. **(1)**

Word Bank

cool	cold	frozen

4. A ____ **cool** ____ breeze is welcome after the day's heat. **(1 point)**

5. You should wear a hat on a ____ **cold** ____ and snowy day. **(1)**

6. When the pond is ____ **frozen** ____, we can skate on it. **(1)**

Proofread for Spelling

Proofread the invitation. Circle the six misspelled words. Then write the correct spellings on the lines below.

Dear Kara,

You are invited to my (paurty). It will be in the (parke) on Center Street. It is not (heard) to find. We will (starrt) from my house at 12:00. My mother will drive us in her (kar). We will be home before (dirk).

Your friend,

Angie

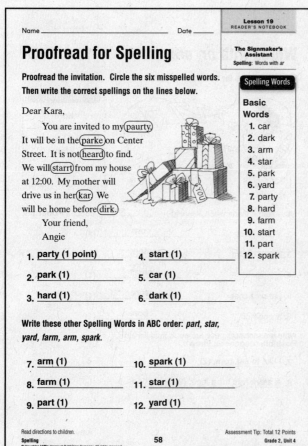

Spelling Words

Basic Words
1. car
2. dark
3. arm
4. star
5. park
6. yard
7. party
8. hard
9. farm
10. start
11. part
12. spark

1. **party (1 point)**   4. **start (1)**
2. **park (1)**   5. **car (1)**
3. **hard (1)**   6. **dark (1)**

Write these other Spelling Words in ABC order: *part, star, yard, farm, arm, spark.*

7. **arm (1)**   10. **spark (1)**
8. **farm (1)**   11. **star (1)**
9. **part (1)**   12. **yard (1)**

Writing Proper Nouns

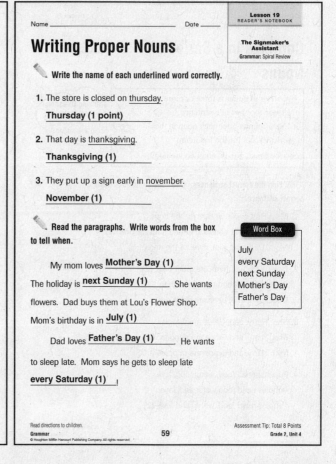 Write the name of each underlined word correctly.

1. The store is closed on thursday.

Thursday (1 point)

2. That day is thanksgiving.

Thanksgiving (1)

3. They put up a sign early in november.

November (1)

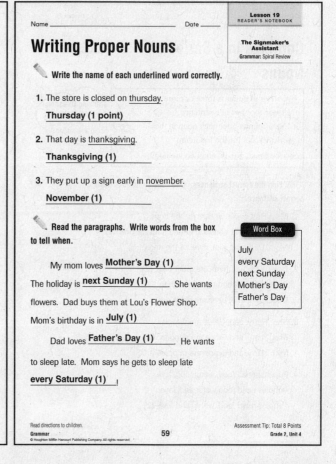 Read the paragraphs. Write words from the box to tell when.

My mom loves **Mother's Day (1)**. The holiday is **next Sunday (1)**. She wants flowers. Dad buys them at Lou's Flower Shop. Mom's birthday is in **July (1)**.

Dad loves **Father's Day (1)**. He wants to sleep late. Mom says he gets to sleep late **every Saturday (1)**.

Word Box

July
every Saturday
next Sunday
Mother's Day
Father's Day

Conventions

Not Correct	Correct
The sports shop opened on May 8 1998.	The sports shop opened on May 8, 1998.

Not Correct	Correct
The soccer ball was made in Detroit Michigan.	The soccer ball was made in Detroit, Michigan.

✏️ **Proofread the sentences for missing commas. Rewrite each sentence correctly.**

1. The sports store opened on March 15 2005.

   The sports store opened on March 15, 2005. (1 point)

2. It is in Charleston South Carolina.

   It is in Charleston, South Carolina. (1)

3. Mr. Thomas sold ice skates on December 1 2006.

   Mr. Thomas sold ice skates on December 1, 2006. (1)

4. He sold beach balls on June 5 2007.

   He sold beach balls on June 5, 2007. (1)

5. He sold shells from Daytona Beach Florida.

   He sold shells from Daytona Beach, Florida. (1)

Words with *or, ore*

Write words to complete the sentences. Use words from the box.

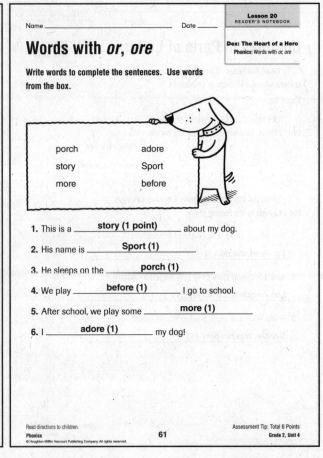

porch	adore
story	Sport
more	before

1. This is a ____**story (1 point)**____ about my dog.

2. His name is ____**Sport (1)**____

3. He sleeps on the ____**porch (1)**____

4. We play ____**before (1)**____ I go to school.

5. After school, we play some ____**more (1)**____

6. I ____**adore (1)**____ my dog!

Commas in a Series of Nouns

- A **series of nouns** is three or more nouns that appear together in a sentence.
- Use a comma after each noun in the series except for the last noun.

Sparky, Spike, Rover, and Leo are dogs.

Thinking Question
Are there three or more nouns being listed in a series?

✏️ **Find the correct sentences. Circle the commas in each correct sentence.**

1. Mom Dad, and Kim care for the dogs.
   Mom, Dad, and Kim care for the dogs. **(2 points)**
   Mom, Dad, and, Kim, care for the dogs.

2. Dogs, cats, and birds are great pets. **(2)**
   Dogs cats and birds are great pets.
   Dogs, cats, and, birds are great pets.

3. Max, Harry, and, Grace are puppies.
   Max, Harry, and Grace are puppies. **(2)**
   Max, Harry, and Grace, are puppies.

4. Puppies need food, water, and, love.
   Puppies need food water and, love.
   Puppies need food, water, and love. **(2)**

Words with *or, ore*

Write a word from the box to answer each riddle.

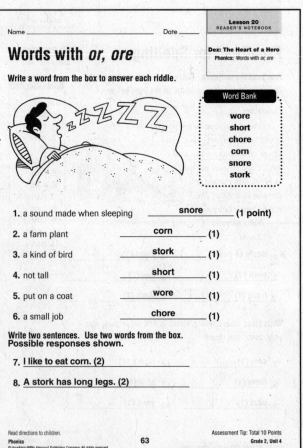

Word Bank
- wore
- short
- chore
- corn
- snore
- stork

1. a sound made when sleeping ____**snore**____ **(1 point)**

2. a farm plant ____**corn**____ **(1)**

3. a kind of bird ____**stork**____ **(1)**

4. not tall ____**short**____ **(1)**

5. put on a coat ____**wore**____ **(1)**

6. a small job ____**chore**____ **(1)**

Write two sentences. Use two words from the box.
Possible responses shown.

7. **I like to eat corn. (2)**

8. **A stork has long legs. (2)**

Words with *or, ore*

Sort the Basic Words.

Spelling Words

or Words	*ore* Words
1. corn (1 point)	9. shore (1)
2. fork (1)	10. store (1)
3. morning (1)	11. tore (1)
4. short (1)	12. score (1)
5. horn (1)	
6. forget (1)	
7. born (1)	
8. story (1)	

Basic Words
1. horn
2. story
3. fork
4. score
5. store
6. corn
7. morning
8. shore
9. short
10. born
11. tore
12. forget

Review Words
13. for
14. more

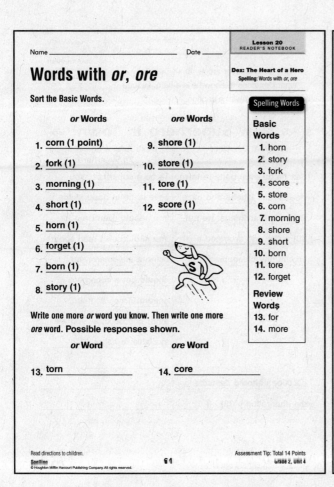

Write one more *or* word you know. Then write one more *ore* word. Possible responses shown.

or Word	*ore* Word
13. torn	14. core

Assessment Tip: Total 14 Points
Grade 2, Unit 4

Commas in a Series of Verbs

- A **series of verbs** is three or more verbs that appear together in a sentence.
- Use a comma after each verb in a series except the last verb.

Hamster runs, leaps, and waves.

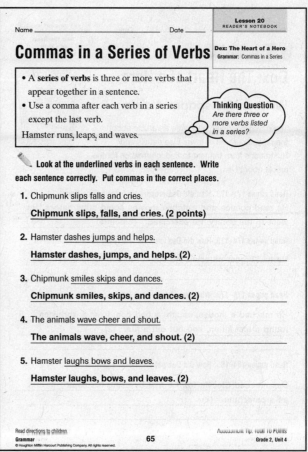

Thinking Question
Are there three or more verbs listed in a series?

Look at the underlined verbs in each sentence. Write each sentence correctly. Put commas in the correct places.

1. Chipmunk slips falls and cries.
   Chipmunk slips, falls, and cries. (2 points)

2. Hamster dashes jumps and helps.
   Hamster dashes, jumps, and helps. (2)

3. Chipmunk smiles skips and dances.
   Chipmunk smiles, skips, and dances. (2)

4. The animals wave cheer and shout.
   The animals wave, cheer, and shout. (2)

5. Hamster laughs bows and leaves.
   Hamster laughs, bows, and leaves. (2)

Assessment Tip: Total 10 Points
Grade 2, Unit 4

Focus Trait: Organization Interesting Beginnings

Uninteresting Beginning	Interesting Beginning
Once there was a cat named Freddy.	Freddy was a fluffy black cat. He was so smart that he solved mysteries for his friends.

Write two different beginnings for a story about a deep-sea diving dog. Make each beginning interesting. Check the one you like better. Possible responses shown.

1. **One day Flipper ran to the beach. He was very happy because he loved playing with the fish in the waves.**

   (5 points)

2. **All day long, Flipper the dog stood and watched the fish. He wished he could play with them. (5)**

Assessment Tip: Total 10 Points
Grade 2, Unit 4

Cumulative Review

Read the clue. Circle the word that matches.

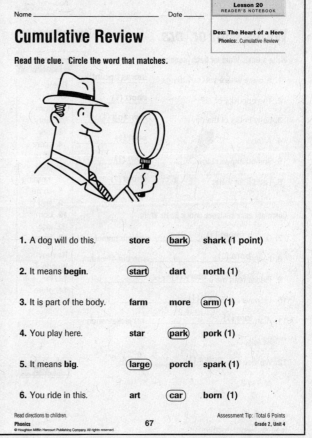

1. A dog will do this.   store   (bark)   shark (1 point)

2. It means **begin**.   (start)   dart   north (1)

3. It is part of the body.   farm   more   (arm) (1)

4. You play here.   star   (park)   pork (1)

5. It means **big**.   (large)   porch   spark (1)

6. You ride in this.   art   (car)   born (1)

Assessment Tip: Total 6 Points
Grade 2, Unit 4

Panel 1 (page 68)

Name _____ Date _____

Reader's Guide

Dex: The Heart of a Hero

Write a Newspaper Article

The newspaper wants to write an article about the new superhero in town. Use details and illustrations from the text to find information for the article about Dex.

Read pages 171–173. How did Dex prepare for being a superhero?

He read comics and watched movies about superheroes. He went to the library. He exercised. **(2 points)**

Read pages 174–175. How did Dex know he was ready to be a superhero?

He had bigger muscles. He could run and jump better. **(2)**

Read pages 178–179. What were some ways Dex helped?

He rescued a mouse, caught a bad dog, fixed a sprinkler, found a lost kitten, and put out a fire. **(2)**

Read pages 184–185. How did Dex get Cleevis as a partner?

Dex rescued Cleevis from a tree by using his cape as a parachute. **(2)**

Panel 2 (page 69)

Name _____ Date _____

Write a newspaper article about Dex. Tell what Dex does to show he is a hero. Include an illustration with a caption.

❧ New Superhero in Town! ❧

What Dex Does	Dex's Advice on Becoming a Superhero
Dex helps everybody in town. He rescues kittens and mice. He finds lost things. He put out a fire and arranged a community cleanup. **(5)**	To be a superhero, you have to be in good shape. You should exercise a lot. You should also read about being a superhero. You should get a superhero uniform. This will help other people know you are available to help. **(5)**
(Captions should describe the illustration.) **(5)**	

Panel 3 (page 70)

Name _____ Date _____

Lesson 20
READER'S NOTEBOOK
Dex: The Heart of a Hero
Spelling: Words with or, ore

Words with *or, ore*

Write a Basic Word for each meaning.

1. A place where you buy things — store **(1 point)**
2. The opposite of *tall* — short **(1)**
3. Early hours of the day — morning **(1)**
4. A food — corn **(1)**
5. Something you blow — horn **(1)**
6. Land near water — shore **(1)**

Complete each sentence with a Basic Word.

7. Do not forget **(1)** your homework!
8. I was born **(1)** on the 4th of July.
9. Please read me a story **(1)**.
10. I always use a fork **(1)** to eat.
11. Alan tore **(1)** his jacket when he fell.
12. We won by a score **(1)** of 3 to 2.

Spelling Words

Basic Words
1. horn
2. story
3. fork
4. score
5. store
6. corn
7. morning
8. shore
9. short
10. born
11. tore
12. forget

Review Words
13. for
14. more

RAMS ◎ EAGLES

Panel 4 (page 71)

Name _____ Date _____

Lesson 20
READER'S NOTEBOOK
Dex: The Heart of a Hero
Grammar: Commas in a Series

Commas in a Series

Draw a line under each correct sentence.

1. Super Cat visits the park, school, and, playground.
   Super Cat visits the park, school, and playground. **(1 point)**
   Super Cat, visits the, park, school and playground.

2. She saves a butterfly, worm, and ladybug. **(1)**
   She saves a, butterfly, worm, and ladybug.
   She saves a butterfly, worm and ladybug.

3. Mama Papa, and Baby Cat, are happy!
   Mama, Papa and Baby, Cat are happy!
   Mama, Papa, and Baby Cat are happy! **(1)**

Write each sentence. Use commas correctly.

4. The penguins waddle jump and slide.
   The penguins waddle, jump, and slide. **(2)**

5. They dive splash and swim.
   They dive, splash, and swim. **(2)**

6. People watch point and smile.
   People watch, point, and smile. **(2)**

Name _____ Date _____

Prefix *over-*

Read each sentence. Fill in the blank with one of the
words in the box.

Word Box

overlooked	overcrowded	overboard
overeat	overdue	overflowed

1. I don't want to **overeat (1 point)** _____ at
   dinner. I want to save room for dessert!

2. Too many people came to the party, so the room
   was **overcrowded (1)** _____

3. Tom can't find his book on the shelf. Maybe he
   overlooked (1) _____ it.

4. I poured too much milk in my cup, and it
   overflowed (1) _____

5. The movies we rented are **overdue (1)** _____
   We should have returned them last week.

6. I went on a boat ride last week, and my sunglasses
   fell **overboard (1)** _____!

Name _____ Date _____

Proofread for Spelling

Proofread the ad. Cross out the five misspelled words.
Then write the correct spellings in the margin.

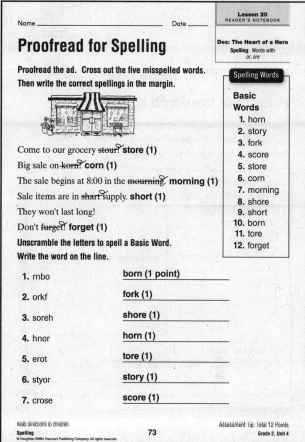

Come to our grocery ~~stour.~~ **store (1)**

Big sale on ~~korn!~~ **corn (1)**

The sale begins at 8:00 in the ~~mourning.~~ **morning (1)**

Sale items are in ~~shart~~ supply. **short (1)**

They won't last long!

Don't ~~furget!~~ **forget (1)**

Unscramble the letters to spell a Basic Word.
Write the word on the line.

1. rnbo **born (1 point)**
2. orkf **fork (1)**
3. soreh **shore (1)**
4. hnor **horn (1)**
5. erot **tore (1)**
6. styor **story (1)**
7. crose **score (1)**

Spelling Words

**Basic
Words**
1. horn
2. story
3. fork
4. score
5. store
6. corn
7. morning
8. shore
9. short
10. born
11. tore
12. forget

Name _____ Date _____

Writing Book Titles

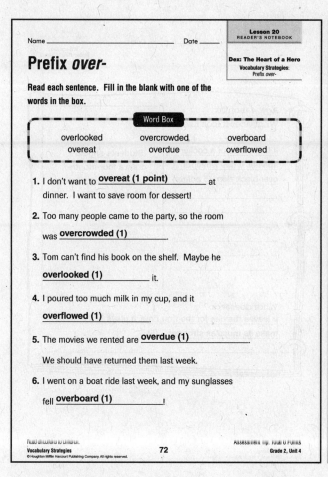 Rewrite each sentence. Write the book titles correctly.
Remember to use capital letters when needed.

1. My favorite book is the cat in the hat.
   My favorite book is <u>The Cat in the Hat</u>**. (1 point)**

2. Did Dr. Rames write the book taking care of pets?
   Did Dr. Rames write the book <u>Taking Care of Pets</u>**? (1)**

Fix the mistakes in the paragraph. Write the
paragraph correctly.

Mr. Grady owns a book store. Today, Lynn buys
the book caring for dogs. Mr. Grady also sells her
another book. This one is called how to keep a bird.

**Mr. Grady owns a book store. Today, Lynn buys the
book** <u>Caring for Dogs</u>**. Mr. Grady also sells her
another book. This one is called** <u>How to Keep a Bird</u>**. (4)**

Name _____ Date _____

Sentence Fluency

Short, Choppy Sentences	Smoother Sentence with Commas
Sam read the story. Izzy read the story. Mario read the story.	Sam, Izzy, and Mario read the story.

Short, Choppy Sentences	Smoother Sentence with Commas
The monkeys had bananas. The monkeys had apples. The monkeys had carrots.	The monkeys had bananas, apples, and carrots.

Read each group of sentences. Combine the three
sentences. Use commas correctly.

1. The monkeys climbed trees.
   The monkeys climbed vines.
   The monkeys climbed ropes.
   The monkeys climbed trees, vines, and ropes. (3 points)

2. Owl watched the monkeys.
   Ant watched the monkeys.
   Tiger watched the monkeys.
   Owl, Ant, and Tiger watched the monkeys. (3)

3. The monkeys jumped on the rocks.
   The monkeys climbed on the rocks.
   The monkeys ate on the rocks.
   The monkeys jumped, climbed, and ate on the rocks. (3)

Name _____ Date _____

Unit 4
READER'S NOTEBOOK
**Where Do
Polar Bears Live?**
Segment 1
Independent Reading

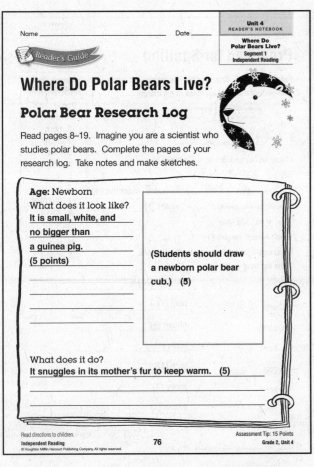

Where Do Polar Bears Live?

Polar Bear Research Log

Read pages 8–19. Imagine you are a scientist who studies polar bears. Complete the pages of your research log. Take notes and make sketches.

Age: Newborn

What does it look like?
It is small, white, and
no bigger than
a guinea pig.
(5 points)
_____
_____
_____

(Students should draw
a newborn polar bear
cub.) (5)

What does it do?
It snuggles in its mother's fur to keep warm. (5)
_____

Name _____ Date _____

Unit 4
READER'S NOTEBOOK
**Where Do
Polar Bears Live?**
Segment 1
Independent Reading

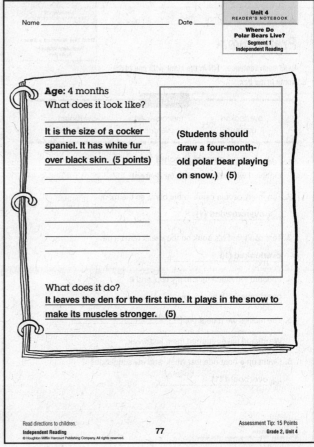

Age: 4 months
What does it look like?
_____
It is the size of a cocker
spaniel. It has white fur
over black skin. (5 points)
_____
_____
_____

(Students should
draw a four-month-
old polar bear playing
on snow.) (5)

What does it do?
It leaves the den for the first time. It plays in the snow to
make its muscles stronger. (5)

Name _____ Date _____

Unit 4
READER'S NOTEBOOK
**Where Do
Polar Bears Live?**
Segment 2
Independent Reading

Where Do Polar Bears Live?

Arctic Scrapbook

Read pages 20–28. You took an Artic tour!
When you came home, you had a lot of photographs.
Now you are going to make a scrapbook with a page
for each arctic animal. Draw a picture of each animal.
Then write what the animal looks like and what it does.

(Students should draw a
seal.) (5 points)

Seal

Arctic seals are gray and smooth. They use their

flippers to make breathing holes in the ice. (5)

Name _____ Date _____

Unit 4
READER'S NOTEBOOK
**Where Do
Polar Bears Live?**
Segment 2
Independent Reading

(Students should draw
an arctic fox.) (5 points)

Arctic Fox

Today we saw an arctic fox.

The artic fox is small and has white fur. Sometimes it steals

meat from polar bears. (5)

Name _____ Date _____

Unit 4
READER'S NOTEBOOK

Where Do
Polar Bears Live?
Segment 3
Independent Reading

Where Do Polar Bears Live?

Help Save the Polar Bears!

Read pages 29–35. Each year, the Arctic ice melts and freezes. However, less ice freezes every year. Write reasons why this is a problem for polar bears.

Polar bears need ice because they hunt on ice. **(5 points)**

With less ice, polar bears catch fewer seals. **(5)**

The Arctic ice is shrinking, and this hurts polar bears.

Bears are getting thinner and less healthy. **(5)**

Many polar bears die before they can have cubs. **(5)**

80

Assessment Tip: 20 Points

Grade 2, Unit 4

Unit 4
READER'S NOTEBOOK

Where Do
Polar Bears Live?
Segment 3
Independent Reading

The author provides interesting facts about polar bears. Use pages 29–35 to create an animal fact card about polar bears. Draw a picture and write facts.

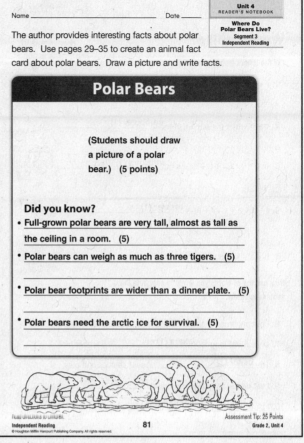

Polar Bears

(Students should draw a picture of a polar bear.) **(5 points)**

Did you know?

• Full-grown polar bears are very tall, almost as tall as the ceiling in a room. **(5)**

• Polar bears can weigh as much as three tigers. **(5)**

• Polar bear footprints are wider than a dinner plate. **(5)**

• Polar bears need the arctic ice for survival. **(5)**

81

Assessment Tip: 25 Points

Grade 2, Unit 4

Words with *er*

Circle the word that fits in each sentence.
Underline the letters that stand for the *er* sound.
Then write the word to complete the sentence.

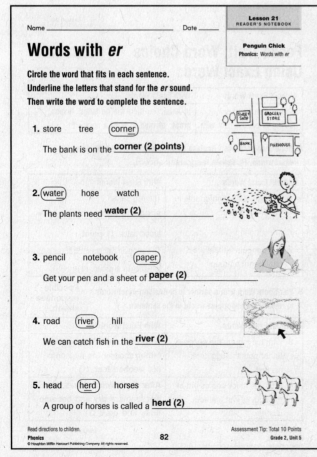

1. store   tree   (corner)

    The bank is on the _corner_ **(2 points)**

2. (water)   hose   watch

    The plants need _water_ **(2)**

3. pencil   notebook   (paper)

    Get your pen and a sheet of _paper_ **(2)**

4. road   (river)   hill

    We can catch fish in the _river_ **(2)**

5. head   (herd)   horses

    A group of horses is called a _herd_ **(2)**

82

Assessment Tip: Total 10 Points

Grade 2, Unit 5

How Things Look

An **adjective** is a word that tells how something looks.
Adjectives can tell size, color, shape, or how many.
Penguins look short.

Thinking Question
Which word tells more about how something looks?

Write the adjective from the box that best fits each sentence. Use the clues in ( ).

round	small	four	black

1. I see _four_ **(1 point)** penguins on the ice.
   (tell how many)

2. The penguins stand in a _round_ **(1)** circle.
   (tell shape)

3. They are _black_ **(1)** and white. (tell color)

4. The baby penguin is _small_ **(1)**. (tell size)

83

Assessment Tip: Total 4 Points

Grade 2, Unit 5

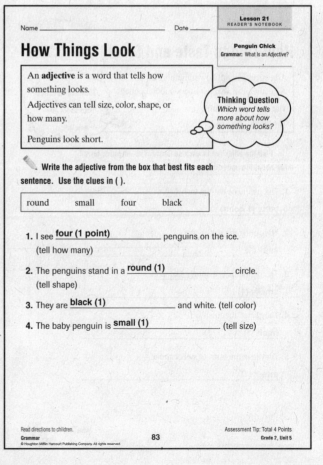

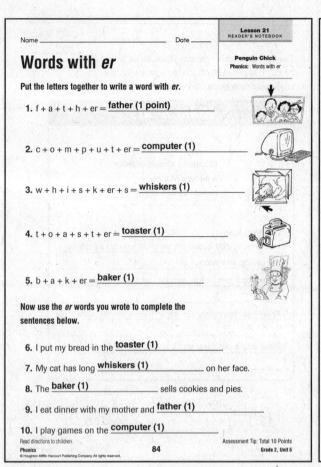

Words with *er*

Put the letters together to write a word with *er*.

1. f + a + t + h + er = __father (1 point)__

2. c + o + m + p + u + t + er = __computer (1)__

3. w + h + i + s + k + er + s = __whiskers (1)__

4. t + o + a + s + t + er = __toaster (1)__

5. b + a + k + er = __baker (1)__

Now use the *er* words you wrote to complete the sentences below.

6. I put my bread in the __toaster (1)__

7. My cat has long __whiskers (1)__ on her face.

8. The __baker (1)__ sells cookies and pies.

9. I eat dinner with my mother and __father (1)__

10. I play games on the __computer (1)__

Words with *er*

Sort the Spelling Words.

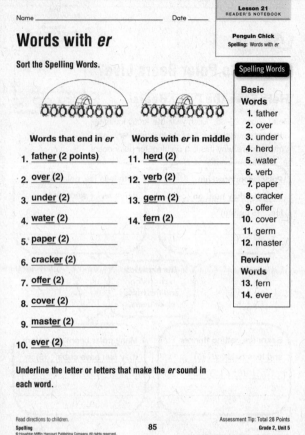

Words that end in *er*

1. __father (2 points)__
2. __over (2)__
3. __under (2)__
4. __water (2)__
5. __paper (2)__
6. __cracker (2)__
7. __offer (2)__
8. __cover (2)__
9. __master (2)__
10. __ever (2)__

Words with *er* in middle

11. __herd (2)__
12. __verb (2)__
13. __germ (2)__
14. __fern (2)__

Underline the letter or letters that make the *er* sound in each word.

Spelling Words

Basic Words
1. father
2. over
3. under
4. herd
5. water
6. verb
7. paper
8. cracker
9. offer
10. cover
11. germ
12. master

Review Words
13. fern
14. ever

How Things Taste and Smell

Adjectives can tell how something tastes.
Adjectives can also tell how something smells.
The ocean smells fishy.
The water tastes salty.

Thinking Question
Which word tells more about how something tastes or smells?

Find the adjective in each sentence. The adjective tells more about the underlined word. Write the adjective.

1. The penguins eat the tasty <u>fish</u>.
   __tasty (1 point)__

2. They drink the salty <u>water</u>.
   __salty (1)__

3. The penguins like smelly <u>seafood</u>.
   __smelly (1)__

4. They smell the fresh <u>air</u>.
   __fresh (1)__

5. They love the taste of sweet <u>squid</u>.
   __sweet (1)__

Focus Trait: Word Choice Using Exact Words

Without Exact Words	With Exact Words
In Antarctica there is <u>nothing</u> to build a nest with.	In Antarctica there are **no twigs, leaves, grass, or mud** to build a nest with.

A. Read each sentence. Replace each underlined word with more exact words. Possible responses shown.

Without Exact Words	With Exact Words
1. The egg stays <u>comfortable</u> in the brood patch.	The egg stays **snug and warm** in the brood patch. **(1 point)**
2. The penguin fathers <u>are</u> together in a group.	The penguin fathers **stand** together in a group. **(1)**

B. Pair/Share Work with a partner to brainstorm exact words to replace the underlined words in the sentence.

Possible responses shown.

Without Exact Words	With Exact Words
3. With his <u>mouth</u>, the penguin father <u>puts</u> the egg onto his <u>feet</u>.	**With his beak, the penguin father scoops the egg onto his webbed feet. (1)**
4. After the chick <u>comes out of the egg</u>, its wet feathers <u>change</u>.	**After the chick hatches, its wet feathers dry and become fluffy and gray. (1)**

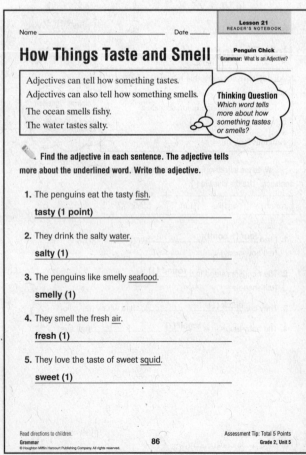

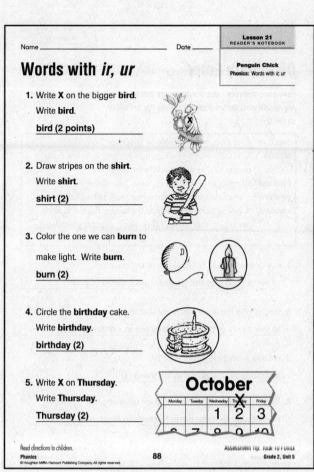

Words with *ir, ur*

1. Write **X** on the bigger **bird**.
   Write **bird**.

   bird (2 points) _____

2. Draw stripes on the **shirt**.
   Write **shirt**.

   shirt (2) _____

3. Color the one we can **burn** to
   make light. Write **burn**.

   burn (2) _____

4. Circle the **birthday** cake.
   Write **birthday**.

   birthday (2) _____

5. Write **X** on **Thursday**.
   Write **Thursday**.

   Thursday (2) _____

October

Monday	Tuesday	Wednesday	Thursday	Friday
	1	2 X	3	

Read directions to children. Assessment Tip: Total 10 Points

Reader's Guide

Penguin Chick

Make a Scrapbook

Make a scrapbook for the baby penguin. Draw and
write about what happens as the chick grows.

Read pages 214–217. Draw and write about what happened today.

Today, your mom laid your egg. Dad keeps you snuggly inside a brood patch. Mom goes fishing. (5 points)

Read page 218. Draw and write about what happened today.

Today, you pecked out of your egg. You aren't ready for the cold yet, so you stay in the brood patch. You are so cute when you whistle to your dad. (5)

Read directions to children. Assessment Tip: 10 Points

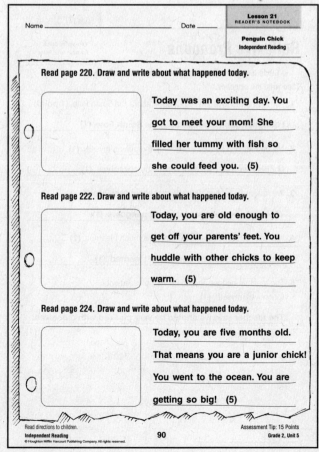

Read page 220. Draw and write about what happened today.

Today was an exciting day. You got to meet your mom! She filled her tummy with fish so she could feed you. (5)

Read page 222. Draw and write about what happened today.

Today, you are old enough to get off your parents' feet. You huddle with other chicks to keep warm. (5)

Read page 224. Draw and write about what happened today.

Today, you are five months old. That means you are a junior chick! You went to the ocean. You are getting so big! (5)

Read directions to children. Assessment Tip: 15 Points

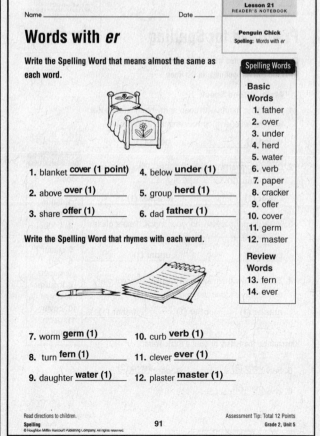

Words with *er*

Write the Spelling Word that means almost the same as
each word.

1. blanket **cover (1 point)**   4. below **under (1)**

2. above **over (1)**   5. group **herd (1)**

3. share **offer (1)**   6. dad **father (1)**

Write the Spelling Word that rhymes with each word.

7. worm **germ (1)**   10. curb **verb (1)**

8. turn **fern (1)**   11. clever **ever (1)**

9. daughter **water (1)**   12. plaster **master (1)**

Spelling Words

Basic Words
1. father
2. over
3. under
4. herd
5. water
6. verb
7. paper
8. cracker
9. offer
10. cover
11. germ
12. master

Review Words
13. fern
14. ever

Read directions to children. Assessment Tip: Total 12 Points

How Things Feel and Sound

✏️ Write the adjective from the box that best fits each sentence. Use the clues in ( ).

| howling | icy | loud | slippery |

1. Penguins stand in the **howling (1 point)** _____ wind. (sound)

2. The father penguin has a **loud (1)** _____ voice. (sound)

3. Penguins swim in **icy (1)** _____ oceans. (feel)

4. They catch **slippery (1)** _____ fish with their beaks. (feel)

✏️ Find the adjective in each sentence. Write the word that tells more about the underlined word.

5. The penguins hear splashing <u>water</u>.
splashing (1) _____

6. They step on the pointy <u>rocks</u>.
pointy (1) _____

7. Penguin chicks have fluffy <u>feathers</u>.
fluffy (1) _____

8. The penguins make whistling <u>sounds</u>.
whistling (1) _____

Name _____ Date _____

Lesson 21
READER'S NOTEBOOK

Penguin Chick
Vocabulary Strategies:
Dictionary Entry

Dictionary Entry

Read each sentence. Use the dictionary entries to help you decide what the word means. Write the definition on the line.

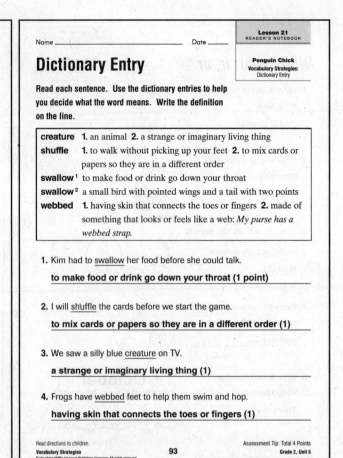

creature	1. an animal 2. a strange or imaginary living thing
shuffle	1. to walk without picking up your feet 2. to mix cards or papers so they are in a different order
swallow¹	to make food or drink go down your throat
swallow²	a small bird with pointed wings and a tail with two points
webbed	1. having skin that connects the toes or fingers 2. made of something that looks or feels like a web: *My purse has a webbed strap.*

1. Kim had to <u>swallow</u> her food before she could talk.

to make food or drink go down your throat (1 point)

2. I will <u>shuffle</u> the cards before we start the game.

to mix cards or papers so they are in a different order (1)

3. We saw a silly blue <u>creature</u> on TV.

a strange or imaginary living thing (1)

4. Frogs have <u>webbed</u> feet to help them swim and hop.

having skin that connects the toes or fingers (1)

Proofread for Spelling

Circle the misspelled words in the items below. Then write the correct spellings on the lines.

Make a Good Snack

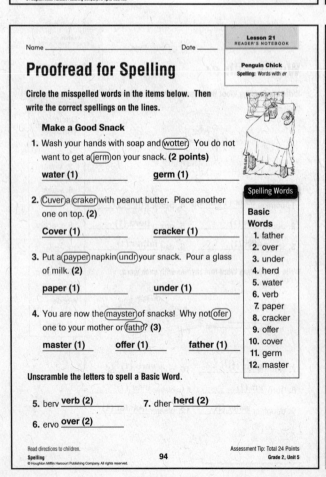

1. Wash your hands with soap and ⟨wotter⟩ You do not want to get a ⟨germ⟩ on your snack. **(2 points)**

water (1) _____   **germ (1)** _____

2. ⟨Cuver⟩ a ⟨craker⟩ with peanut butter. Place another one on top. **(2)**

Cover (1) _____   **cracker (1)** _____

3. Put a ⟨payper⟩ napkin ⟨undr⟩ your snack. Pour a glass of milk. **(2)**

paper (1) _____   **under (1)** _____

4. You are now the ⟨mayster⟩ of snacks! Why not ⟨ofer⟩ one to your mother or ⟨fathr⟩? **(3)**

master (1) _____   **offer (1)** _____   **father (1)** _____

Unscramble the letters to spell a Basic Word.

5. berv **verb (2)** _____   7. dher **herd (2)** _____

6. ervo **over (2)** _____

Spelling Words

Basic Words
1. father
2. over
3. under
4. herd
5. water
6. verb
7. paper
8. cracker
9. offer
10. cover
11. germ
12. master

Reflexive Pronouns

✏️ Circle the correct pronoun to complete each sentence. Then write the sentence.

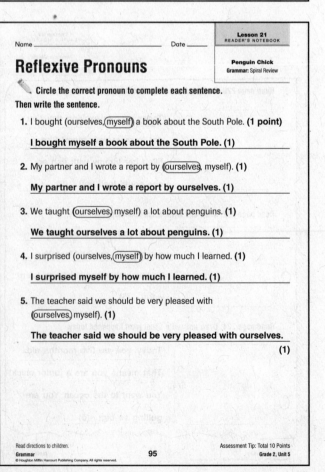

1. I bought (ourselves, ⟨myself⟩) a book about the South Pole. **(1 point)**

I bought myself a book about the South Pole. (1)

2. My partner and I wrote a report by (⟨ourselves⟩, myself). **(1)**

My partner and I wrote a report by ourselves. (1)

3. We taught (⟨ourselves⟩, myself) a lot about penguins. **(1)**

We taught ourselves a lot about penguins. (1)

4. I surprised (ourselves, ⟨myself⟩) by how much I learned. **(1)**

I surprised myself by how much I learned. (1)

5. The teacher said we should be very pleased with (⟨ourselves⟩, myself). **(1)**

The teacher said we should be very pleased with ourselves.
(1)

Left Top — Sentence Fluency

Name _____ Date _____

Sentence Fluency

Short, Choppy Sentences	Longer, Smooth Sentence
The penguins were hungry. The penguins were tired.	The penguins were hungry and tired.

Read each pair of sentences. Join the sentences using **and** between the two adjectives. Write the new sentence.

1. The penguin was cold.
   The penguin was wet.
   The penguin was cold and wet. (1 point)

2. The rain was heavy.
   The rain was pounding.
   The rain was heavy and pounding. (1)

3. The egg was warm.
   The egg was covered.
   The egg was warm and covered. (1)

4. The sky was cloudy.
   The sky was dark.
   The sky was cloudy and dark. (1)

Read directions to children.
Grammar
Assessment Tip: Total 4 Points
96
Grade 2, Unit 5
© Houghton Mifflin Harcourt Publishing Company. All rights reserved.

Right Top — Homophones

Name _____ Date _____

Homophones

Read the two homophones in each box. Then choose the word that goes on each line. Read the completed sentences.

1. I **rode (1 point)** _____ my bike on a bumpy **road (1)** _____

   | rode |
   | road |

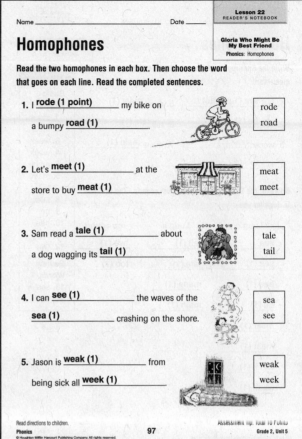

2. Let's **meet (1)** _____ at the store to buy **meat (1)** _____

   | meat |
   | meet |

3. Sam read a **tale (1)** _____ about a dog wagging its **tail (1)** _____

   | tale |
   | tail |

4. I can **see (1)** _____ the waves of the **sea (1)** _____ crashing on the shore.

   | sea |
   | see |

5. Jason is **weak (1)** _____ from being sick all **week (1)** _____

   | weak |
   | week |

Read directions to children.
Phonics
Assessment Tip: Total 10 Points
97
Grade 2, Unit 5
© Houghton Mifflin Harcourt Publishing Company. All rights reserved.

Left Bottom — Adjectives

Name _____ Date _____

Adjectives

- An **adjective** is a word that tells more about another word.
- Numbers are special adjectives that tell how many.

Julian made <u>one</u> kite.
Gloria tied <u>two</u> wishes to her kite.

Thinking Question
Which word tells how many?

Draw a line under each adjective that tells how many. Write the noun it tells about.

1. Gloria had <u>two</u> pigtails. **pigtails (1 point)**

2. Julian tied <u>five</u> wishes to his kite. **wishes (1)**

3. Gloria and Julian walked <u>six</u> blocks. **blocks (1)**

4. Julian counted <u>twelve</u> rocks from his collection.
   rocks (1)

5. They found <u>one</u> nest. **nest (1)**

Read directions to children.
Grammar
Assessment Tip: Total 5 Points
98
Grade 2, Unit 5
© Houghton Mifflin Harcourt Publishing Company. All rights reserved.

Right Bottom — Homophones

Name _____ Date _____

Homophones

Choose a word from the box to complete each sentence. Write the word on the line. Read each completed sentence.

Word Bank

be	blew	rode	weak	two
bee	main	road	sea	too
blue	mane	week	see	

1. The wind **blew (1 point)** _____ the door open.
2. Please save **two (1)** _____ seats at lunch.
3. This flower has a **bee (1)** _____ on it!
4. Tim **rode (1)** _____ his dad's bike.
5. There are seven days in one **week (1)** _____
6. I like to swim in the salty **sea (1)** _____
7. What is the **main (1)** _____ idea on that page?
8. There is **too (1)** _____ much noise.
9. My favorite color is **blue (1)** _____
10. It is too dark to **see (1)** _____

Read directions to children.
Phonics
Assessment Tip: Total 10 Points
99
Grade 2, Unit 5
© Houghton Mifflin Harcourt Publishing Company. All rights reserved.

Homophones

Gloria Who Might Be My Best Friend
Spelling: Homophones

Write the Spelling Word that sounds the same as the given word.

Spelling Words

Basic Words

1. meet
2. meat
3. week
4. weak
5. mane
6. main
7. tail
8. tale
9. be
10. bee
11. too
12. two

Review Words

13. sea
14. see

1. sea __see (1 points)__   5. meet __meat (1)__

2. bee __be (1)__   6. tail __tale (1)__

3. week __weak (1)__   7. mane __main (1)__

4. two __too (1)__

Now sort the Spelling Words by vowel sounds. The first one is done for you.

Long *e*	Long *a*	*oo* sound
sea	tail (1)	two (1)
see (1)	tale (1)	too (1)
bee (1)	mane (1)	
be (1)	main (1)	
meet (1)		
meat (1)		
week (1)		
weak (1)		

Read directions to children.
Spelling
© Houghton Mifflin Harcourt Publishing Company. All rights reserved.
100
Assessment Tip: Total 20 Points
Grade 2, Unit 5

Adjectives with -*er* and -*est*

Gloria Who Might Be My Best Friend
Grammar: Using Adjectives

- Add -er to adjectives to compare **two** people, animals, places, or things.
- Add -est to compare **more than two** people, animals, places, or things.

Jan is tall.
Beth is taller than Jan.
Nina is the tallest friend of all.

Thinking Question
How many people, animals, places, or things are being compared?

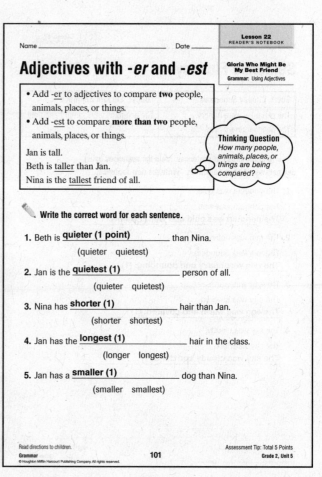

Write the correct word for each sentence.

1. Beth is __quieter (1 point)__ than Nina.
   (quieter   quietest)

2. Jan is the __quietest (1)__ person of all.
   (quieter   quietest)

3. Nina has __shorter (1)__ hair than Jan.
   (shorter   shortest)

4. Jan has the __longest (1)__ hair in the class.
   (longer   longest)

5. Jan has a __smaller (1)__ dog than Nina.
   (smaller   smallest)

Read directions to children.
Grammar
© Houghton Mifflin Harcourt Publishing Company. All rights reserved.
101
Assessment Tip: Total 5 Points
Grade 2, Unit 5

Focus Trait: Organization Details

Gloria Who Might Be My Best Friend
Writing: Informative Writing

A. Read each paragraph. Cross out the detail that does not support the main idea.

1. Gloria and Julian are different in some ways.
   ~~They both know how to fly a kite.~~
   Gloria is a fast runner, but Julian runs slowly.
   Gloria can turn a cartwheel, but Julian can't. **(1 point)**

2. Gloria and Julian are alike in some ways.
   ~~Julian knows the best way to make wishes, and Gloria doesn't.~~
   They like playing outside.
   They go to the same school. **(1)**

B. Read each main idea. Give a detail that supports the main idea.

Pair/Share Work with a partner to brainstorm possible details for each main idea. Possible responses shown.

Main Idea	Detail
3. Doctors and nurses are alike in many ways.	They both work in hospitals. (1)
4. Cats and dogs are alike in some ways.	They both have four legs. (1)

Read directions to children.
Writing
© Houghton Mifflin Harcourt Publishing Company. All rights reserved.
102
Assessment Tip: Total 4 Points
Grade 2, Unit 5

Base Words and Endings -er, -est

Gloria Who Might Be My Best Friend
Phonics: Base Words and Endings -er, -est

Follow the direction for each question.

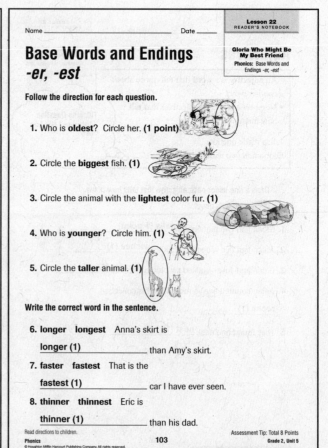

1. Who is **oldest**? Circle her. **(1 point)**

2. Circle the **biggest** fish. **(1)**

3. Circle the animal with the **lightest** color fur. **(1)**

4. Who is **younger**? Circle him. **(1)**

5. Circle the **taller** animal. **(1)**

Write the correct word in the sentence.

6. longer   longest   Anna's skirt is
   __longer (1)__ than Amy's skirt.

7. faster   fastest   That is the
   __fastest (1)__ car I have ever seen.

8. thinner   thinnest   Eric is
   __thinner (1)__ than his dad.

Read directions to children.
Phonics
© Houghton Mifflin Harcourt Publishing Company. All rights reserved.
103
Assessment Tip: Total 8 Points
Grade 2, Unit 5

Name _____ Date _____

Lesson 22
READER'S NOTEBOOK

Gloria Who Might Be
My Best Friend
Independent Reading

Reader's Guide

Gloria Who Might Be My Best Friend

Gloria Retells the Story

Now Gloria is going to tell the story of meeting Julian. What will she say? Use the text to help Gloria tell and illustrate the story.

Read pages 248–249. How would Gloria tell this part of the story?

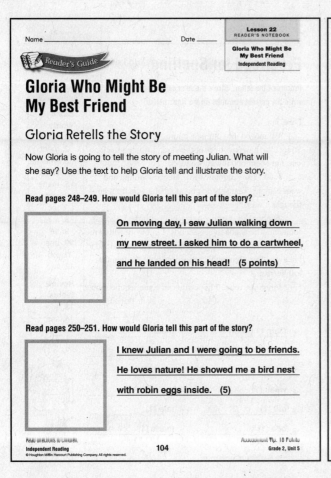

On moving day, I saw Julian walking down my new street. I asked him to do a cartwheel, and he landed on his head! (5 points)

Read pages 250–251. How would Gloria tell this part of the story?

I knew Julian and I were going to be friends. He loves nature! He showed me a bird nest with robin eggs inside. (5)

Read directions to children.
Independent Reading
104
Assessment Tip: 10 Points
Grade 2, Unit 5
© Houghton Mifflin Harcourt Publishing Company. All rights reserved.

Name _____ Date _____

Lesson 22
READER'S NOTEBOOK

Gloria Who Might Be
My Best Friend
Independent Reading

Read pages 254–255. Think about what Gloria might wish for. Draw and write about her two wishes.

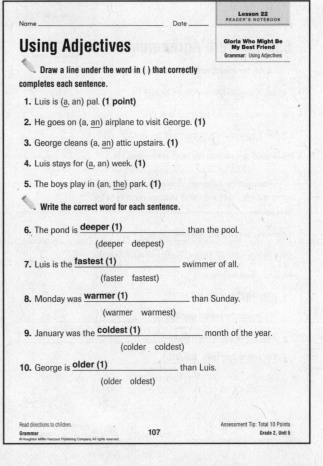

I wished that Julian and I would be best friends. I wished that my family would never move again. (5)

Read pages 257–261. How would Gloria tell this part of the story?

We flew our kite until the wishes flew off the tail. When we brought the kite down, Julian asked me if I wished we would be friends. He was right! (5)

Read directions to children.
Independent Reading
105
Assessment Tip: 10 Points
Grade 2, Unit 5
© Houghton Mifflin Harcourt Publishing Company. All rights reserved.

Name _____ Date _____

Lesson 22
READER'S NOTEBOOK

Gloria Who Might Be
My Best Friend
Spelling: Homophones

Homophones

Circle the correct Spelling Word to complete each sentence. Write the Spelling Word on the line.

(1 point)

1. A horse has a (mane, main).   **mane**

2. Our town has one (mane, main) street.   **main (1)**

3. I like to eat (meat, meet).   **meat (1)**

4. It is fun to (meat, meet) a new friend.   **meet (1)**

5. Seven days make a (week, weak).   **week (1)**

6. A (week, weak) person is not strong.   **weak (1)**

7. I read a (tail, tale) about a cat with a long (tail, tale).

   tale (1)   **tail (1)**

8. Who will (bee, be) afraid of a (bee, be)?

   be (1)   **bee (1)**

9. You can (sea, see) the (sea, see) at the beach.

   see (1)   **sea (1)**

10. (Too, Two) hippos are (too, two) big for the pond.

   Two (1)   **too (1)**

Spelling Words

Basic Words
1. meet
2. meat
3. week
4. weak
5. mane
6. main
7. tail
8. tale
9. be
10. bee
11. too
12. two

Review Words
13. sea
14. see

Read directions to children.
Spelling
106
Assessment Tip: Total 14 Points
Grade 2, Unit 5
© Houghton Mifflin Harcourt Publishing Company. All rights reserved.

Name _____ Date _____

Lesson 22
READER'S NOTEBOOK

Gloria Who Might Be
My Best Friend
Grammar: Using Adjectives

Using Adjectives

Draw a line under the word in ( ) that correctly completes each sentence.

1. Luis is (a, an) pal. **(1 point)**

2. He goes on (a, an) airplane to visit George. (1)

3. George cleans (a, an) attic upstairs. (1)

4. Luis stays for (a, an) week. (1)

5. The boys play in (an, the) park. (1)

Write the correct word for each sentence.

6. The pond is **deeper (1)** _____ than the pool.
   (deeper   deepest)

7. Luis is the **fastest (1)** _____ swimmer of all.
   (faster   fastest)

8. Monday was **warmer (1)** _____ than Sunday.
   (warmer   warmest)

9. January was the **coldest (1)** _____ month of the year.
   (colder   coldest)

10. George is **older (1)** _____ than Luis.
   (older   oldest)

Read directions to children.
Grammar
107
Assessment Tip: Total 10 Points
Grade 2, Unit 5
© Houghton Mifflin Harcourt Publishing Company. All rights reserved.

Name _____ Date _____

Lesson 22
READER'S NOTEBOOK

Gloria Who Might Be
My Best Friend
Vocabulary Strategies: Idioms

Idioms

Read each sentence. Choose the meaning from the box that could replace the underlined words. Write the meaning on the line.

Meanings

stay cheerful   very special to him   understands what to do
does her best   tight and uncomfortable

1. Kim's grandpa is proud of her. She is the apple of his eye.

   very special to him (1 point)

2. Sally has been at her job for a long time, so she knows the ropes.

   understands what to do (1)

3. Jen had a good day at school. She always puts her best foot forward.

   does her best (1)

4. Jay is sad, so Mel told him to keep his chin up.

   stay cheerful (1)

5. I am so nervous! My stomach is tied in knots.

   tight and uncomfortable (1)

Read directions to children.
Vocabulary Strategies
© Houghton Mifflin Harcourt Publishing Company. All rights reserved.
108
Assessment Tip: Total 5 Points
Grade 2, Unit 5

Name _____ Date _____

Lesson 22
READER'S NOTEBOOK

Gloria Who Might Be
My Best Friend
Spelling: Homophones

Proofread for Spelling

Proofread the letter. Circle the misspelled words. Then write the correct spellings on the lines below.

Dear Jen,

We moved into our new house. It is on (Mane) Street. We have (too) trees in the yard. I wanted to climb one, but Mom said it was (two) (week).

Lucky likes our new yard. He runs around and wags his (tale). That silly dog bit at a (be). I wonder if he thought it was (meet) to eat.

This (weak) I start my new school. I hope I'll (meat) someone who wants to (bee) friends. I know we will have story time, and I think my new teacher is going to read a (tail) every day. Remember the story about the lion that lost his (main)?

I miss you a lot. I hope you can come see me soon.

Your Friend,
Max

Spelling Words

Basic Words
1. meet
2. meat
3. week
4. weak
5. mane
6. main
7. tail
8. tale
9. be
10. bee
11. too
12. two

Review Words
13. sea
14. see

1. **Main (1 point)**
2. **two (1)**
3. **too (1)**
4. **weak (1)**
5. **tail (1)**
6. **bee (1)**
7. **meat (1)**
8. **week (1)**
9. **meet (1)**
10. **be (1)**
11. **tale (1)**
12. **mane (1)**

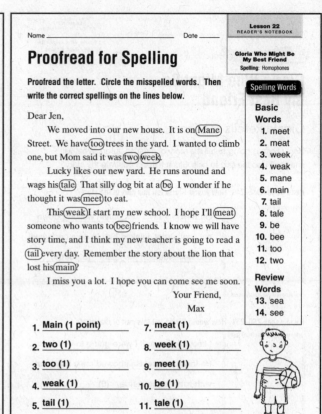

Read directions to children.
Spelling
© Houghton Mifflin Harcourt Publishing Company. All rights reserved.
109
Assessment Tip: Total 12 Points
Grade 2, Unit 5

Name _____ Date _____

Lesson 22
READER'S NOTEBOOK

Gloria Who Might Be
My Best Friend
Grammar: Spiral Review

Subject-Verb Agreement

Circle the correct verb to go with each subject.

1. She (play, **plays**) with me. **(1 point)**

2. He (wish, **wishes**) for good luck. **(1)**

3. We (**throw**, throws) a penny in the fountain. **(1)**

4. They (**hope**, hopes) her wish comes true. **(1)**

Proofread the paragraph. Circle the four verbs with the wrong endings. Then write each sentence correctly on the lines below.

Julia is my best friend. She (laugh) at my jokes.

We (watches) baseball games. She (give) me sandwiches.

We (shares) our toys, too.

1. **She laughs at my jokes. (1)**

2. **We watch baseball games. (1)**

3. **She gives me sandwiches. (1)**

4. **We share our toys, too. (1)**

Read directions to children.
Grammar
© Houghton Mifflin Harcourt Publishing Company. All rights reserved.
110
Assessment Tip: Total 8 Points
Grade 2, Unit 5

Name _____ Date _____

Lesson 22
READER'S NOTEBOOK

Gloria Who Might Be
My Best Friend
Grammar: Connect to Writing

Ideas

My friend has a new dog.
His dog is smaller than my dog.
His dog is the smallest of all the dogs.

Rewrite the paragraph. Replace each underlined adjective with words from the box that compare.

the fastest of all	longer than my arm
stronger today than yesterday	the highest of all the kites

My friend Bob makes a kite. The tail is long. His kite looks like a bird. Bob takes the bird kite to the park. The wind is strong. Many people are flying their kites. The bird kite is fast. It flies high.

My friend Bob makes a kite. The tail is longer than my arm. His kite looks like a bird. Bob takes the bird kite to the park. The wind is stronger today than yesterday. Many people are flying their kites. The bird kite is the fastest of all. It flies the highest of all the kites. (4 points)

Read directions to children.
Grammar
© Houghton Mifflin Harcourt Publishing Company. All rights reserved.
111
Assessment Tip: Total 4 Points
Grade 2, Unit 5

Suffixes -y, -ly, -ful

Circle the word that matches each picture. Write the word and underline the suffix.

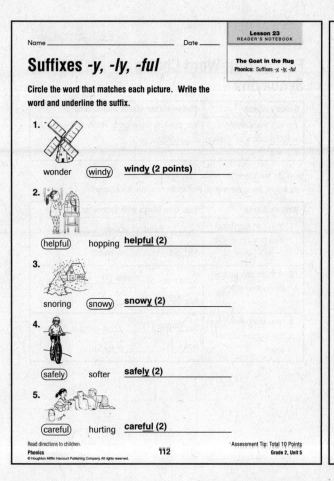

1. wonder (windy) **windy (2 points)**

2. (helpful) hopping **helpful (2)**

3. snoring (snowy) **snowy (2)**

4. (safely) softer **safely (2)**

5. (careful) hurting **careful (2)**

Read directions to children.
Phonics
112
Assessment Tip: Total 10 Points
Grade 2, Unit 5
© Houghton Mifflin Harcourt Publishing Company. All rights reserved.

Have, *Has*, and *Had*

- *Have*, *has*, and *had* are **irregular verbs**.
- Use *have* and *has* to tell about present time.
- Use *had* to tell about something that happened in the past.

Subject	Present	Past
We	have	had
Glenda	has	had
He, She, It	has	had
Ken and Marti	have	had
They	have	had

Jean **has** a new rug now.
Dee and Ben **have** a red rug now.
We **had** a blue rug years ago.

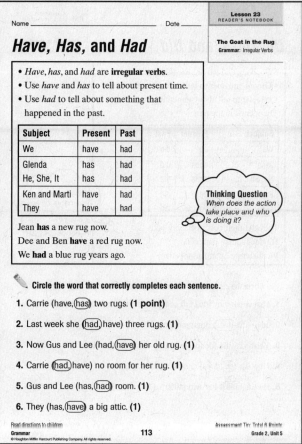

Thinking Question
When does the action take place and who is doing it?

Circle the word that correctly completes each sentence.

1. Carrie (have, (has)) two rugs. **(1 point)**

2. Last week she ((had,) have) three rugs. **(1)**

3. Now Gus and Lee (had, (have)) her old rug. **(1)**

4. Carrie ((had,) have) no room for her rug. **(1)**

5. Gus and Lee (has, (had)) room. **(1)**

6. They (has, (have)) a big attic. **(1)**

Read directions to children.
Grammar
113
Assessment Tip: Total 6 Points
Grade 2, Unit 5
© Houghton Mifflin Harcourt Publishing Company. All rights reserved.

Suffixes -y, -ly, -ful

Choose a word from the box to complete each sentence. Then read each sentence aloud with a partner.

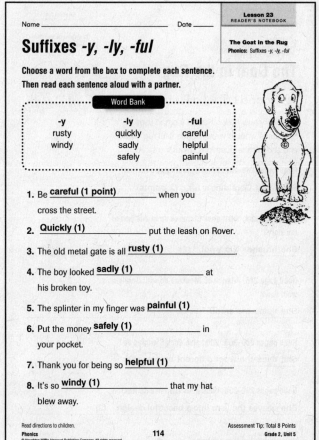

Word Bank

-y	-ly	-ful
rusty	quickly	careful
windy	sadly	helpful
	safely	painful

1. Be **careful (1 point)** when you cross the street.

2. **Quickly (1)** put the leash on Rover.

3. The old metal gate is all **rusty (1)**

4. The boy looked **sadly (1)** at his broken toy.

5. The splinter in my finger was **painful (1)**

6. Put the money **safely (1)** in your pocket.

7. Thank you for being so **helpful (1)**

8. It's so **windy (1)** that my hat blew away.

Read directions to children.
Phonics
114
Assessment Tip: Total 8 Points
Grade 2, Unit 5
© Houghton Mifflin Harcourt Publishing Company. All rights reserved.

Suffixes -ly, -ful

Sort the Basic Words by the suffixes *-ly* and *-ful*.

-ly	-ful

Word + ly

1. **sadly (2 points)**
2. **slowly (2)**
3. **kindly (2)**
4. **safely (2)**
5. **weakly (2)**

Word + ful

6. **helpful (2)**
7. **hopeful (2)**
8. **thankful (2)**
9. **wishful (2)**
10. **useful (2)**
11. **painful (2)**
12. **mouthful (2)**

Underline the suffix in each Basic Word.

Spelling Words

Basic Words
1. helpful
2. sadly
3. hopeful
4. thankful
5. slowly
6. wishful
7. kindly
8. useful
9. safely
10. painful
11. mouthful
12. weakly

Read directions to children.
Spelling
115
Assessment Tip: Total 24 Points
Grade 2, Unit 5
© Houghton Mifflin Harcourt Publishing Company. All rights reserved.

Do, Does, and Did

- *Do*, *does*, and *did* are **irregular verbs**.
- Use *do* and *does* to tell about present time.
- Use *did* to tell about something that happened in the past.

Subject	Present	Past
We	do	did
Janet	does	did
He, She, It	does	did
Pedro and Sam	do	did
They	do	did

Thinking Question
When does the action take place and who is doing it?

They **did** their best work with Jake.
He **does** square patterns.
We **do** striped patterns together.

✎ Circle the correct word for each sentence.

1. Last week they (do, (did)) some patterns with Jake. **(1 point)**

2. Jake (do, (does)) great patterns. **(1)**

3. Yesterday, he (do, (did)) squares and triangles. **(1)**

4. Now we ((do,) does) circles together. **(1)**

5. He (do, (does)) his own pattern. **(1)**

Read directions to children.
Grammar
© Houghton Mifflin Harcourt Publishing Company. All rights reserved.
116
Assessment Tip: Total 5 Points
Grade 2, Unit 5

Focus Trait: Word Choice Synonyms

Writer's Words	Students' Own Words with Synonyms
You can <u>make</u> wool <u>beautiful</u> colors by <u>soaking</u> it in <u>dye</u>.	You can <u>turn</u> wool <u>pretty</u> colors by <u>dipping</u> it in <u>coloring</u>.

Read the words a writer wrote. Then rewrite the sentence in your own words, using synonyms. Possible responses shown.

Writer's Words	Your Own Words with Synonyms
1. You can <u>spin</u> wool into <u>threads</u> of yarn.	You can **twist (1 point)** wool into **strings (1)** of yarn.
2. A loom can be <u>built</u> using four <u>poles</u>.	A loom can be **made (1)** using four **sticks (1)**.
3. You <u>start</u> weaving at the <u>bottom</u> of the loom.	You **begin (1)** weaving at the **base (1)** of the loom.

Read directions to children.
Writing
© Houghton Mifflin Harcourt Publishing Company. All rights reserved.
117
Assessment Tip: Total 6 Points
Grade 2, Unit 5

Syllables -tion, -ture

Read the two words in each item below. Think about how the two words are alike. Then write the missing *-tion* or *-ture* word from the Word Bank that fits with each pair of words.

Word Bank

-tion	-ture
lotion	creature
vacation	picture
fraction	capture
nation	nature

1. trip, travel, **vacation (1 point)**

2. animal, beast, **creature (1)**

3. piece, part of, **fraction (1)**

4. grab, catch, **capture (1)**

5. a drawing, a painting, a **picture (1)**

6. weather, plants, **nature (1)**

7. city, state, **nation (1)**

8. sunblock, hand cream, **lotion (1)**

Read directions to children.
Phonics
© Houghton Mifflin Harcourt Publishing Company. All rights reserved.
118
Assessment Tip: Total 8 Points
Grade 2, Unit 5

📖 **Reader's Guide**

The Goat in the Rug

Draw and Label a Picture

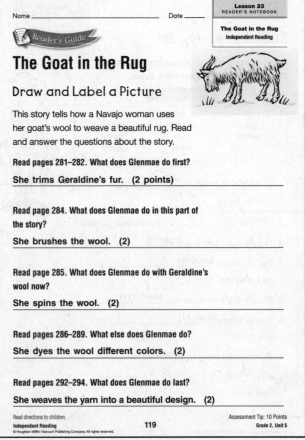

This story tells how a Navajo woman uses her goat's wool to weave a beautiful rug. Read and answer the questions about the story.

Read pages 281–282. What does Glenmae do first?

She trims Geraldine's fur. **(2 points)**

Read page 284. What does Glenmae do in this part of the story?

She brushes the wool. **(2)**

Read page 285. What does Glenmae do with Geraldine's wool now?

She spins the wool. **(2)**

Read pages 286–289. What else does Glenmae do?

She dyes the wool different colors. **(2)**

Read pages 292–294. What does Glenmae do last?

She weaves the yarn into a beautiful design. **(2)**

Read directions to children.
Independent Reading
© Houghton Mifflin Harcourt Publishing Company. All rights reserved.
119
Assessment Tip: 10 Points
Grade 2, Unit 5

In this story, Glenmae uses many tools. Find four tools in the story. Write and draw them in the order they are used. Write a sentence telling what Glenmae does with each tool.

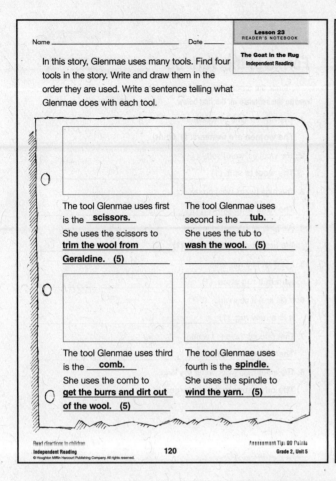

The tool Glenmae uses first is the **scissors.**

She uses the scissors to **trim the wool from Geraldine. (5)**

The tool Glenmae uses second is the **tub.**

She uses the tub to **wash the wool. (5)**

The tool Glenmae uses third is the **comb.**

She uses the comb to **get the burrs and dirt out of the wool. (5)**

The tool Glenmae uses fourth is the **spindle.**

She uses the spindle to **wind the yarn. (5)**

Read directions to children.
Independent Reading
© Houghton Mifflin Harcourt Publishing Company. All rights reserved.
120
Assessment Tip: 20 Points
Grade 2, Unit 5

Suffixes -ly, -ful

Write the Spelling Word that matches each meaning.

1. In a slow way ___ slowly (1 point)
2. Wishing for something ___ wishful (1)
3. In a way with no energy ___ weakly (1)
4. Having hope ___ hopeful (1)
5. In a sad way ___ sadly (1)
6. Giving help ___ helpful (1)
7. Being kind ___ kindly (1)
8. Being put to use ___ useful (1)
9. In a way that won't hurt you ___ safely (1)
10. A lot of food in your mouth ___ mouthful (1)
11. Full of thanks ___ thankful (1)
12. Full of pain ___ painful (1)

Spelling Words

Basic Words
1. helpful
2. sadly
3. hopeful
4. thankful
5. slowly
6. wishful
7. kindly
8. useful
9. safely
10. painful
11. mouthful
12. weakly

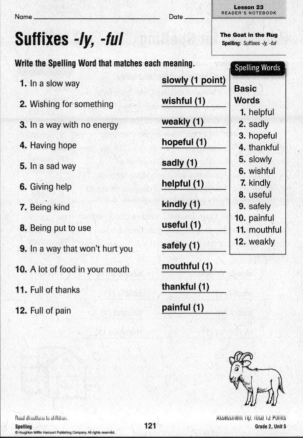

Read directions to children.
Spelling
© Houghton Mifflin Harcourt Publishing Company. All rights reserved.
121
Assessment Tip: Total 12 Points
Grade 2, Unit 5

Irregular Verbs

Circle the verb that correctly completes each sentence.

1. Last week the goat and lamb (have, **had**) long hair. **(1 point)**
2. Yesterday they (have, **had**) a hair cut. **(1)**
3. The lamb (**has**, have) short hair now. **(1)**
4. The goat (**has**, have) short hair, too. **(1)**
5. Now we (**have**, had) wool to make a rug. **(1)**

Write the correct verb to finish each sentence.

6. Gerry **does (1 point)** ___ something fun.
   (do does)
7. Tonya and Raj **do (1)** ___ a dance on the rug.
   (do does)
8. They **did (1)** ___ their favorite dance yesterday.
   (do did)
9. Gerry **did (1)** ___ his best when he jumped.
   (did do)
10. He **does (1)** ___ his best right now.
    (do does)

Read directions to children.
Grammar
© Houghton Mifflin Harcourt Publishing Company. All rights reserved.
122
Assessment Tip: Total 10 Points
Grade 2, Unit 5

Name _____ Date _____

Lesson 23
READER'S NOTEBOOK

The Goat in the Rug
Vocabulary Strategies:
Compound Words

Compound Words

Draw a line between the words that make up each compound word in the Word Bank. Use what you know about the shorter words to predict the compound word's meaning. Complete each sentence by writing the compound word whose meaning fits the best.

Word Bank

door|mat   rose|bush   back|yard   door|bell
mail|box   sand|box   side|walk   trash|can

1. The children sat in the **sandbox (2 points)** ___ and filled the pails with sand.
2. "Let's go to the **backyard (2)** ___," said Robert. "I want to climb the oak tree."
3. Mr. Hendricks wiped his feet on the **doormat (2)** ___ before going into the house.
4. We thought we heard the **doorbell (2)** ___ ring, but nobody was there.
5. Larry found two letters in his **mailbox (2)** ___.
6. The **trashcan (2)** ___ is full. I better empty it.
7. "Ouch," said Theresa. "This **rosebush (2)** ___ has a lot of thorns.
8. Sometimes Steve skateboards on the **sidewalk (2)** ___

Read directions to children.
Vocabulary Strategies
© Houghton Mifflin Harcourt Publishing Company. All rights reserved.
123
Assessment Tip: Total 16 Points
Grade 2, Unit 5

Proofread for Spelling

The Goat in the Rug
Spelling: Suffixes -ly, -ful

Proofread Bert's story. Circle the eight misspelled words.
Then write the correct spellings on the lines below.

Spelling Words

Last week we went to visit my Grandpa's farm. I
couldn't wait, but my dad kept driving (slowlee)! When
we finally arrived, Grandpa took me to the barn.

In the corner of a pen, I saw a goat breathing
(weakly). (Saddly), Grandpa said it was sick. The vet gave
the goat some pills. The goat ate them with a
(mothful) of corn. Grandpa was (hopful) that the goat
would get well. I stayed (safly) out of the pen. It would
be (paynful) if the goat kicked me.

After dinner, Grandpa and I went to check on the
goat. It was running around in its pen! Grandpa and I
were happy and (tankful) that the goat was feeling better.

(8 points)

Basic Words
1. helpful
2. sadly
3. hopeful
4. thankful
5. slowly
6. wishful
7. kindly
8. useful
9. safely
10. painful
11. mouthful
12. weakly

1. __slowly (1 point)__   5. __hopeful (1)__
2. __weakly (1)__   6. __safely (1)__
3. __sadly (1)__   7. __painful (1)__
4. __mouthful (1)__   8. __thankful (1)__

Read directions to children.
Spelling
© Houghton Mifflin Harcourt Publishing Company. All rights reserved.
124
Assessment Tip: Total 16 Points
Grade 2, Unit 5

Forms of the Verb *be*

The Goat in the Rug
Grammar: Spiral Review

Circle the correct form of the verb *be*. Then
rewrite the sentence on the line below.

1. The women (are, is) weavers.
   The women are weavers. (1 point)

2. The wool (is, were) soft.
   The wool is soft. (1)

3. The rugs (were, was) pretty.
   The rugs were pretty. (1)

4. We (are, is) interested in rugs.
   We are interested in rugs. (1)

5. I (am, is) in a rug store.
   I am in a rug store. (1)

6. It (is, are) a new rug.
   It is a new rug. (1)

7. That (are, is) the one I want.
   That is the one I want. (1)

8. The other rugs (was, were) too large.
   The other rugs were too large. (1)

Read directions to children.
Grammar
© Houghton Mifflin Harcourt Publishing Company. All rights reserved.
125
Assessment Tip: Total 8 Points
Grade 2, Unit 5

Conventions

The Goat in the Rug
Grammar: Connect to Writing

Wrong	Right
We has a new rug.	We have a new rug.

Read the paragraphs. Find six verb mistakes. Then
rewrite each sentence. Make sure each verb matches the
subject in the sentence.

Sue Makes Rugs

Sue (have) a loom now. She likes to weave rugs. We
(has) a rug from her now. I watch Sue work. She (do) a lot
to get ready to weave.

Last week, Sue needed wool. Yesterday, Sue (do) a
trade with the owner of the wool store. Now the owner
(have) a rug, too. Now Sue (have) enough wool for many
rugs! **(6 points)**

Sue has a loom now. She likes to weave rugs. We have a

rug from her now. I watch Sue work. She does a lot to get ready

to weave.

Last week, Sue needed wool. Yesterday, Sue did a trade

with the owner of the wool store. Now the owner has a rug, too.

Now Sue has enough wool for many rugs! (6 points)

Read directions to children.
Grammar
© Houghton Mifflin Harcourt Publishing Company. All rights reserved.
126
Assessment Tip: Total 12 Points
Grade 2, Unit 5

Prefixes

Half-Chicken
Phonics: Prefixes re-, un-, over-, pre-, mis-

Make words with prefixes. Read the base word.
Then add the prefix at the top of the column and
write the new word.

	un-	re-
1. lock	unlock (1 point)	relock (1)
2. tie	untie (1)	retie (1)
3. pin	unpin (1)	repin (1)
4. fold	unfold (1)	refold (1)
5. pack	unpack (1)	repack (1)

Complete each sentence. Add a prefix from the box to the base
word at the end of the sentence. Write the new word on the line.

over-	pre-	mis-

6. Set an alarm clock so you do not
   oversleep (2) _____ sleep

7. Before the real test, we will have a
   pretest (2) _____ test

8. Be careful not to **misspell (2)** _____
   any words. **spell**

Read directions to children.
Phonics
© Houghton Mifflin Harcourt Publishing Company. All rights reserved.
127
Assessment Tip: Total 16 Points
Grade 2, Unit 5

Irregular Action Verbs

• *Run, come, sit, hide,* and *tell* are **irregular verbs**. You do not add an *-ed* ending to these verbs to tell about the past.

Thinking Question
Is the action happening now or did it happen in the past?

Happening Now	Happened in the Past
The ducks **come** to the pond.	The ducks **came** to the pond.
The chipmunks **run** away.	The chipmunks **ran** away.
The pigs **sit** in the mud.	The pigs **sat** in the mud.
The children **hide** in the field.	The children **hid** in the field.
The parents **tell** a story.	The parents **told** a story.

Read and circle the word that tells when the action happens. Write each sentence using the correct verb.

1. The cows (come, came) from the fields.   **now**

   The cows come from fields. (1 point)

2. The children (run, ran) down the path.   **now**

   The children run down the path. (1)

3. They (sit, sat) in the field.   **past**

   They sat in the field. (1)

4. They all (hide, hid) in the dark.   **past**

   They all hid in the dark. (1)

Prefixes

Read each word. Then write the prefix and base word on the lines. (1 point each)

1. unsafe   un _____   safe _____
2. recheck   re _____   check _____
3. retell   re _____   tell _____
4. overeat   over _____   eat _____
5. unwise   un _____   wise _____
6. repaint   re _____   paint _____

Add the prefix *re-*, *mis-*, or *pre-* to the base word at the end of each sentence. Write the new word on the line to complete the sentence.

7. I **preheat (2)** _____ the oven before

   I bake.   **heat**

8. I listen carefully so I won't

   misunderstand (2) _____   **understand**

9. I will study again and **retake (2)** _____

   the test.   **take**

Prefixes *re-* and *un-*

Sort the Basic Words by the prefixes *re-* and *un-*. Underline the prefix in each word.

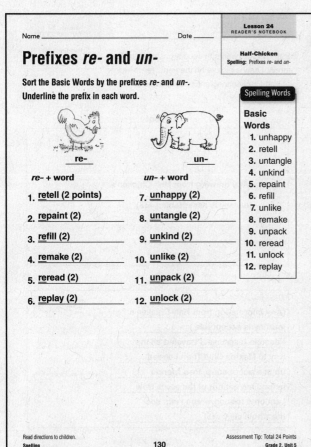

Spelling Words

Basic Words
1. unhappy
2. retell
3. untangle
4. unkind
5. repaint
6. refill
7. unlike
8. remake
9. unpack
10. reread
11. unlock
12. replay

re-   **un-**

re- + word

1. retell (2 points)
2. repaint (2)
3. refill (2)
4. remake (2)
5. reread (2)
6. replay (2)

un- + word

7. unhappy (2)
8. untangle (2)
9. unkind (2)
10. unlike (2)
11. unpack (2)
12. unlock (2)

See, Saw and *Go, Went*

• *See* and *go* are **irregular verbs**. Do not add an *-ed* ending to these verbs to tell about the past.
• *See* tells about an action happening now. *Saw* tells about an action in the past.
• *Go* tells about an action happening now. *Went* tells about an action in the past.

Thinking Question
Is the action happening now or did it happen in the past?

Happening Now	Happened in the Past
The squirrels **go** up a tree.	The squirrels **went** up a tree.
The squirrels **see** their food.	The squirrels **saw** their food.

Read the word that tells when the action happens. Write each sentence using the correct verb.

1. The chicks (see, saw) their mother.   **now**

   The chicks see their mother. (1 point)

2. The chicks (go, went) with their mother.   **now**

   The chicks go with their mother. (1)

3. All of the chickens (see, saw) the chicks.   **past**

   All of the chickens saw the chicks. (1)

4. The chickens (go, went) quickly to their nests.   **past**

   The chickens went quickly to their nests. (1)

Focus Trait: Ideas
Exact Details

Sentence	Sentence with Exact Details
Animals live on this ranch.	**Horses, pigs, chickens, and cows** live on this ranch.

A. Read each sentence. Add exact details to make each
sentence clearer and more interesting. **Possible responses shown.**

Sentence	Sentence with Exact Details
1. The hen ate.	The **red** hen ate seed from the ground. **(2 points)**
2. The chicks gathered around their mother.	The **tiny** chicks gathered around their mother **in the** barnyard. **(2)**

B. Read each sentence. Look at the picture on pages 320–321
of *Half-Chicken*. Add exact details to make each
sentence clearer. **Possible responses shown.**

Sentence	Sentence with Exact Details
3. Everyone came to see.	**Horses, cows, chickens, and the rancher came to see Half-Chicken leave the ranch. (2)**
4. Plants grew in the field.	**Golden wheat and green trees grew in the field. (2)**

Silent Consonants

Write a word from the sentence to answer the question.

1. Would you **kneel** or **knit** a hat? <u>knit (1 point)</u>
2. Would you **crumb** or **climb** a hill? <u>climb (1)</u>
3. Would you **knob** or **knock** on a door? <u>knock (1)</u>
4. Could you bend a **wrong** or a **wrist**? <u>wrist (1)</u>
5. Would you tie a **knot** or a **knife**? <u>knot (1)</u>
6. Is a **gnat** or a **gnu** very small? <u>gnat (1)</u>
7. Would a **comb** or a **lamb** eat grass? <u>lamb (1)</u>
8. Would you **wrench** or **wrap** a gift? <u>wrap (1)</u>

Use words from above to write two new sentences.
Possible responses shown.

9. <u>Dad needs to climb a ladder to reach that shelf. (2)</u>

10. <u>I will wrap her birthday present. (2)</u>

Reader's Guide

Half-Chicken

Draw and Label a Picture

This story tells about a very special chicken and his
trip to Mexico City. Reread pages from the story and
write what happened at each part of the trip.

Read page 321. Why does Half-Chicken decide to go on a trip?
He thinks he is very special and that he should be a part of
the viceroy's court in Mexico City. **(2 points)**

Read pages 323–324. Who does he help along the way?
He helps the stream by removing some branches. He makes
a fire larger. He untangles the wind from some bushes. **(2)**

Read pages 327–329. What happens in the viceroy's court?
The chef puts him into a soup pot. The water and fire help
rescue him. The cook throws him out the window. **(2)**

Read pages 330–331. Where does Half-Chicken end up staying?
The wind blows Half-Chicken to the top of a building. He
stays on top where he can see the city. **(2)**

Half-Chicken wants to send a postcard to his
family. Draw a picture on the front. Tell the story
of Half-Chicken's adventure on the back.

Front

(Any drawing from Half-Chicken's

journey is acceptable.) (5)

Back

Dear Family,
(Any information from Half-Chicken's
journey is acceptable.)
Possible response: I traveled all the
way to Mexico City! Then I ended
up in a pot of soup. New friends
helped me get out of the soup. Now
I am on a rooftop where I can see
the whole city! (5)

Mrs. Chicken and Family
The Ranch
Countryside, Mexico City

Prefixes *re-* and *un-*

Write the Basic Word that matches each meaning.

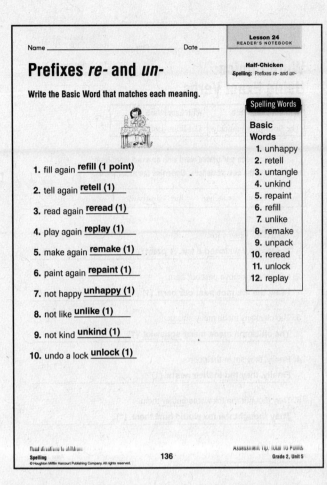

1. fill again **refill (1 point)**

2. tell again **retell (1)**

3. read again **reread (1)**

4. play again **replay (1)**

5. make again **remake (1)**

6. paint again **repaint (1)**

7. not happy **unhappy (1)**

8. not like **unlike (1)**

9. not kind **unkind (1)**

10. undo a lock **unlock (1)**

Spelling Words

Basic Words
1. unhappy
2. retell
3. untangle
4. unkind
5. repaint
6. refill
7. unlike
8. remake
9. unpack
10. reread
11. unlock
12. replay

Irregular Action Verbs

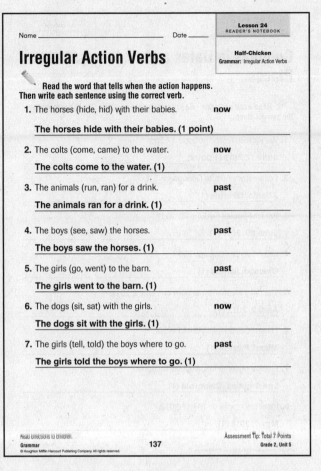

Read the word that tells when the action happens. Then write each sentence using the correct verb.

1. The horses (hide, hid) with their babies. **now**

   The horses hide with their babies. (1 point)

2. The colts (come, came) to the water. **now**

   The colts come to the water. (1)

3. The animals (run, ran) for a drink. **past**

   The animals ran for a drink. (1)

4. The boys (see, saw) the horses. **past**

   The boys saw the horses. (1)

5. The girls (go, went) to the barn. **past**

   The girls went to the barn. (1)

6. The dogs (sit, sat) with the girls. **now**

   The dogs sit with the girls. (1)

7. The girls (tell, told) the boys where to go. **past**

   The girls told the boys where to go. (1)

Antonyms

Circle the two words that are antonyms in each sentence.

1. James put his (wet) shirt in the sun so it would get (dry). **(2 points)**

2. Cindy put the (soft) pillow on the (hard) chair. **(2)**

3. Nathan filled a (tall) glass with water and sat down to do his (short) paper. **(2)**

4. Amy used her (strong) arms to pull down the (weak) and broken branches of the tree. **(2)**

Circle the two words in each group that are antonyms.

5. (swift)   steady   (slow) **(2)**

6. high   (full)   (empty) **(2)**

7. (cold)   (hot)   cloudy **(2)**

8. (sunny)   hilly   (cloudy) **(2)**

9. before   (over)   (under) **(2)**

10. (smooth)   (bumpy)   brush **(2)**

Proofread for Spelling

Proofread the newspaper article. Circle the eight misspelled words. Then write the correct spellings on the lines below. (1 point each)

New at the Ranch

The Wild Bill Ranch is getting a new prize bull named Ollie.

This morning, ranch hands arrived to (unpak) a huge crate. Out came a very (unhapi) bull.

"It might seem (unkined) to put Ollie in a crate," said the rancher. "But it was the best way to keep him safe. Once we (unlok) the crate and (untanglel) Ollie from his blanket, he will soon forget about it. Ollie's new space is (unlik) the small pen he once called home."

Watch tonight's news to see a (repla) of Ollie's arrival. You can buy the book that (reteels) Ollie's story.

1. **unpack (1)**   5. **untangle (1)**

2. **unhappy (1)**   6. **unlike (1)**

3. **unkind (1)**   7. **replay (1)**

4. **unlock (1)**   8. **retells (1)**

Spelling Words

Basic Words
1. unhappy
2. retell
3. untangle
4. unkind
5. repaint
6. refill
7. unlike
8. remake
9. unpack
10. reread
11. unlock
12. replay

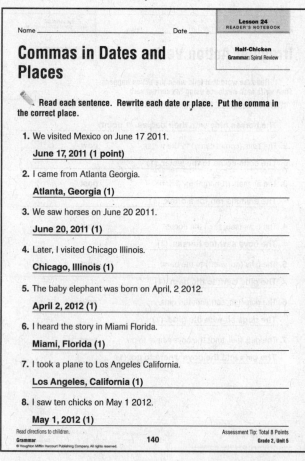
Commas in Dates and Places

Read each sentence. Rewrite each date or place. Put the comma in the correct place.

1. We visited Mexico on June 17 2011.

   June 17, 2011 (1 point)

2. I came from Atlanta Georgia.

   Atlanta, Georgia (1)

3. We saw horses on June 20 2011.

   June 20, 2011 (1)

4. Later, I visited Chicago Illinois.

   Chicago, Illinois (1)

5. The baby elephant was born on April, 2 2012.

   April 2, 2012 (1)

6. I heard the story in Miami Florida.

   Miami, Florida (1)

7. I took a plane to Los Angeles California.

   Los Angeles, California (1)

8. I saw ten chicks on May 1 2012.

   May 1, 2012 (1)

Read directions to children.
Grammar
140
Assessment Tip: Total 8 Points
Grade 2, Unit 5
© Houghton Mifflin Harcourt Publishing Company. All rights reserved.

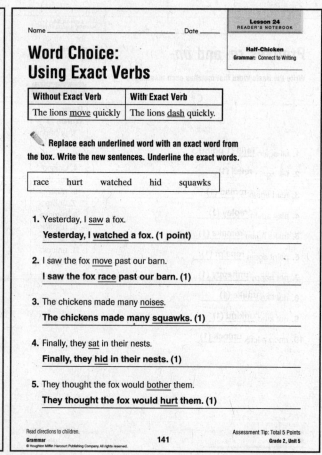
Word Choice: Using Exact Verbs

Without Exact Verb	With Exact Verb
The lions <u>move</u> quickly	The lions <u>dash</u> quickly.

Replace each underlined word with an exact word from the box. Write the new sentences. Underline the exact words.

race	hurt	watched	hid	squawks

1. Yesterday, I <u>saw</u> a fox.

   Yesterday, I <u>watched</u> a fox. (1 point)

2. I saw the fox <u>move</u> past our barn.

   I saw the fox <u>race</u> past our barn. (1)

3. The chickens made many <u>noises</u>.

   The chickens made many <u>squawks</u>. (1)

4. Finally, they <u>sat</u> in their nests.

   Finally, they <u>hid</u> in their nests. (1)

5. They thought the fox would <u>bother</u> them.

   They thought the fox would <u>hurt</u> them. (1)

Read directions to children.
Grammar
141
Assessment Tip: Total 5 Points
Grade 2, Unit 5
© Houghton Mifflin Harcourt Publishing Company. All rights reserved.

Words with *au, aw, al, o, a*

Complete the puzzle with words that have the vowel sound you hear in *saw*.

Read each clue. Then choose a word from the box.

Word Bank

toss	straw	tall	paw	salt
frost	pause	lost	soft	lawn

(1 point each)

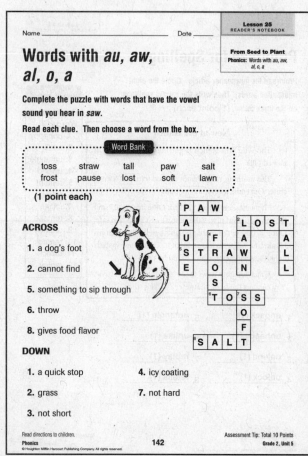

ACROSS

1. a dog's foot

2. cannot find

5. something to sip through

6. throw

8. gives food flavor

DOWN

1. a quick stop

2. grass

3. not short

4. icy coating

7. not hard

Read directions to children.
Phonics
142
Assessment Tip: Total 10 Points
Grade 2, Unit 5
© Houghton Mifflin Harcourt Publishing Company. All rights reserved.

Say, Said and *Eat, Ate*

- The verbs *say* and *eat* are **irregular verbs**.
- *Say* tells about an action happening now. *Said* tells about an action in the past.
- *Eat* tells about an action happening now. *Ate* tells about an action in the past.

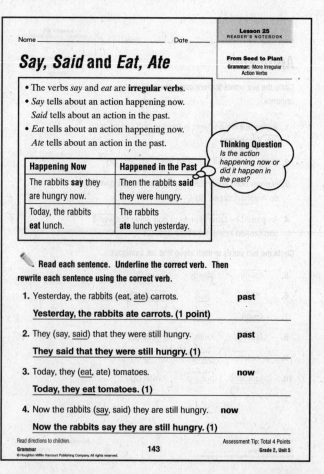

Thinking Question
Is the action happening now or did it happen in the past?

Happening Now	Happened in the Past
The rabbits **say** they are hungry now.	Then the rabbits **said** they were hungry.
Today, the rabbits **eat** lunch.	The rabbits **ate** lunch yesterday.

Read each sentence. Underline the correct verb. Then rewrite each sentence using the correct verb.

1. Yesterday, the rabbits (eat, <u>ate</u>) carrots.   **past**

   Yesterday, the rabbits ate carrots. (1 point)

2. They (say, <u>said</u>) that they were still hungry.   **past**

   They said that they were still hungry. (1)

3. Today, they (<u>eat</u>, ate) tomatoes.   **now**

   Today, they eat tomatoes. (1)

4. Now the rabbits (<u>say</u>, said) they are still hungry.   **now**

   Now the rabbits say they are still hungry. (1)

Read directions to children.
Grammar
143
Assessment Tip: Total 4 Points
Grade 2, Unit 5
© Houghton Mifflin Harcourt Publishing Company. All rights reserved.

Words with *au, aw, al, o, a*

In each row, circle the words that have the /aw/ sound as in *saw*.

1. (flaw) (hog) some (ball) (soft) **(4 points)**

2. (talk) cold (drawn) hang (launch) **(3)**

3. smoke (salt) (small) (faucet) (off) **(4)**

4. (toss) (awful) cane pale (water) **(3)**

5. (mall) (chalk) (jaw) (autumn) (yawn) **(5)**

Circle the word that completes the sentence and write it on the line.

6. Paul and I went for a __**walk (1)**__
   frost   (walk)

7. A __**hawk (1)**__ _____ sat on a high branch.
   haul   (hawk)

8. I saw its sharp __**claws (1)**__
   (claws)   clogs

Words with *aw, al, o*

Sort the Spelling Words by the /aw/ sound spelled *al, aw,* and *o.*

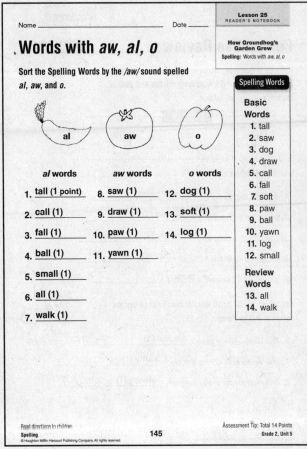

al   aw   o

al words	*aw* words	*o* words
1. **tall** (1 point)	8. **saw** (1)	12. **dog** (1)
2. **call** (1)	9. **draw** (1)	13. **soft** (1)
3. **fall** (1)	10. **paw** (1)	14. **log** (1)
4. **ball** (1)	11. **yawn** (1)	
5. **small** (1)		
6. **all** (1)		
7. **walk** (1)		

Spelling Words

Basic Words
1. tall
2. saw
3. dog
4. draw
5. call
6. fall
7. soft
8. paw
9. ball
10. yawn
11. log
12. small

Review Words
13. all
14. walk

Give, Gave and *Take, Took*

- The verbs *give* and *take* are **irregular verbs**.
- *Give* tells about an action happening now. *Gave* tells about an action in the past.
- *Take* tells about an action happening now. *Took* tells about an action in the past.

Happening Now	Happened in the Past
They **give** the gardener seeds now.	Last fall they **gave** the gardener seeds.
They **take** the vegetables home now.	They **took** the vegetables home yesterday.

Thinking Question
Is the action happening now or did it happen in the past?

✏ Read each sentence. Underline the correct verb. Then rewrite each sentence using the correct verb.

1. Last year, the children (give, <u>gave</u>) me seeds.   **past**
   Last year, the children gave me seeds. (1 point)

2. I (take, <u>took</u>) the seeds to my garden last spring.   **past**
   I took the seeds to my garden last spring. (1)

3. All that summer, I (give, <u>gave</u>) the plants water.   **past**
   All that summer, I gave the plants water. (1)

4. Now I (<u>take</u>, took) vegetables from my garden.   **now**
   Now I take vegetables from my garden. (1)

Focus Trait: Voice
Using Your Own Words

Original Sentences	Writer's Own Words
Plants such as pumpkins, zucchini, yellow squash, and sunflowers grow very big. Their seeds need to be planted far apart to give them room to grow.	Some plants are very big. They need extra room to grow. Be careful not to plant their seeds close together.

Read each original sentence or set of sentences. Paraphrase each by using different words to give the same information.   **Possible responses shown.**

Original Sentences	Your Own Words
1. Sometimes it is hard to find potatoes in a garden because they grow underground.	**Potatoes grow underground. This is why you might have trouble finding them. (1 point)**
2. Rabbits eat only plants. They use their long ears to listen for animals that might eat them.	**Rabbits don't eat meat. Their long ears help protect them from other animals. (1)**
3. Bees and butterflies carry pollen from flower to flower.	**Some insects move pollen from flower to flower. They pick up pollen from one plant and then carry it to another. (1)**
4. Some scientists believe the tomato first came from Mexico.	**Some experts think that tomatoes grew first in Mexico. (1)**
5. Thousands of types of apples exist.	**There are more than 7,500 different kinds of apples. (1)**

Cumulative Review

Read each question. Make a word that answers each question by choosing a word from the box and adding the suffix -y, -ly, or -ful to it.

> **Word Bank**
>
> hand   rock   neat
> skill   bump

Which word describes . . .

1. a place with rocks? __rocky (1 point)__

2. someone with a skill? __skillful (1)__

3. working in a neat way? __neatly (1)__

4. an amount held in a hand? __handful (1)__

5. a road with bumps? __bumpy (1)__

Add -y, -ly, or -ful to the word in bold print so that the sentence makes sense.

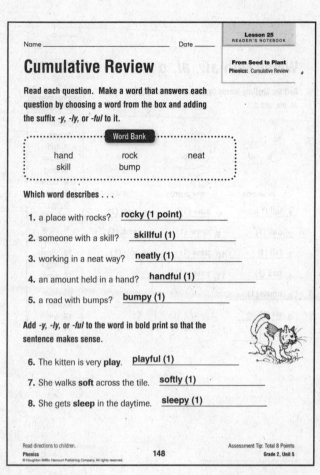

6. The kitten is very **play**. __playful (1)__

7. She walks **soft** across the tile. __softly (1)__

8. She gets **sleep** in the daytime. __sleepy (1)__

Read directions to children.
Phonics
© Houghton Mifflin Harcourt Publishing Company. All rights reserved.
148
Assessment Tip: Total 8 Points
Grade 2, Unit 5

Reader's Guide

From Seed to Plant

Scientist's Notebook

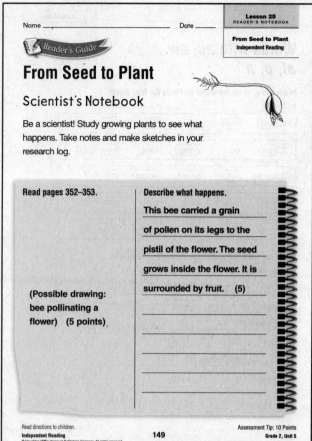

Be a scientist! Study growing plants to see what happens. Take notes and make sketches in your research log.

Read pages 352–353.	Describe what happens.
(Possible drawing: bee pollinating a flower) (5 points)	This bee carried a grain of pollen on its legs to the pistil of the flower. The seed grows inside the flower. It is surrounded by fruit. (5)

Read directions to children.
Independent Reading
© Houghton Mifflin Harcourt Publishing Company. All rights reserved.
149
Assessment Tip: 10 Points
Grade 2, Unit 5

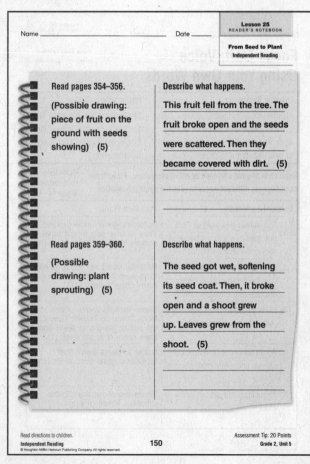

Read pages 354–356.	Describe what happens.
(Possible drawing: piece of fruit on the ground with seeds showing) (5)	This fruit fell from the tree. The fruit broke open and the seeds were scattered. Then they became covered with dirt. (5)
Read pages 359–360. (Possible drawing: plant sprouting) (5)	Describe what happens. The seed got wet, softening its seed coat. Then, it broke open and a shoot grew up. Leaves grew from the shoot. (5)

Read directions to children.
Independent Reading
© Houghton Mifflin Harcourt Publishing Company. All rights reserved.
150
Assessment Tip: 20 Points
Grade 2, Unit 5

Words with *aw, al, o*

Write the Spelling Word that belongs in each group.

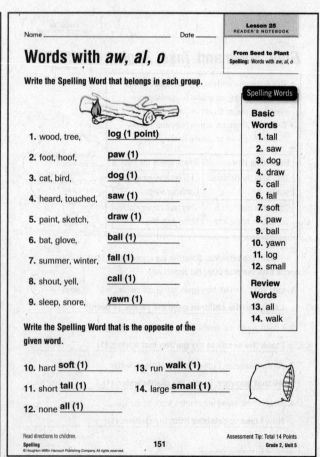

1. wood, tree, __log (1 point)__

2. foot, hoof, __paw (1)__

3. cat, bird, __dog (1)__

4. heard, touched, __saw (1)__

5. paint, sketch, __draw (1)__

6. bat, glove, __ball (1)__

7. summer, winter, __fall (1)__

8. shout, yell, __call (1)__

9. sleep, snore, __yawn (1)__

Write the Spelling Word that is the opposite of the given word.

10. hard __soft (1)__

11. short __tall (1)__

12. none __all (1)__

13. run __walk (1)__

14. large __small (1)__

> **Spelling Words**
>
> **Basic Words**
> 1. tall
> 2. saw
> 3. dog
> 4. draw
> 5. call
> 6. fall
> 7. soft
> 8. paw
> 9. ball
> 10. yawn
> 11. log
> 12. small
>
> **Review Words**
> 13. all
> 14. walk

Read directions to children.
Spelling
© Houghton Mifflin Harcourt Publishing Company. All rights reserved.
151
Assessment Tip: Total 14 Points
Grade 2, Unit 5

More Irregular Action Verbs

Read each sentence. Use the clue and underline the correct verb. Then rewrite each sentence using the correct verb that tells about now or the past.

1. The farmers (say, <u>said</u>) they planted corn.   **past**

   The farmers said they planted corn. (1 point)

2. Today, the children (<u>eat</u>, ate) a lot of corn.   **now**

   Today, the children eat a lot of corn. (1)

3. The farmers (<u>say</u>, said) they can bring more corn.   **now**

   The farmers say they can bring more corn. (1)

4. We (give, <u>gave</u>) vegetables to our friends.   **past**

   We gave vegetables to our friends. (1)

5. They (<u>give</u>, gave) us fruit from their trees.   **now**

   They give us fruit from their trees. (1)

6. We (<u>take</u>, took) two apples from the basket.   **now**

   We take two apples from the basket. (1)

Using Context

Use clues in the sentence to find the meaning of the underlined word. Then find the word's meaning in the box. Write the definition on the line.

> **Word Bank**
>
> something that helps plants grow   move quickly
> take small bites   speak with anger
> someone who lives nearby   lucky

1. I like to <u>nibble</u> the carrot. I eat it like a bunny.

   take small bites (2 points)

2. Lisa is very late. She has to <u>rush</u> to catch the school

   bus. **move quickly (2)**

3. Please don't <u>scold</u> me. I did not mean to drop the

   cup. **speak with anger (2)**

4. Jake is our <u>neighbor</u>. He walks to my house to play.

   someone who lives nearby (2)

5. Dad uses <u>fertilizer</u> in the garden. He wants the plants

   to be healthy.   **something that helps plants grow (2)**

6. My sister has the flu. I feel very <u>fortunate</u> that I

   didn't catch it. **lucky (2)**

Proofread for Spelling

Proofread this journal entry. Circle the eight misspelled words. Then write the correct spellings on the lines below.

April 10, 2010

   I think spring is here. Today I (sow) a robin. I have not seen one since last (fal). I like spring because I spend more time outside.

   I like to plant seeds in the (sawft) mud of Mom's flower garden. Then I (drow) pictures of the flowers on (smoll) cards and place the signs at the head of each row.

   My dog Max likes to help, but just one paw can smash my plants. Mom will call him away to chase his ball. Sometimes Max will just sit near me and (yown) in the sun.

   Soon my plants will grow (toll). Then I will sit on a (lawg) and smell my flowers. **(8 points)**

> **Spelling Words**
>
> **Basic Words**
> 1. tall
> 2. saw
> 3. dog
> 4. draw
> 5. call
> 6. fall
> 7. soft
> 8. paw
> 9. ball
> 10. yawn
> 11. log
> 12. small

1. **saw (1point)**   5. **small (1)**

2. **fall (1)**   6. **yawn (1)**

3. **soft (1)**   7. **tall (1)**

4. **draw (1)**   8. **log (1)**

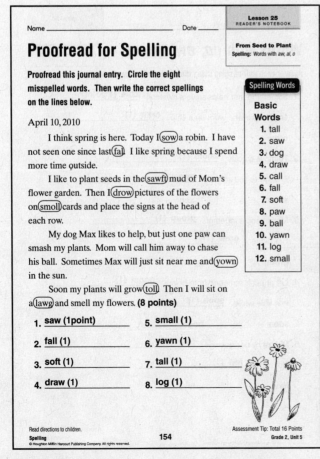

Commas in a Series

Draw a line under each correct sentence.

1. Mom's garden has tomatoes, peppers and squash.
   <u>Mom's garden has tomatoes, peppers, and squash.</u> **(1 point)**

2. <u>She planted on Sunday, Monday, and Tuesday.</u> **(1)**
   She planted, on Sunday Monday and Tuesday.

3. We helped her dig plant, and water.
   <u>We helped her dig, plant, and water.</u> **(1)**

4. I planted the carrots celery and eggplant.
   <u>I planted the carrots, celery, and eggplant.</u> **(1)**

5. We saw, bees, birds and butterflies on the plants.
   <u>We saw bees, birds, and butterflies on the plants.</u> **(1)**

6. <u>We will have vegetables in June, July, and August.</u> **(1)**
   We will have vegetables in, June July and, August.

Sentence Fluency

Incorrect
Last week she **gives** me a bag of carrots.
I **taked** the carrots home.

Correct
Last week she **gave** me a bag of carrots.
I **took** the carrots home.

✏ Read this story about last summer. Write the paragraph correctly. Change each underlined verb to tell about the past.

My Summer Garden

Last year, I grew a garden. I <u>take</u> seeds and put them in the ground. I <u>gived</u> them water. Mom and Dad <u>say</u> we could pick the vegetables when they grow. Soon, the garden grew. I <u>give</u> eggplant to Mom. I <u>take</u> carrots for myself. We <u>eat</u> it all. Yum!

Last year, I grew a garden. I took seeds and put them in the ground. I gave them water. Mom and Dad said we could pick the vegetables when they grow. Soon, the garden grew. I gave eggplant to Mom. I took carrots for myself. We ate it all. Yum!

(6 points)

Words with *oo, ew, ue, ou*

Put these letters together to write words with the vowel sound you hear in *zoo*.

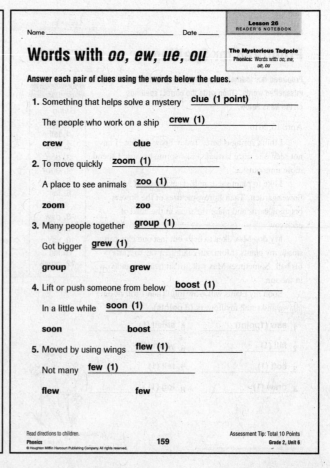

1. m + oo + n   **moon (1 point)**
2. s + ou + p   **soup (1)**
3. c + h + ew   **chew (1)**
4. b + l + ue   **blue (1)**
5. p + oo + l   **pool (1)**

Now use the words you wrote above to complete the sentences below.

6. Did you see the **moon (1)** _____ and the stars last night?
7. We swim in the **pool (1)** _____.
8. I ate a bowl of hot **soup (1)** _____.
9. The sun is shining in the **blue (1)** _____ sky.
10. Our puppy likes to **chew (1)** _____ on socks.

Contractions with *not*

- A **contraction** is a short way of writing two words.
- An **apostrophe** (') shows where letters were left out.

Two Words	Contraction
do not	don't
does not	doesn't
is not	isn't
cannot	can't

Thinking Question
Which two words are being put together to make a contraction?

✏ Write contractions for the underlined words.

1. I <u>do not</u> believe my eyes!   **don't (1 point)**
2. Your pet <u>is not</u> friendly.   **isn't (1)**
3. I <u>cannot</u> believe your pig can fly.   **can't (1)**
4. Your pig <u>does not</u> have wings.   **doesn't (1)**
5. I <u>do not</u> know how it can fly!   **don't (1)**
6. Our art teacher <u>does not</u> come on Tuesdays.
   doesn't (1)

Words with *oo, ew, ue, ou*

Answer each pair of clues using the words below the clues.

1. Something that helps solve a mystery   **clue (1 point)**
   The people who work on a ship   **crew (1)**

   crew   clue

2. To move quickly   **zoom (1)**
   A place to see animals   **zoo (1)**

   zoom   zoo

3. Many people together   **group (1)**
   Got bigger   **grew (1)**

   group   grew

4. Lift or push someone from below   **boost (1)**
   In a little while   **soon (1)**

   soon   boost

5. Moved by using wings   **flew (1)**
   Not many   **few (1)**

   flew   few

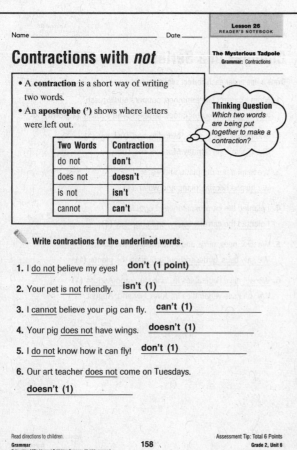

Words with *oo* (ew, oo, ou)

Name _____ Date _____

Lesson 26
READER'S NOTEBOOK

The Mysterious Tadpole
Spelling: Words with oo
(ew, oo, ou)

Sort the words by the spelling for the vowel sound in *moon*.

With *oo*	With *ew*	With *ou*
1. <u>root</u> (2 points)	9. <u>crew</u> (2)	14. <u>you</u> (2)
2. sp<u>oo</u>n (2)	10. f<u>ew</u> (2)	
3. bl<u>oo</u>m (2)	11. gr<u>ew</u> (2)	
4. r<u>oo</u>m (2)	12. st<u>ew</u> (2)	
5. b<u>oo</u>st (2)	13. fl<u>ew</u> (2)	
6. sc<u>oo</u>p (2)		
7. z<u>oo</u> (2)		
8. n<u>oo</u>n (2)		

Spelling Words

Basic Words
1. root
2. crew
3. spoon
4. few
5. bloom
6. grew
7. room
8. you
9. stew
10. boost
11. scoop
12. flew

Review Words
13. zoo
14. noon

Underline the letters in each word that make the vowel sound in *moon*.

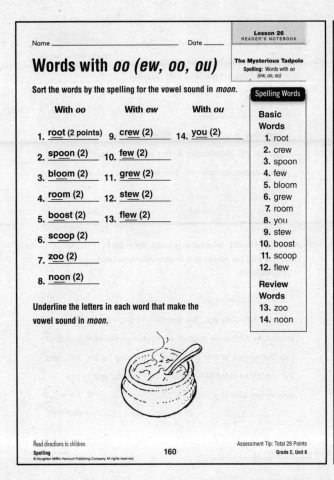

Read directions to children.
Spelling
© Houghton Mifflin Harcourt Publishing Company. All rights reserved.
160
Assessment Tip: Total 28 Points
Grade 2, Unit 6

Contractions with Pronouns

- A **contraction** is a word made by putting two words together.
- An **apostrophe** replaces the letter or letters that were left out.
- Many contractions are made by joining a **pronoun** and a **verb**.

Two Words	Contraction
I am	I'm
You will	You'll
She will	She'll
We are	We're
They are	They're
She is	She's
It is	It's

Thinking Question
Which two words are being put together to make a contraction?

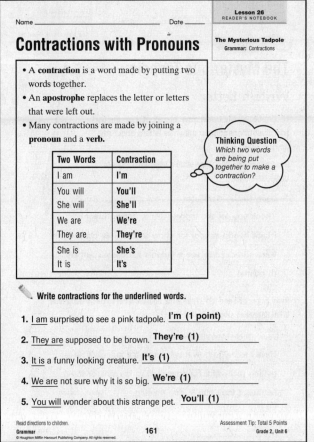

Write contractions for the underlined words.

1. <u>I am</u> surprised to see a pink tadpole. **I'm (1 point)** _____
2. <u>They are</u> supposed to be brown. **They're (1)** _____
3. <u>It is</u> a funny looking creature. **It's (1)** _____
4. <u>We are</u> not sure why it is so big. **We're (1)** _____
5. <u>You will</u> wonder about this strange pet. **You'll (1)** _____

Read directions to children.
Grammar
© Houghton Mifflin Harcourt Publishing Company. All rights reserved.
161
Assessment Tip: Total 5 Points
Grade 2, Unit 6

Focus Trait: Word Choice
Sense Words and Details

Without Sense Words and Details	With Sense Words and Details
Louis saw a tadpole.	Louis saw a **huge spotted** tadpole.

A. Complete each sentence, using sense words and details. Use the hint in ( ) to help you. **Possible responses shown.**

Without Sense Words and Details	With Sense Words and Details
1. Louis touched Alphonse's skin. (touch)	Louis touched Alphonse's **smooth, slippery** skin. **(1 point)**
2. Louis smelled the water. (smell)	Louis smelled the **fishy** water. **(1)**

B. Read each weak sentence. Rewrite each sentence. Add sense words and details.

Pair/Share Work with a partner to brainstorm powerful words.

Possible responses shown.

Weak Language	Powerful Language
3. Alphonse ate a snack.	Alphonse ate a sweet, chewy snack. **(2)**
4. Louis heard a sound.	Louis heard a loud popping sound. **(2)**

Read directions to children.
Writing
© Houghton Mifflin Harcourt Publishing Company. All rights reserved.
162
Assessment Tip: Total 6 Points
Grade 2, Unit 6

Cumulative Review

Add the suffix *-y*, *-ly*, or *-ful* to each word. Write the word on the line and read each completed sentence.

1. **rain**: I painted my bedroom one **rainy (2 points)** _____ day.
2. **slow**: I painted **slowly (2)** _____.
3. **care**: I was **careful (2)** _____ not to spill.
4. **hope**: Mom was **hopeful (2)** _____ that I would finish by noon.
5. **quick**: I tried painting **quickly (2)** _____.
6. **mess**: It was **messy (2)** _____.

Add the prefix to each base word. Then write the new word on the line.

7. re + paint = **repaint (2)** _____
8. un + cover = **uncover (2)** _____
9. over + look = **overlook (2)** _____
10. pre + mix = **premix (2)** _____
11. mis + match = **mismatch (2)** _____

Read directions to children.
Phonics
© Houghton Mifflin Harcourt Publishing Company. All rights reserved.
163
Assessment Tip: Total 22 Points
Grade 2, Unit 6

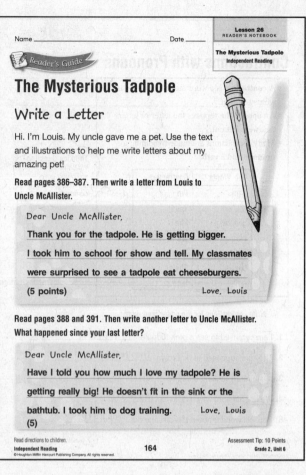

The Mysterious Tadpole

Write a Letter

Hi. I'm Louis. My uncle gave me a pet. Use the text and illustrations to help me write letters about my amazing pet!

Read pages 386–387. Then write a letter from Louis to Uncle McAllister.

> Dear Uncle McAllister,
>
> Thank you for the tadpole. He is getting bigger.
> I took him to school for show and tell. My classmates
> were surprised to see a tadpole eat cheeseburgers.
> (5 points)   Love, Louis

Read pages 388 and 391. Then write another letter to Uncle McAllister. What happened since your last letter?

> Dear Uncle McAllister,
>
> Have I told you how much I love my tadpole? He is
> getting really big! He doesn't fit in the sink or the
> bathtub. I took him to dog training.   Love, Louis
> (5)

Read pages 397–399. Write another letter from Louis to Uncle McAllister. Let him know what happened on these pages.

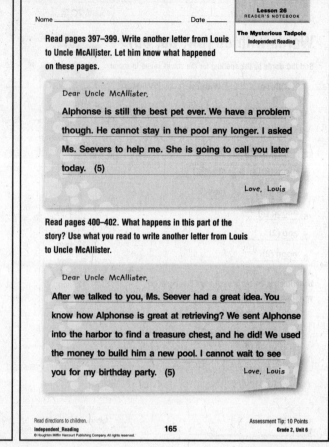

> Dear Uncle McAllister,
>
> Alphonse is still the best pet ever. We have a problem
> though. He cannot stay in the pool any longer. I asked
> Ms. Seevers to help me. She is going to call you later
> today. (5)
>   Love, Louis

Read pages 400–402. What happens in this part of the story? Use what you read to write another letter from Louis to Uncle McAllister.

> Dear Uncle McAllister,
>
> After we talked to you, Ms. Seever had a great idea. You
> know how Alphonse is great at retrieving? We sent Alphonse
> into the harbor to find a treasure chest, and he did! We used
> the money to build him a new pool. I cannot wait to see
> you for my birthday party. (5)   Love, Louis

Name _____ Date _____

Lesson 26
READER'S NOTEBOOK

The Mysterious Tadpole
Spelling: Words with oo
(ew, oo, ou)

Words with *oo* (ew, oo, ou)

Write the Spelling Word that matches each meaning.

1. not many **few (1 point)**
2. got bigger **grew (1)**
3. animal park **zoo (1)**
4. raise **boost (1)**
5. midday **noon (1)**
6. pick up **scoop (1)**

Spelling Words

Basic Words
1. root
2. crew
3. spoon
4. few
5. bloom
6. grew
7. room
8. you
9. stew
10. boost
11. scoop
12. flew

Review Words
13. zoo
14. noon

Write the Basic Word that belongs in each group.

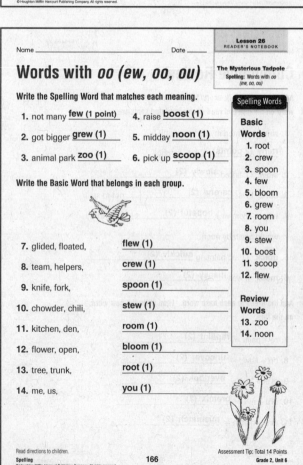

7. glided, floated, **flew (1)**
8. team, helpers, **crew (1)**
9. knife, fork, **spoon (1)**
10. chowder, chili, **stew (1)**
11. kitchen, den, **room (1)**
12. flower, open, **bloom (1)**
13. tree, trunk, **root (1)**
14. me, us, **you (1)**

Contractions

Write the contraction for each underlined word or words.

1. Tina knows that cats <u>do not</u> talk. **don't (1 point)**
2. She <u>is not</u> sure why her cat can sing. **isn't (1)**
3. Tina <u>cannot</u> tell people about the cat. **can't (1)**
4. She <u>does not</u> think anyone will believe her.
   doesn't (1)

Write each sentence. Write a contraction in place of the underlined words.

5. <u>We are</u> tadpoles in a pond.
   We're tadpoles in a pond. (2)
6. <u>They are</u> afraid of us.
   They're afraid of us. (2)
7. <u>You will</u> see that I am small.
   You'll see that I am small. (2)
8. But <u>I am</u> going to be ten feet tall!
   But I'm going to be ten feet tall! (2)

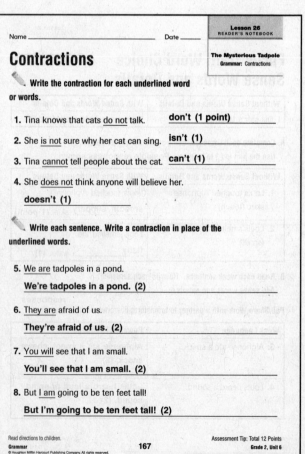

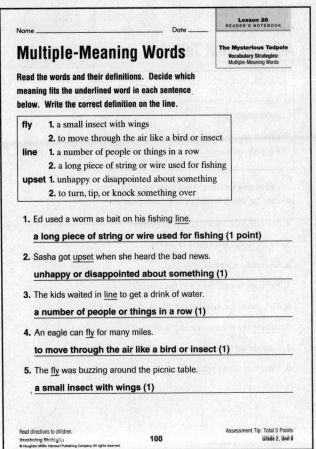

Multiple-Meaning Words

Read the words and their definitions. Decide which
meaning fits the underlined word in each sentence
below. Write the correct definition on the line.

fly	**1.** a small insect with wings
	2. to move through the air like a bird or insect
line	**1.** a number of people or things in a row
	2. a long piece of string or wire used for fishing
upset	**1.** unhappy or disappointed about something
	2. to turn, tip, or knock something over

1. Ed used a worm as bait on his fishing <u>line</u>.

   a long piece of string or wire used for fishing (1 point)

2. Sasha got <u>upset</u> when she heard the bad news.

   unhappy or disappointed about something (1)

3. The kids waited in <u>line</u> to get a drink of water.

   a number of people or things in a row (1)

4. An eagle can <u>fly</u> for many miles.

   to move through the air like a bird or insect (1)

5. The <u>fly</u> was buzzing around the picnic table.

   a small insect with wings (1)

Read directions to children.
Vocabulary Strategies
© Houghton Mifflin Harcourt Publishing Company. All rights reserved.
100
Assessment Tip: Total 5 Points
Grade 2, Unit 6

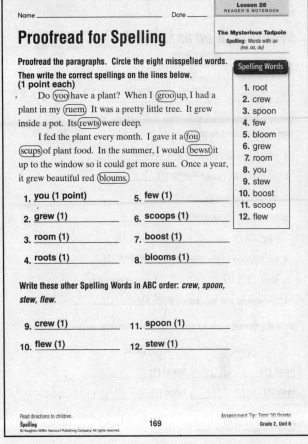

Proofread for Spelling

Lesson 26
READER'S NOTEBOOK

The Mysterious Tadpole
Spelling: Words with oo
(ew, oo, ou)

Proofread the paragraphs. Circle the eight misspelled words.
Then write the correct spellings on the lines below.
(1 point each)

   Do yoo have a plant? When I groo up, I had a
plant in my ruem. It was a pretty little tree. It grew
inside a pot. Its rewts were deep.

   I fed the plant every month. I gave it a fou
scups of plant food. In the summer, I would bewst it
up to the window so it could get more sun. Once a year,
it grew beautiful red bloums.

Spelling Words
1. root
2. crew
3. spoon
4. few
5. bloom
6. grew
7. room
8. you
9. stew
10. boost
11. scoop
12. flew

1. **you (1 point)** 5. **few (1)**

2. **grew (1)** 6. **scoops (1)**

3. **room (1)** 7. **boost (1)**

4. **roots (1)** 8. **blooms (1)**

Write these other Spelling Words in ABC order: *crew, spoon,
stew, flew.*

9. **crew (1)** 11. **spoon (1)**

10. **flew (1)** 12. **stew (1)**

Read directions to children.
Spelling
© Houghton Mifflin Harcourt Publishing Company. All rights reserved.
169
Assessment Tip: Total 20 Points
Grade 2, Unit 6

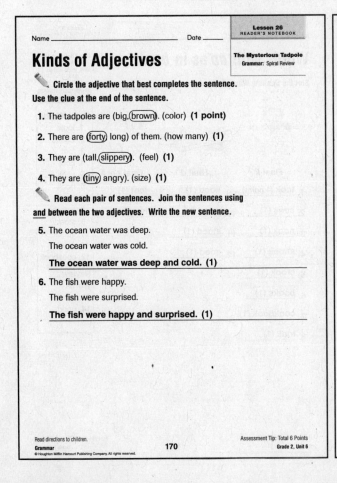

Kinds of Adjectives

Circle the adjective that best completes the sentence.
Use the clue at the end of the sentence.

1. The tadpoles are (big, brown). (color) **(1 point)**

2. There are (forty, long) of them. (how many) **(1)**

3. They are (tall, slippery). (feel) **(1)**

4. They are (tiny, angry). (size) **(1)**

Read each pair of sentences. Join the sentences using
and between the two adjectives. Write the new sentence.

5. The ocean water was deep.

   The ocean water was cold.

   The ocean water was deep and cold. (1)

6. The fish were happy.

   The fish were surprised.

   The fish were happy and surprised. (1)

Read directions to children.
Grammar
© Houghton Mifflin Harcourt Publishing Company. All rights reserved.
170
Assessment Tip: Total 6 Points
Grade 2, Unit 6

Contractions

Incorrect	Correct
The mysterious horse is'nt growing.	The mysterious horse isn't growing.
H'es getting smaller!	He's getting smaller!

Read the paragraph. Circle five mistakes with
contractions. Copy the story and write the contractions correctly.

The Mysterious Horse

Im going to tell you a story. I once knew a pony
named Lou. He was'nt a big pony. And he did'nt get
any bigger, either. One day he started to shrink. H'es
still getting smaller today. I think one day hel'l be the
smallest horse in the world!

I'm going to tell you a story. I once knew a pony named Lou.

He wasn't a big pony. And he didn't get any bigger, either.

One day he started to shrink. He's still getting smaller today.

I think one day he'll be the smallest horse in the world! (10 points)

Read directions to children.
Grammar
© Houghton Mifflin Harcourt Publishing Company. All rights reserved.
171
Assessment Tip: Total 10 Points
Grade 2, Unit 6

Words with *oo* as in *book*

Word Bank

cookbook	cook	took
good	cookies	looking

Write a word from the box to complete each sentence. Then read each completed sentence.

1. My father and I like to **cook (1 point)** _____

2. Last Saturday I was **looking (1)** _____

   for something to do.

3. "Let's bake oatmeal **cookies (1)** _____,"

   said Dad.

4. We followed all the steps in the **cookbook (1)** _____

5. Mom **took (1)** _____ one of our treats.

6. She agreed that they tasted **good (1)** _____

Write two rhyming words for each word below. **Possible responses shown.**

cook   **good**

book **(1)**   wood **(1)**

look **(1)**   hood **(1)**

Adverbs That Tell How

- An **adverb** describes a verb.

- **Adverbs** can tell about how something is done.

We lined up <u>quickly</u>.

We got off the bus <u>slowly</u>.

Thinking Questions
Which word tells how the action was done?

Read each sentence. Think about the action. Then underline the adverb that tells how the action was done.

1. The bus driver spoke <u>loudly</u>. **(1 point)**

2. He <u>carefully</u> called each name. **(1)**

3. She raised her hand <u>shyly</u>. **(1)**

4. He <u>nicely</u> helped her climb the steps. **(1)**

5. They got to the museum <u>quickly</u>. **(1)**

6. <u>Quietly</u>, the children asked questions. **(1)**

7. They looked at the dinosaurs <u>together</u>. **(1)**

8. Then they talked <u>softly</u>. **(1)**

Words with *oo* as in *book*

Word Bank

brook	hoof	hook	good	football
look	wood	foot	woof	cookies

Read the words below. Think about how the words in each group are alike. Then choose an *oo* word from the box that goes with each group. Write the word on the line.

1. hand, eye, **foot (1 point)** _____

2. kickball, baseball, **football (1)** _____

3. nice, fine, **good (1)** _____

4. mane, tail, **hoof (1)** _____

5. moo, chirp, **woof (1)** _____

6. creek, stream, **brook (1)** _____

7. pies, cakes, **cookies (1)** _____

8. see, peek, **look (1)** _____

9. brick, glass, **wood (1)** _____

10. bait, pole, **hook (1)** _____

Words with *oo* as in *book*

Sort the Spelling Words by final consonants.

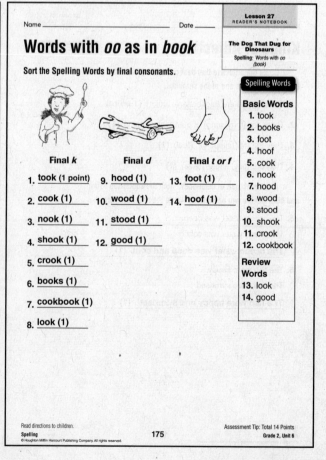

Final *k*   **Final *d***   **Final *t* or *f***

1. **took (1 point)**   9. **hood (1)**   13. **foot (1)**

2. **cook (1)**   10. **wood (1)**   14. **hoof (1)**

3. **nook (1)**   11. **stood (1)**

4. **shook (1)**   12. **good (1)**

5. **crook (1)**

6. **books (1)**

7. **cookbook (1)**

8. **look (1)**

Spelling Words

Basic Words
1. took
2. books
3. foot
4. hoof
5. cook
6. nook
7. hood
8. wood
9. stood
10. shook
11. crook
12. cookbook

Review Words
13. look
14. good

Name _____ Date _____

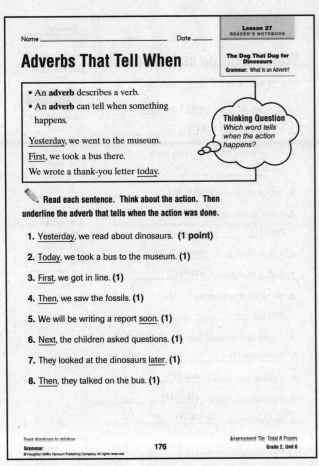

Adverbs That Tell When

- An **adverb** describes a verb.
- An **adverb** can tell when something happens.

<u>Yesterday</u>, we went to the museum.

<u>First</u>, we took a bus there.

We wrote a thank-you letter <u>today</u>.

Thinking Question
Which word tells when the action happens?

✏️ **Read each sentence. Think about the action. Then underline the adverb that tells when the action was done.**

1. <u>Yesterday</u>, we read about dinosaurs. **(1 point)**

2. <u>Today</u>, we took a bus to the museum. **(1)**

3. <u>First</u>, we got in line. **(1)**

4. <u>Then</u>, we saw the fossils. **(1)**

5. We will be writing a report <u>soon</u>. **(1)**

6. <u>Next</u>, the children asked questions. **(1)**

7. They looked at the dinosaurs <u>later</u>. **(1)**

8. <u>Then</u>, they talked on the bus. **(1)**

Name _____ Date _____

Focus Trait: Organization
Introduction and Conclusion

The **introduction sentence** of a book report tells about the book and gives an opinion about the book.

Sentences that give **reasons** tell facts to support the opinion.

The **conclusion sentence** sums up the information and tells the opinion in a different way.

Label the introduction sentence, the sentences that give reasons, and the conclusion sentence.

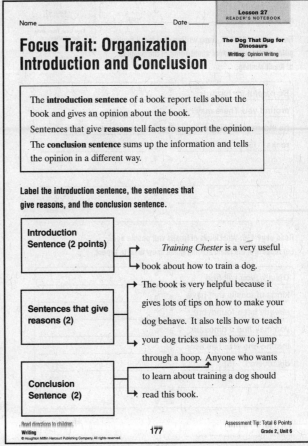

Introduction Sentence (2 points)	→ *Training Chester* is a very useful book about how to train a dog.
Sentences that give reasons (2)	→ The book is very helpful because it gives lots of tips on how to make your dog behave. It also tells how to teach your dog tricks such as how to jump through a hoop. Anyone who wants to learn about training a dog should
Conclusion Sentence (2)	→ read this book.

Name _____ Date _____

Possessive Nouns

Read the sentences. Draw a circle around each word that shows who or what owns something.

1. The (bike's) tire is flat. **(1 point)**

2. We laughed at the (seals') tricks. **(1)**

3. The (ladies') club has a meeting today. **(1)**

4. The little (rabbit's) tail is white and fluffy. **(1)**

5. The (book's) pages are torn. **(1)**

6. The (girls') team has a game on Thursday. **(1)**

Now write each word you circled under the right heading.

One	More Than One
bike's (1)	seals' (1)
rabbit's (1)	ladies' (1)
book's (1)	girls' (1)

Name _____ Date _____

📓 **Reader's Guide**

The Dog That Dug for Dinosaurs

Create a Fossil Hunting Guide

Use the text and illustrations to help Digger complete a fossil hunting guide.

Read pages 425–426.
Describe fossils and the tools needed to find them.

Read pages 427–428.
Explain to readers how to find fossils.

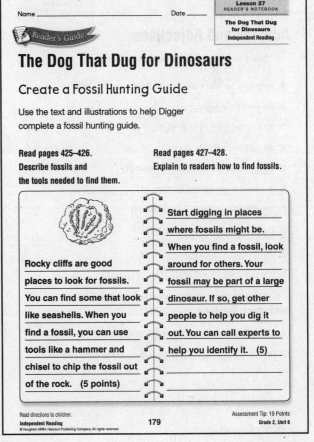

Rocky cliffs are good places to look for fossils. You can find some that look like seashells. When you find a fossil, you can use tools like a hammer and chisel to chip the fossil out of the rock. **(5 points)**

Start digging in places where fossils might be. When you find a fossil, look around for others. Your fossil may be part of a large dinosaur. If so, get other people to help you dig it out. You can call experts to help you identify it. **(5)**

Read pages 434–435. Keep writing your fossil hunting guide. Tell your readers about some of the dangers of fossil hunting.

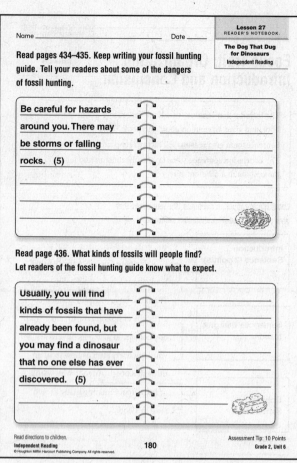

Be careful for hazards around you. There may be storms or falling rocks. **(5)**

Read page 436. What kinds of fossils will people find? Let readers of the fossil hunting guide know what to expect.

Usually, you will find kinds of fossils that have already been found, but you may find a dinosaur that no one else has ever discovered. **(5)**

Read directions to children.
Independent Reading
© Houghton Mifflin Harcourt Publishing Company. All rights reserved.
180
Assessment Tip: 10 Points
Grade 2, Unit 6

Words with *oo* as in *book*

Write the Basic Word that matches each clue.

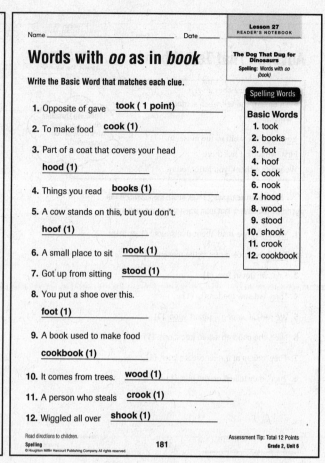

Spelling Words

Basic Words
1. took
2. books
3. foot
4. hoof
5. cook
6. nook
7. hood
8. wood
9. stood
10. shook
11. crook
12. cookbook

1. Opposite of gave   **took (1 point)**

2. To make food   **cook (1)**

3. Part of a coat that covers your head
   hood (1)

4. Things you read   **books (1)**

5. A cow stands on this, but you don't.
   hoof (1)

6. A small place to sit   **nook (1)**

7. Got up from sitting   **stood (1)**

8. You put a shoe over this.
   foot (1)

9. A book used to make food
   cookbook (1)

10. It comes from trees.   **wood (1)**

11. A person who steals   **crook (1)**

12. Wiggled all over   **shook (1)**

Read directions to children.
Spelling
© Houghton Mifflin Harcourt Publishing Company. All rights reserved.
181
Assessment Tip: Total 12 Points
Grade 2, Unit 6

Adverbs and Adjectives

Draw a line under the adverb that tells how or when.

1. <u>Yesterday</u>, we saw a show about dinosaurs. **(1 point)**

2. We went there <u>together</u>. **(1)**

3. We listened <u>carefully</u> to all the facts. **(1)**

4. We took notes <u>quietly</u>. **(1)**

5. <u>Today</u>, we are talking about the show. **(1)**

6. Our teacher <u>quickly</u> lists the facts. **(1)**

7. <u>Tomorrow</u>, we will write our papers. **(1)**

8. <u>Then</u>, we will share our reports. **(1)**

9. We will speak <u>clearly</u>. **(1)**

10. The others will listen <u>politely</u>. **(1)**

Choose the adverb or adjective that best completes each sentence. Underline it.

11. We watched the dog run (<u>quickly</u>, quick) to the dirt area. **(2)**

12. He was (<u>careful</u>, carefully) while digging for the old bones. **(2)**

Read directions to children.
Grammar
© Houghton Mifflin Harcourt Publishing Company. All rights reserved.
182
Assessment Tip: Total 14 Points
Grade 2, Unit 6

Shades of Meaning

Read the story. Complete each sentence by writing the word that fits better.

Tina and Larry went on a hike. They stopped at a creek

to ___**eat (1 point)**___ their lunch. Tina took her boots off.
     (eat   gobble)

She put her feet in the creek. "This feels good," she said. "The

water is ___**cool (1)**___ "
        (freezing   cool)

"Look at that ___**tiny (1)**___ animal," said
              (tiny   small)

Larry. "It's the size of a mouse. I think it's a chipmunk." He

___**broke (1)**___ a peanut and tossed it to the chipmunk.
(broke   smashed)

From the top of a hill, the children ___**spotted (1)**___
                                    (saw   spotted)

another hiker. "Hey," said Tina, "that's Rob. He likes to hike

too." She ___**yelled (1)**___ to get Rob's attention. Soon
         (screamed   yelled)

the three friends were hiking together.

"We should turn around," said Lawrence. "I'm

___**worried (1)**___ we might not get home in time for dinner.
(worried   scared)

I'm starving. I want to eat a ___**giant (1)**___ hamburger."
                             (large   giant)

Read directions to children.
Vocabulary Strategies
© Houghton Mifflin Harcourt Publishing Company. All rights reserved.
183
Assessment Tip: Total 8 Points
Grade 2, Unit 6

Proofread for Spelling

Proofread the story. Circle the eight misspelled words. Then write the correct spellings on the lines below.

Spelling Words

1. took
2. books
3. foot
4. hoof
5. cook
6. nook
7. hood
8. wood
9. stood
10. shook
11. crook
12. cookbook

Review Words
13. look
14. good

    I had a funny dream. I dreamed I was sitting in a nook next to an old fireplace. I could smell the (wud) fire. Near the door, (stud) a huge cook. I knew because he wore an apron and held a (cookbuck)

    He came over and (shok) my hand. Then he pulled a hood over his head and started cooking breakfast. It smelled (gud.) I saw that his right (foat) was not in a shoe, but was a (huf!) He smiled at me. He looked like a character from one of my story (boaks!) **(8 points)**

1. **wood** (1)   5. **good** (1)

2. **stood** (1)   6. **foot** (1)

3. **cookbook** (1)   7. **hoof** (1)

4. **shook** (1)   8. **books** (1)

Write these other Spelling Words in ABC order: took, cook, nook, hood, look, crook.

9. **cook** (1)   12. **look** (1)

10. **crook** (1)   13. **nook** (1)

11. **hood** (1)   14. **took** (1)

Read directions to children.
Spelling   184
© Houghton Mifflin Harcourt Publishing Company. All rights reserved.
Assessment Tip: Total 22 Points
Grade 2, Unit 6

Using Adjectives

✏ **Circle the word that correctly completes the sentence.**

1. I found (a, an) fossil today. **(1 point)**

2. It is the (bigger, biggest) fossil I have ever seen. **(1)**

3. It may be (a, an) leg bone of a dinosaur. **(1)**

4. The other bone I found was (shorter, shortest). **(1)**

✏ **Rewrite the paragraph. Add -er or -est to each underlined adjective. Write the new paragraph on the lines below.**

    I have the great dog in the world. His name is Chester. Chester digs in the park with his dog friends. Chester is small than his friend Chelsie, but he is the fast of all the dogs. He and his friend Luke find bones. The bone Chester finds is long than the others.

    I have the **greatest** dog in the world. His name is Chester.

Chester digs in the park with his dog friends. He is **smaller** than

his friend Chelsie, but he is the **fastest** of all the dogs. He and

his friend Luke find bones. The bone Chester finds is **longer**

than the others. **(4 points)**

Read directions to children.
Grammar   185
© Houghton Mifflin Harcourt Publishing Company. All rights reserved.
Assessment Tip: Total 8 Points
Grade 2, Unit 6

Adverbs

You can combine sentences that describe the same action. Use *and* to join the adverbs.

The tourists walked quickly. The tourists walked quietly.	The tourists walked quickly <u>and</u> quietly.
They are digging today. They are digging tomorrow.	They are digging today <u>and</u> tomorrow.

✏ **Read each pair of sentences. Use *and* to join the adverbs and write the new sentence.**

1. We read about dinosaurs yesterday.
   We read about dinosaurs today.

   We read about dinosaurs yesterday and today. **(1 point)**

2. I wrote my notes neatly.
   I wrote my notes carefully.

   I wrote my notes neatly and carefully. (1)

3. I'm going to study today.
   I'm going to study tomorrow.

   I'm going to study today and tomorrow. (1)

4. I will answer the test questions slowly.
   I will answer the test questions correctly.

   I will answer the test questions slowly and correctly. (1)

Read directions to children.
Grammar   186
© Houghton Mifflin Harcourt Publishing Company. All rights reserved.
Assessment Tip: Total 4 Points
Grade 2, Unit 6

Words with *ow, ou*

Put these letters together to write words with *ow* and *ou*. Then read each word aloud.

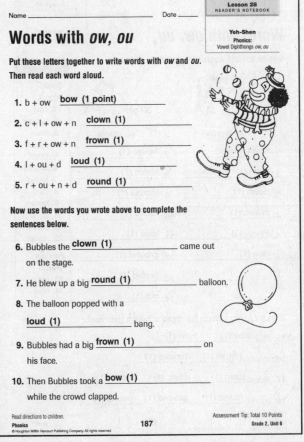

1. b + ow   **bow (1 point)**

2. c + l + ow + n   **clown (1)**

3. f + r + ow + n   **frown (1)**

4. l + ou + d   **loud (1)**

5. r + ou + n + d   **round (1)**

Now use the words you wrote above to complete the sentences below.

6. Bubbles the **clown (1)** came out on the stage.

7. He blew up a big **round (1)** balloon.

8. The balloon popped with a **loud (1)** bang.

9. Bubbles had a big **frown (1)** on his face.

10. Then Bubbles took a **bow (1)** while the crowd clapped.

Read directions to children.
Phonics   187
© Houghton Mifflin Harcourt Publishing Company. All rights reserved.
Assessment Tip: Total 10 Points
Grade 2, Unit 6

Nouns Ending with 's

- A **possessive noun** shows that a person, animal, or thing owns or has something.
- When a noun names one person or thing, add an **apostrophe (')** and an **s** to that noun to show ownership. This makes the noun a possessive noun.

The <u>fish's</u> scales were shiny.

Thinking Question
Who or what in the sentence owns or has something?

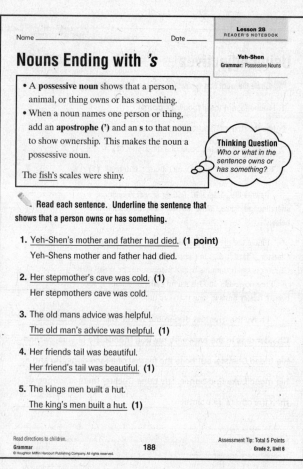

Read each sentence. Underline the sentence that shows that a person owns or has something.

1. <u>Yeh-Shen's mother and father had died.</u> **(1 point)**
   Yeh-Shens mother and father had died.

2. <u>Her stepmother's cave was cold.</u> **(1)**
   Her stepmothers cave was cold.

3. The old mans advice was helpful.
   <u>The old man's advice was helpful.</u> **(1)**

4. Her friends tail was beautiful.
   <u>Her friend's tail was beautiful.</u> **(1)**

5. The kings men built a hut.
   <u>The king's men built a hut.</u> **(1)**

Read directions to children.
Grammar
© Houghton Mifflin Harcourt Publishing Company. All rights reserved.
188
Assessment Tip: Total 5 Points
Grade 2, Unit 6

Words with *ow, ou*

Word Bank

couch	crowd	crown	found	frown
howl	mouth	ouch	round	shout

Write a word from the box that matches each clue.

1. A part of your face _____ **mouth (1 point)**
2. A sound a dog might make _____ **howl (1)**
3. A large group of people _____ **crowd (1)**
4. A long seat for sitting _____ **couch (1)**
5. To yell loudly _____ **shout (1)**
6. Something a queen has _____ **crown (1)**
7. The shape of a ball _____ **round (1)**
8. The face a grouch makes _____ **frown (1)**
9. What you say when you get hurt _____ **ouch (1)**
10. Got something you were looking for _____ **found (1)**

Read directions to children.
Phonics
© Houghton Mifflin Harcourt Publishing Company. All rights reserved.
189
Assessment Tip: Total 10 Points
Grade 2, Unit 6

Words with *ow, ou*

Sort the Spelling Words by the spellings *ow* and *ou*.

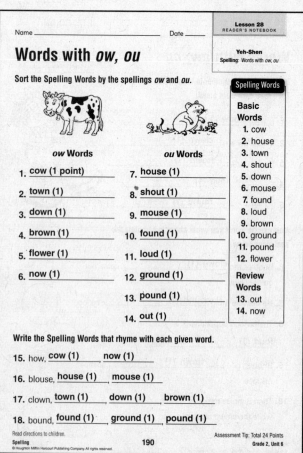

Spelling Words

Basic Words
1. cow
2. house
3. town
4. shout
5. down
6. mouse
7. found
8. loud
9. brown
10. ground
11. pound
12. flower

Review Words
13. out
14. now

ow Words
1. cow (1 point)
2. town (1)
3. down (1)
4. brown (1)
5. flower (1)
6. now (1)

ou Words
7. house (1)
8. shout (1)
9. mouse (1)
10. found (1)
11. loud (1)
12. ground (1)
13. pound (1)
14. out (1)

Write the Spelling Words that rhyme with each given word.

15. how, cow (1) , now (1)
16. blouse, house (1) , mouse (1)
17. clown, town (1) , down (1) , brown (1)
18. bound, found (1) , ground (1) , pound (1)

Read directions to children.
Spelling
© Houghton Mifflin Harcourt Publishing Company. All rights reserved.
190
Assessment Tip: Total 24 Points
Grade 2, Unit 6

Nouns Ending with s'

- A **possessive noun** shows that a person, animal, or thing owns or has something.
- When a noun names more than one and ends in **s**, add just an **apostrophe (')** after the **s** to show ownership.

The <u>musicians'</u> show was great.

Thinking Question
Who or what in the sentence owns something?

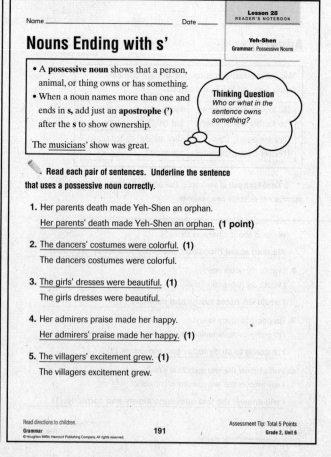

Read each pair of sentences. Underline the sentence that uses a possessive noun correctly.

1. Her parents death made Yeh-Shen an orphan.
   <u>Her parents' death made Yeh-Shen an orphan.</u> **(1 point)**

2. <u>The dancers' costumes were colorful.</u> **(1)**
   The dancers costumes were colorful.

3. <u>The girls' dresses were beautiful.</u> **(1)**
   The girls dresses were beautiful.

4. Her admirers praise made her happy.
   <u>Her admirers' praise made her happy.</u> **(1)**

5. <u>The villagers' excitement grew.</u> **(1)**
   The villagers excitement grew.

Read directions to children.
Grammar
© Houghton Mifflin Harcourt Publishing Company. All rights reserved.
191
Assessment Tip: Total 5 Points
Grade 2, Unit 6

Focus Trait: Ideas
Details That Don't Belong

Opinion: *Yeh-Shen was lonely.*

Details:
1. She has no time to play with other children.
2. Her one special friend was a fish.
3. Yeh-Shen lost her slipper.

Detail 3 does not belong. It does not support the opinion.

✏️ Read each opinion and the details that follow. Cross out the detail that does not support the opinion.

1. **Opinion:** Jin should not have cooked Yeh-Shen's fish friend.

   Details: The fish meant a lot to Yeh-Shen.
   ~~Jin went to the pond and caught the fish.~~ **(2 points)**
   Yeh-Shen's friendship with the fish did not keep her from doing her work.

2. **Opinion:** It was good that Yeh-Shen followed the old man's advice.

   Details: ~~A traveler found Yeh-Shen's slipper.~~ **(2)**
   Yeh-Shen's wish was granted.
   The bones of the fish had special powers.

3. **Opinion:** The king's treatment of Jin and Jun-li was too harsh.

   Details: Jin and Jun-Li could never come to the castle.
   Jin and Jun-Li had to stay in their cave.
   ~~Jin and Jun-Li went to the festival.~~ **(2)**

Read directions to children.
Writing
© Houghton Mifflin Harcourt Publishing Company. All rights reserved.
192
Assessment Tip: Total 6 Points
Grade 2, Unit 6

Cumulative Review

Fill in the blanks.

Word Bank
bloom
crew
toss
yawn
shook

1. It rhymes with **moss**.
   It begins like **took**. toss (1 point)

2. It rhymes with **moo**.
   It begins like **cross**. crew (1)

3. It rhymes with **book**.
   It begins like **show**. shook (1)

4. It rhymes with **room**.
   It begins like **blue**. bloom (1)

5. It rhymes with **fawn**.
   It begins like **yes**. yawn (1)

Now use words you wrote above to complete the sentences below.

6. Many flowers bloom (1) in the spring.

7. A good crew (1) makes a ship run smoothly.

8. When it got late, Tony started to yawn (1)

Read directions to children.
Phonics
© Houghton Mifflin Harcourt Publishing Company. All rights reserved.
193
Assessment Tip: Total 8 Points
Grade 2, Unit 6

Reader's Guide

Yeh-Shen

Write a Travel Brochure

Travelers want to take a tour and visit each place in Yeh-Shen's story. Tell why each place is important and draw a picture.

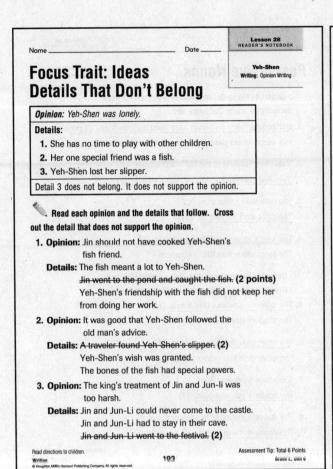

Read page 458.

The first stop on our tour is the cave where Yeh-Shen lived with her mean stepmother and lazy stepsister.
(5 points)

(Drawings should relate to the children's written descriptions.)

Read pages 459–460.

The second stop on our tour is the pond where Yeh-Shen met her friend the fish and the old man who told her to bury the fish bones. **(5)**

Read directions to children.
Independent Reading
© Houghton Mifflin Harcourt Publishing Company. All rights reserved.
194
Assessment Tip: 10 Points
Grade 2, Unit 6

Read page 462–463.

The next stop on our tour is the festival area. This is where Yeh-Shen enjoyed an evening in her beautiful clothes and where she lost her slipper. **(5)**

Read page 464.

The last stop on our tour is the hut where the missing slipper is placed. The king's men saw Yeh-Shen here when she tried to get her slipper back. **(5)**

Think about the whole story.

After this tour, many visitors say they have learned an important lesson: kindness is rewarded in the end. **(5)**

Read directions to children.
Independent Reading
© Houghton Mifflin Harcourt Publishing Company. All rights reserved.
195
Assessment Tip: 15 Points
Grade 2, Unit 6

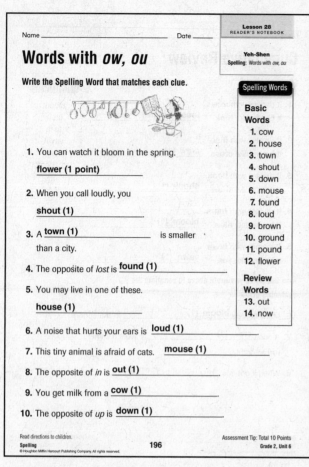

Words with *ow, ou*

Write the Spelling Word that matches each clue.

1. You can watch it bloom in the spring.
   flower (1 point)

2. When you call loudly, you
   shout (1)

3. A town (1) _____ is smaller than a city.

4. The opposite of *lost* is found (1)

5. You may live in one of these.
   house (1)

6. A noise that hurts your ears is loud (1)

7. This tiny animal is afraid of cats. mouse (1)

8. The opposite of *in* is out (1)

9. You get milk from a cow (1)

10. The opposite of *up* is down (1)

Spelling Words

Basic Words
1. cow
2. house
3. town
4. shout
5. down
6. mouse
7. found
8. loud
9. brown
10. ground
11. pound
12. flower

Review Words
13. out
14. now

Read directions to children.
Spelling
© Houghton Mifflin Harcourt Publishing Company. All rights reserved.
196
Assessment Tip: Total 10 Points
Grade 2, Unit 6

Possessive Nouns

Underline the sentence that uses a possessive noun correctly for nouns that name one.

1. Her stepmother's demands were hard on Yeh-Shen. **(1 point)**
   Her stepmothers demands were hard on Yeh-Shen.

2. Yeh-Shen listened to the old mans advice.
   Yeh-Shen listened to the old man's advice. **(1)**

3. The girls wish came true.
   The girl's wish came true. **(1)**

4. The king's voice was full of kindness. **(1)**
   The kings voice was full of kindness.

Underline the sentence that uses a possessive noun correctly for nouns that name more than one.

5. The slippers' size was very small. **(1)**
   The slippers size was very small.

6. The other girls' feet were too big. **(1)**
   The other girls feet were too big.

7. The soldiers job was hard.
   The soldiers' job was hard. **(1)**

8. The dancers movements were graceful.
   The dancers' movements were graceful. **(1)**

Read directions to children.
Grammar
© Houghton Mifflin Harcourt Publishing Company. All rights reserved.
197
Assessment Tip: Total 8 Points
Grade 2, Unit 6

Classify and Categorize

Name _____ Date _____

Lesson 28
READER'S NOTEBOOK

Yeh-Shen
Vocabulary Strategies:
Classify and Categorize

Word Bank

prince	fairy godmother	stepsister
fish friend	king	girl
wise old man	traveler	

Read each word above. Write each word in the best category.

Characters in Fairy Tales	
	fairy godmother (1 point)
	fish friend (1)
	wise old man (1)

Characters in Real Life	
	prince (1)
	stepsister (1)
	king (1)
	girl (1)
	traveler (1)

Read directions to children.
Vocabulary Strategies
© Houghton Mifflin Harcourt Publishing Company. All rights reserved.
198
Assessment Tip: Total 8 Points
Grade 2, Unit 6

Proofread for Spelling

Proofread the sentences. Circle the misspelled word. Then write the word correctly on the line.

1. When you see your present, you'll (showt) with joy!
   shout (2 points)

2. Is that a stuffed (mowse)? mouse (2)

3. I have never seen a (flouwer) shop like that one!
   flower (2)

4. That restaurant has the best waffles in (toun.)
   town (2)

5. I have never seen her (howse) house (2)

6. All of his clothes are (broun) brown (2)

7. It takes a good (caw) to make good milk.
   cow (2)

8. Come on (doun) to the kitchen for dinner!
   down (2)

9. I (fownd) the book that I lost. found (2)

10. She dropped her sandwich on the (grownd)
    ground (2)

Spelling Words
1. cow
2. house
3. town
4. shout
5. down
6. mouse
7. found
8. loud
9. brown
10. ground
11. pound
12. flower

Read directions to children.
Spelling
© Houghton Mifflin Harcourt Publishing Company. All rights reserved.
199
Assessment Tip: Total 20 Points
Grade 2, Unit 6

Lesson 28
READER'S NOTEBOOK

Yeh-Shen
Grammar: Spiral Review

Irregular Verbs

Circle the word that correctly completes the sentence.

1. Yeh-Shen (have, (had)) lots of chores. **(1 point)**

2. She (do, (did)) her work well. **(1)**

3. Yen-Shen ((had) have) no help. **(1)**

4. Jin and Jun-li ((did) does) no work. **(1)**

Read the paragraph. Underline the six mistakes.
Then rewrite the paragraph. Make sure each verb matches
the subject in the sentence.

Long ago, Yeh-Shen <u>have</u> a hard life. Jin <u>do</u> mean
things to her. Yeh-Shen <u>have</u> only rags to wear. She <u>do</u>
chores all day. Then, Yeh-Shen <u>have</u> a wish. Her wish
came true and at last she <u>do</u> a happy life. **(6)**

Long ago, Yeh-Shen <u>had</u> a hard life. Jin <u>did</u> mean things

to her. Yeh-Shen <u>had</u> only rags to wear. She <u>did</u> chores all day.

Then, Yeh-Shen <u>had</u> a wish. Her wish came true and at last she

<u>had</u> a happy life. **(6)**

_____

_____

Read directions to children.
Grammar
© Houghton Mifflin Harcourt Publishing Company. All rights reserved.
200
Assessment Tip: Total 16 Points
Grade 2, Unit 6

Lesson 28
READER'S NOTEBOOK

Yeh-Shen
Grammar: Connect to Writing

Possessive Nouns

Weak	Strong
The slippers belonging to Yeh-Shen were silk.	Yeh-Shen's slippers were silk.
The advice of the old man was good.	The old man's advice was good.

Rewrite each sentence. Use a possessive noun to
rewrite each underlined group of words. Write the new
sentences on the line.

1. <u>The eyes belonging to the fish</u> were golden.

   The fish's eyes were golden. (2 points)

2. <u>The stepmother of Yeh-Shen</u> was angry.

   Yeh-Shen's stepmother was angry. (2)

3. Yeh-Shen followed <u>the directions of the old man</u>.

   Yeh-Shen followed the old man's directions. (2)

4. <u>The men of the king</u> caught Yeh-Shen.

   The king's men caught Yeh-Shen. (2)

Read directions to children.
Grammar
© Houghton Mifflin Harcourt Publishing Company. All rights reserved.
201
Assessment Tip: Total 8 Points
Grade 2, Unit 6

Lesson 29
READER'S NOTEBOOK

Two of Everything
Phonics: Reading Longer Words:
Long Vowels *a* and *i*

Reading Longer Words: Long Vowels *a* and *i*

Write a word from the box to complete each sentence.

Word Bank

frightened	pasted	kindly
racecar	higher	explained

1. The **kindly (1 point)** _____ woman likes to
   help her neighbors.

2. Dale's **racecar (1)** _____ was speeding
   around the track.

3. Dad **explained (1)** _____ the problem in a
   way I could understand.

4. Were you **frightened (1)** _____ by the
   strange sounds in the middle of the night?

5. We watched the hot air balloon rise
   higher (1) _____ in the sky.

6. Gina **pasted (1)** _____ the photos into
   her scrapbook.

Read directions to children.
Phonics
© Houghton Mifflin Harcourt Publishing Company. All rights reserved.
202
Assessment Tip: Total 6 Points
Grade 2, Unit 6

Lesson 29
READER'S NOTEBOOK

Two of Everything
Grammar: Possessive Pronouns

Pronouns and Ownership

- A **possessive pronoun** shows that a person or
  animal owns or has something.
- *My*, *your*, *his*, and *her* come before a noun to
  show that someone has or owns something.

My <u>mom</u> gets two gifts.

Thinking Question
What noun goes
with the pronoun?

Underline the possessive pronoun in each sentence.
Circle the noun that goes with it.

1. His (presents) are on the table. **(1 point)**

2. Mom also sees gifts from her (children) **(1)**

3. Her (daughter) gives two books. **(1)**

4. Her (son) gives two flowers. **(1)**

5. Mom opens your (gifts) too. **(1)**

6. My (mom) has a good birthday. **(1)**

7. Her (sister) called this morning. **(1)**

8. My (dad) will take her out to dinner tomorrow. **(1)**

Read directions to children.
Grammar
© Houghton Mifflin Harcourt Publishing Company. All rights reserved.
203
Assessment Tip: Total 8 Points
Grade 2, Unit 6

Reading Longer Words: Long Vowels *a* and *i*

Read each clue. Choose the answer from the word pair below.

1. Doing something to have fun ___playing (1 point)___

   Water coming down from the sky ___raining (1)___

   raining   **playing**

2. Talk about things that trouble you ___complain (1)___

   Tell what something means ___explain (1)___

   explain   **complain**

3. Flashes of light during a storm ___lightning (1)___

   Above something else ___higher (1)___

   lightning   **higher**

4. A track that trains run on ___railway (1)___

   A thing that plays music ___radio (1)___

   railway   **radio**

5. Bright and glowing ___shining (1)___

   Moving through the sky with wings ___flying (1)___

   flying   **shining**

Read directions to children.
Phonics
© Houghton Mifflin Harcourt Publishing Company. All rights reserved.
204
Assessment Tip: Total 10 Points
Grade 2, Unit 6

Words with *ai*, *ay*, *igh*, *y*

Sort the Spelling Words by the spelling patterns.

Long *a* Sound	Long *i* Sound
1. aim (2 point)	10. sly (2)
2. snail (2)	11. shy (2)
3. bay (2)	12. bright (2)
4. braid (2)	13. fright (2)
5. ray (2)	14. try (2)
6. always (2)	
7. gain (2)	
8. chain (2)	
9. tray (2)	

Underline the letters in each word that stand for the long *a* or long *i* sound.

Spelling Words

Basic Words
1. aim
2. snail
3. bay
4. braid
5. ray
6. always
7. gain
8. sly
9. chain
10. shy
11. bright
12. fright

Review Words
13. tray
14. try

Read directions to children.
Spelling
© Houghton Mifflin Harcourt Publishing Company. All rights reserved.
205
Assessment Tip: Total 28 Points
Grade 2, Unit 6

More Pronouns and Ownership

- Some **possessive pronouns** stand alone. They are usually at the end of a sentence.
- *Mine*, *yours*, *his*, and *hers* are possessive pronouns.

Which <u>coins</u> are **yours**?

Thinking Question
Which word shows that someone has or owns something?

Underline the possessive pronoun. Circle the noun that shows what is owned.

1. The (pennies) are <u>mine</u>. **(2 points)**
2. The (dimes) are <u>hers</u>. **(2)**
3. The (quarters) are <u>his</u>. **(2)**
4. The (nickels) are <u>yours</u>. **(2)**
5. The (money) is <u>mine</u>. **(2)**
6. Which (bank) is <u>yours</u>? **(2)**
7. That (wallet) is <u>his</u>. **(2)**
8. The (purse) is <u>hers</u>. **(2)**
9. The (dollar) is <u>mine</u>. **(2)**
10. The (coins) are <u>yours</u>. **(2)**

Read directions to children.
Grammar
© Houghton Mifflin Harcourt Publishing Company. All rights reserved.
206
Assessment Tip: Total 20 Points
Grade 2, Unit 6

Focus Trait: Ideas Supporting Reasons

Good writers tell their opinions in responses to literature. They give reasons for their opinions. They support their reasons with examples from the story.

Read the opinion. Then read each reason that supports the opinion. Find an example from *Two of Everything* that supports each reason.

Opinion: The pot makes the Haktaks happy. **Possible responses shown.**

Reason	Example
1. The pot makes them rich.	The pot makes many gold coins. (2 points)
2. The pot helps them get a lot of things they did not have before.	Mr. Haktak brings home many packages. (2)
3. The pot makes them new friends.	It makes a new Mr. Haktak and a new Mrs. Haktak. (2)
4. The pot helps them make other things they need.	It makes a second house with furniture for the new Haktaks. (2)

Read directions to children.
Writing
© Houghton Mifflin Harcourt Publishing Company. All rights reserved.
207
Assessment Tip: Total 8 Points
Grade 2, Unit 6

Top-left panel

Lesson 29
READER'S NOTEBOOK

Two of Everything
Phonics: Vowel Diphthongs *oi, oy*

Words with *oi, oy*

Write the missing *oi* or *oy* word that will complete each sentence.

Word Bank

joined	voice	cowboy
noise	enjoyed	spoiled

1. The __cowboy (1 point)__ sat by the campfire.

2. He had a very nice __voice (1)__ for singing.

3. He __enjoyed (1)__ singing to pass the time.

4. Sometimes the cows __joined (1)__ in.

5. Their mooing __spoiled (1)__ his songs.

6. The lovely singing became frightful __noise (1)__

Read each word you wrote above. Write each one in the correct column below, under the word that has the same vowel spelling.

point	toy
voice (1)	cowboy (1)
joined (1)	enjoyed (1)
spoiled (1)	
noise (1)	

Read directions to children.
Phonics
© Houghton Mifflin Harcourt Publishing Company. All rights reserved.

208

Assessment Tip: Total 12 Points
Grade 2, Unit 6

Top-right panel

Lesson 29
READER'S NOTEBOOK

Two of Everything
Independent Reading

Reader's Guide

Two of Everything

Make a Cartoon

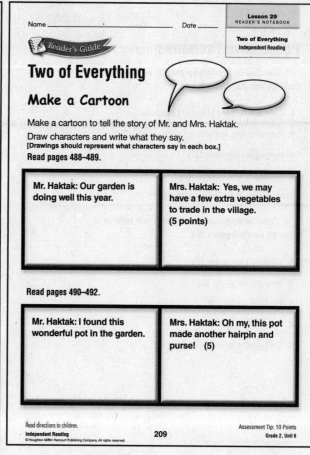

Make a cartoon to tell the story of Mr. and Mrs. Haktak.
Draw characters and write what they say.
[Drawings should represent what characters say in each box.]
Read pages 488–489.

Mr. Haktak: Our garden is doing well this year.	Mrs. Haktak: Yes, we may have a few extra vegetables to trade in the village. (5 points)

Read pages 490–492.

Mr. Haktak: I found this wonderful pot in the garden.	Mrs. Haktak: Oh my, this pot made another hairpin and purse! (5)

Read directions to children.
Independent Reading
© Houghton Mifflin Harcourt Publishing Company. All rights reserved.

209

Assessment Tip: 10 Points
Grade 2, Unit 6

Bottom-left panel

Lesson 29
READER'S NOTEBOOK

Two of Everything
Independent Reading

Read pages 496–497.

Mr. Haktak: Oh my, there are two of you! Ahhhhh... I'm falling.	Mrs. Haktak: Now there are two of you! What will we do? (5)

Read pages 501–502.

Mr. Haktak: I like having two of us.	Mrs. Haktak: Yes, they make great neighbors and friends! (5)

Read directions to children.
Independent Reading
© Houghton Mifflin Harcourt Publishing Company. All rights reserved.

210

Assessment Tip: 10 Points
Grade 2, Unit 6

Bottom-right panel

Lesson 29
READER'S NOTEBOOK

Two of Everything
Spelling: Words with
ai, ay, igh, y

Words with *ai, ay, igh, y*

Write the Spelling Word that means the same as the given word.

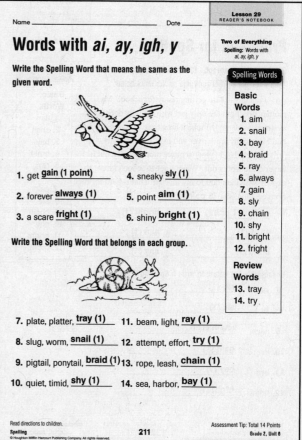

1. get __gain (1 point)__

2. forever __always (1)__

3. a scare __fright (1)__

4. sneaky __sly (1)__

5. point __aim (1)__

6. shiny __bright (1)__

Write the Spelling Word that belongs in each group.

7. plate, platter, __tray (1)__

8. slug, worm, __snail (1)__

9. pigtail, ponytail, __braid (1)__

10. quiet, timid, __shy (1)__

11. beam, light, __ray (1)__

12. attempt, effort, __try (1)__

13. rope, leash, __chain (1)__

14. sea, harbor, __bay (1)__

Spelling Words

Basic Words
1. aim
2. snail
3. bay
4. braid
5. ray
6. always
7. gain
8. sly
9. chain
10. shy
11. bright
12. fright

Review Words
13. tray
14. try

Read directions to children.
Spelling
© Houghton Mifflin Harcourt Publishing Company. All rights reserved.

211

Assessment Tip: Total 14 Points
Grade 2, Unit 6

Possessive Pronouns

✏️ Underline the possessive pronoun in each sentence.
Circle the noun that goes with it.

1. Dana and Dan are my pals. **(2 points)**
2. The twins help you with your homework. **(2)**
3. Her help is with math. **(2)**
4. His help is with reading. **(2)**
5. My friends like to help people. **(2)**

✏️ Underline the possessive pronoun in each sentence.
Circle the noun that goes with it.

6. The skates are mine. **(2)**
7. The hats are yours. **(2)**
8. The bats are his. **(2)**
9. The balls are hers. **(2)**
10. The tickets are mine. **(2)**

Antonyms

Circle the antonyms in each sentence. Then write what
each antonym means.

1. She put one purse into the pot and pulled out two. **(1 point)**
   in or inside; not in (1 point)

2. They worked late filling and emptying the pot. **(1)**
   putting in; taking out (1)

3. The branch swung high and low in the wind. **(1)**
   up; down (1)

4. The tiny mouse wanted to be as huge as a horse. **(1)**
   little; big (1)

5. The chair was heavy, but the pillows were light. **(1)**
   hard to carry; easy to carry (1)

6. Mike was glad to have a rest, but Patty was unhappy. **(1)**
   happy; sad (1)

7. Her dress was colorful, but her coat was faded. **(1)**
   bright, many colors; no color (1)

Proofread for Spelling

Proofread the paragraph. Circle the six misspelled words.
Then write the correct spellings on the lines below.

I am alwas late getting ready for school. My
mother says I am the only girl who actually does move
as slowly as a snayl. I take a long time to brade my hair,
and I brush my teeth over and over until they are
brite. Each day, I aym to move more quickly, but it
never quite works out. When I get to school, I have to
explain why I am late to my teacher. That is hard for me
because I am shi. **(6 points)**

Spelling Words
Basic Words
1. aim
2. snail
3. bay
4. braid
5. ray
6. always
7. gain
8. sly
9. chain
10. shy
11. bright
12. fright

1. **always (1 point)**   4. **bright (1)**
2. **snail (1)**   5. **aim (1)**
3. **braid (1)**   6. **shy (1)**

Unscramble the letters to write a Spelling Word.

7. yar   **ray (1)**
8. lys   **sly (1)**
9. nachi   **chain (1)**
10. inag   **gain (1)**
11. bya   **bay (1)**
12. firght   **fright (1)**

Irregular Verbs

✏️ Write each sentence. Use the past-tense verb.

1. Yesterday, dogs (run, ran) through the park.
   Yesterday, dogs ran through the park. (1 point)

2. Two birds (come, came) after them.
   Two birds came after them. (1)

3. They (go, went) to the lake.
   They went to the lake. (1)

4. They (see, saw) a giant rainbow.
   They saw a giant rainbow. (1)

✏️ Replace each underlined word with a word from the
box. Write the new sentences.

came	went	saw	ran

5. The boys watched two movies.
   The boys saw two movies. (1)

6. They walked to two games.
   They went to two games. (1)

7. They dashed around the field.
   They ran around the field. (1)

8. Then they traveled to my house.
   Then they came to my house. (1)

Possessive Pronouns

Weak	Strong
The teacher gave tests to the **teacher's** class.	The teacher gave tests to **her** class.
The student studied for the **student's** tests.	The student studied for **his** tests.

✎ **Rewrite each paragraph. Replace the underlined words with the possessive pronoun *mine, his, your,* or *her.***

Miss Lee gave two tests today. Miss Lee got papers from <u>Miss Lee's</u> drawer.

Miss Lee said to the students, "Take out <u>the students'</u> pencils."

Dave took out <u>Dave's</u> green pencil. Annette picked up my blue pencil. I said, "That is <u>the one that belongs to me.</u>

Miss Lee gave two tests today. Miss Lee got papers from her drawer.

Miss Lee said to the students, "Take out your pencils."

Dave took out his green pencil. Annette picked up my blue pencil. I said, "That is mine." (4 points)

Read directions to children.
Grammar
© Houghton Mifflin Harcourt Publishing Company. All rights reserved.
216
Assessment Tip: Total 4 Points
Grade 2, Unit 6

Name _____ Date _____

Lesson 30
READER'S NOTEBOOK

Now & Ben
Phonics: Reading Longer Words:
Long o and e

Reading Longer Words: Long *o* and *e*

Read the sentences. Draw a circle around each word that has the long *o* sound spelled *o, oa,* or *ow,* or the long *e* sound spelled *ee* or *ea.*

1. (Rosa) looked out the (window) on the (coldest) day of winter. **(3 points)**
2. She (noticed) (snowflakes) (floating) down. **(3)**
3. (Slowly) the (snow) got (deeper) **(3)**
4. The (snowplow) went by on the (street) **(2)**
5. This might be the biggest (snowstorm) of the (season) **(2)**

Now write each word you circled under the word that has the same spelling for the same vowel sound.

folding	blowing	freezing
Rosa (1)	window (1)	deeper (1)
coldest (1)	snowflakes (1)	street (1)
noticed (1)	Slowly (1)	
	snow (1)	

coasting		meaning
floating (1)	snowplow (1)	season (1)
	snowstorm (1)	

Read directions to children.
Phonics
© Houghton Mifflin Harcourt Publishing Company. All rights reserved.
217
Assessment Tip: Total 26 Points
Grade 2, Unit 6

Name _____ Date _____

Lesson 30
READER'S NOTEBOOK

Now & Ben
Grammar: Adjectives and
Adverbs

Adjectives and Adverbs

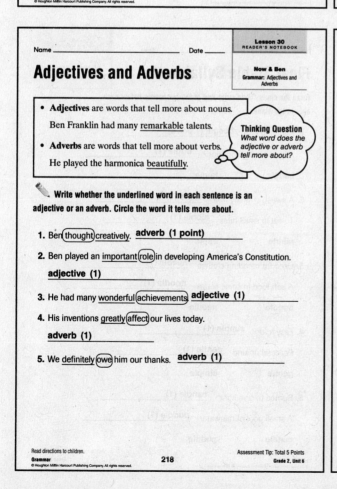

- **Adjectives** are words that tell more about nouns. Ben Franklin had many <u>remarkable</u> talents.

- **Adverbs** are words that tell more about verbs. He played the harmonica <u>beautifully</u>.

Thinking Question
What word does the adjective or adverb tell more about?

✎ **Write whether the underlined word in each sentence is an adjective or an adverb. Circle the word it tells more about.**

1. Ben (thought) <u>creatively</u>. **adverb (1 point)**
2. Ben played an <u>important</u> (role) in developing America's Constitution. **adjective (1)**
3. He had many <u>wonderful</u> (achievements) **adjective (1)**
4. His inventions <u>greatly</u> (affect) our lives today. **adverb (1)**
5. We <u>definitely</u> (owe) him our thanks. **adverb (1)**

Read directions to children.
Grammar
© Houghton Mifflin Harcourt Publishing Company. All rights reserved.
218
Assessment Tip: Total 5 Points
Grade 2, Unit 6

Name _____ Date _____

Lesson 30
READER'S NOTEBOOK

Now & Ben
Phonics: Reading Longer Words:
Long Vowels o and e

Reading Longer Words: Long Vowels *o* and *e*

Fill in the blank.

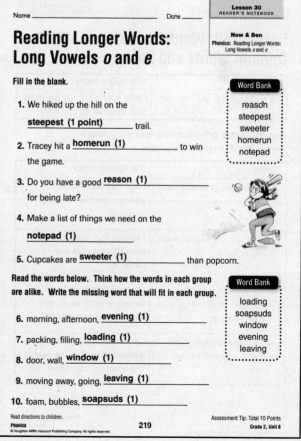

Word Bank
reason
steepest
sweeter
homerun
notepad

1. We hiked up the hill on the **steepest (1 point)** trail.
2. Tracey hit a **homerun (1)** to win the game.
3. Do you have a good **reason (1)** for being late?
4. Make a list of things we need on the **notepad (1)**
5. Cupcakes are **sweeter (1)** than popcorn.

Read the words below. Think how the words in each group are alike. Write the missing word that will fit in each group.

Word Bank
loading
soapsuds
window
evening
leaving

6. morning, afternoon, **evening (1)**
7. packing, filling, **loading (1)**
8. door, wall, **window (1)**
9. moving away, going, **leaving (1)**
10. foam, bubbles, **soapsuds (1)**

Read directions to children.
Phonics
© Houghton Mifflin Harcourt Publishing Company. All rights reserved.
219
Assessment Tip: Total 10 Points
Grade 2, Unit 6

Name _____ Date _____

Lesson 30
READER'S NOTEBOOK

Now & Ben
Spelling: Words with
oa, ow, ee, ea

Words with *oa, ow, ee, ea*

Sort the Spelling Words by the long *e* and long *o* vowel
sounds.

Spelling Words

Basic Words
1. seated
2. keeps
3. speed
4. seen
5. means
6. clean
7. groan
8. roast
9. bowls
10. crow
11. owe
12. grown

Review Words
13. green
14. snow

Long *e* Sound	Long *o* Sound
1. seated (1 point)	8. groan (1)
2. keeps (1)	9. roast (1)
3. speed (1)	10. bowls (1)
4. seen (1)	11. crow (1)
5. means (1)	12. owe (1)
6. clean (1)	13. grown (1)
7. green (1)	14. snow (1)

Now sort the words by how the vowel sound is spelled.

Long *e* Spelled		Long *o* Spelled	
ee	**ea**	**oa**	**ow**
15. keeps (1)	19. seated (1)	22. groan (1)	24. bowls (1)
16. speed (1)	20. means (1)	23. roast (1)	25. crow (1)
17. seen (1)	21. clean (1)		26. owe (1)
18. green (1)			27. grown (1)
			28. snow (1)

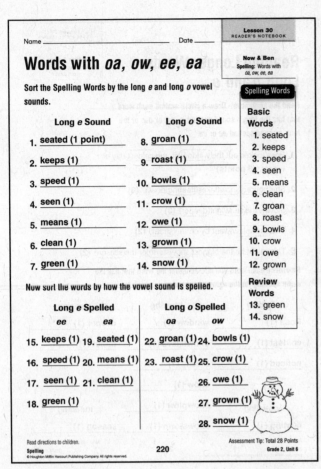

Read directions to children.
Spelling
© Houghton Mifflin Harcourt Publishing Company. All rights reserved.
220
Assessment Tip: Total 28 Points
Grade 2, Unit 6

Name _____ Date _____

Lesson 30
READER'S NOTEBOOK

Now & Ben
Grammar: Adjectives and
Adverbs

Adjectives and Adverbs

- **Adjectives** tell more about nouns.
  Ben Franklin's (quick, quickly) thinking
  solved the problem. noun _____
- **Adverbs** tell more about verbs.
  Ben's fame spread (quick, quickly). verb

> **Thinking Question**
> Is the word I want
> to tell more about a
> noun or a verb?

Write *noun* or *verb* to tell about the underlined word. Then circle
the adjective or adverb in ( ) to correctly complete the sentence.

1. Ben (strong, strongly) promoted the eating of citrus fruit.

   verb (1 point) _____

2. He believed eating fruit would prevent an (awful, awfully) disease.

   noun (1) _____

3. Ben created (beautiful, beautifully) music.

   noun (1) _____

4. His music (deep, deeply) moved many composers.

   verb (1) _____

5. Many people (great, greatly) appreciated Ben's achievements.

   verb (1) _____

Read directions to children.
Grammar
© Houghton Mifflin Harcourt Publishing Company. All rights reserved.
221
Assessment Tip: Total 5 Points
Grade 2, Unit 6

Focus Trait: Word Choice
Opinion Words and Phrases

Opinion	With Opinion Words
Ben Franklin was an important man.	**I think** Ben Franklin was **one of the most important** men in history.

Read each opinion. Add opinion words or phrases to make it
stronger. Possible responses shown.

Opinion	With Opinion Words
1. Ben Franklin was the greatest inventor.	**I feel that** Ben Franklin was our greatest inventor. (2 points)
2. Ben Franklin's hospital made his city better.	**I believe that** Ben Franklin's hospital made his city better. (2)
3. The documents that Ben Franklin helped to write were very important.	**I believe that** Ben Franklin helped to write some very important documents. (2)
4. Ben Franklin's work in the past is important for our future.	**I think that** Ben Franklin's wonderful work in the past is important for our future. (2)

Read directions to children.
Writing
© Houghton Mifflin Harcourt Publishing Company. All rights reserved.
222
Assessment Tip: Total 8 Points
Grade 2, Unit 6

Final Stable Syllable *-le*

Read the clues. Then write one of the two words below each
clue in the blank.

1. A kind of dog   beagle (1 point) _____

   A horn for making music   bugle (1) _____

   beagle   **bugle**

2. A sweet, crunchy fruit   apple (1) _____

   To eat in small bites   nibble (1) _____

   nibble   **apple**

3. Used for mending clothes   needle (1) _____

   A soft food in some soups   noodle (1) _____

   noodle   **needle**

4. Easy to do   simple (1) _____

   Peaceful or kind   gentle (1) _____

   gentle   **simple**

5. Burned to give light   candle (1) _____

   A small pool of rainwater   puddle (1) _____

   candle   **puddle**

Read directions to children.
Phonics
© Houghton Mifflin Harcourt Publishing Company. All rights reserved.
223
Assessment Tip: Total 10 Points
Grade 2, Unit 6

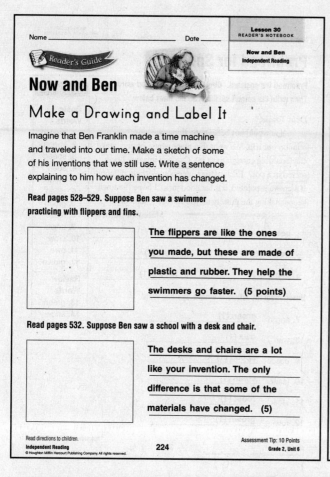

Now and Ben

Make a Drawing and Label It

Imagine that Ben Franklin made a time machine and traveled into our time. Make a sketch of some of his inventions that we still use. Write a sentence explaining to him how each invention has changed.

Read pages 528–529. Suppose Ben saw a swimmer practicing with flippers and fins.

The flippers are like the ones you made, but these are made of plastic and rubber. They help the swimmers go faster. (5 points)

Read pages 532. Suppose Ben saw a school with a desk and chair.

The desks and chairs are a lot like your invention. The only difference is that some of the materials have changed. (5)

Read directions to children.
Independent Reading
© Houghton Mifflin Harcourt Publishing Company. All rights reserved.
224
Assessment Tip: 10 Points
Grade 2, Unit 6

Read page 534. Suppose Ben saw an odometer on a car.

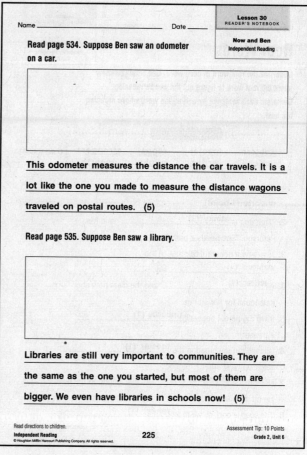

This odometer measures the distance the car travels. It is a lot like the one you made to measure the distance wagons traveled on postal routes. (5)

Read page 535. Suppose Ben saw a library.

Libraries are still very important to communities. They are the same as the one you started, but most of them are bigger. We even have libraries in schools now! (5)

Read directions to children.
Independent Reading
© Houghton Mifflin Harcourt Publishing Company. All rights reserved.
225
Assessment Tip: 10 Points
Grade 2, Unit 6

Name _____ Date _____
Lesson 30
READER'S NOTEBOOK
Now & Ben
Spelling: Words with
oa, ow, ee, ea

Words with *oa, ow, ee, ea*

Write the Basic Word that matches each clue.

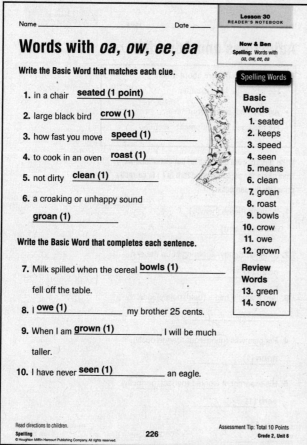

Spelling Words

Basic Words
1. seated
2. keeps
3. speed
4. seen
5. means
6. clean
7. groan
8. roast
9. bowls
10. crow
11. owe
12. grown

Review Words
13. green
14. snow

1. in a chair **seated (1 point)**

2. large black bird **crow (1)**

3. how fast you move **speed (1)**

4. to cook in an oven **roast (1)**

5. not dirty **clean (1)**

6. a croaking or unhappy sound **groan (1)**

Write the Basic Word that completes each sentence.

7. Milk spilled when the cereal **bowls (1)** fell off the table.

8. I **owe (1)** my brother 25 cents.

9. When I am **grown (1)**, I will be much taller.

10. I have never **seen (1)** an eagle.

Read directions to children.
Spelling
© Houghton Mifflin Harcourt Publishing Company. All rights reserved.
226
Assessment Tip: Total 10 Points
Grade 2, Unit 6

Name _____ Date _____
Lesson 30
READER'S NOTEBOOK
Now & Ben
Grammar: Adjectives and
Adverbs

Adjectives and Adverbs

- **Adjectives** are words that tell about nouns.
- **Adverbs** are words that tell about verbs.

Ben was a (careful, carefully) swimmer.
Ben put on the flippers (careful, carefully).

Write *noun* or *verb* to tell about the underlined word. Then circle the adjective or adverb to correctly complete each sentence.

1. Many people admired Ben (great, greatly).
   verb (1 point)

2. Ben solved problems (quick, quickly).
   verb (1)

3. Ben created (useful, usefully) inventions.
   noun (1)

4. Some of Ben's work was (dangerous, dangerously).
   noun (1)

5. Ben shared his inventions (eager, eagerly).
   verb (1)

Read directions to children.
Grammar
© Houghton Mifflin Harcourt Publishing Company. All rights reserved.
227
Assessment Tip: Total 5 Points
Grade 2, Unit 6

Name _____ Date _____
Lesson 30
READER'S NOTEBOOK
Now & Ben
Vocabulary Strategies:
Root Words

Root Words

Underline the root word in each word. Use what you know
about the root word to figure out the word's meaning.
Complete each sentence by writing the word whose meaning
fits best.

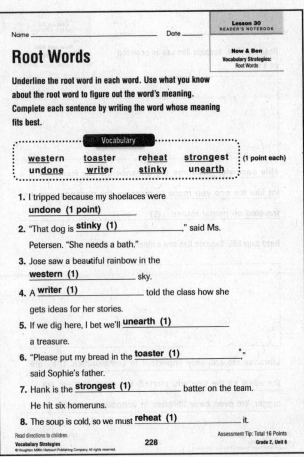

Vocabulary

western   toaster   reheat   strongest   (1 point each)
undone   writer   stinky   unearth

1. I tripped because my shoelaces were
   undone (1 point)

2. "That dog is **stinky (1)** ," said Ms.
   Petersen. "She needs a bath."

3. Jose saw a beautiful rainbow in the
   western (1) sky.

4. A **writer (1)** told the class how she
   gets ideas for her stories.

5. If we dig here, I bet we'll **unearth (1)**
   a treasure.

6. "Please put my bread in the **toaster (1)** ,"
   said Sophie's father.

7. Hank is the **strongest (1)** batter on the team.
   He hit six homeruns.

8. The soup is cold, so we must **reheat (1)** it.

Read directions to children.
Vocabulary Strategies
© Houghton Mifflin Harcourt Publishing Company. All rights reserved.
228
Assessment Tip: Total 16 Points
Grade 2, Unit 6

Name _____ Date _____
Lesson 30
READER'S NOTEBOOK
Now & Ben
Spelling: Words with
oa, ow, ee, ea

Proofread for Spelling

Proofread the postcard. Circle the six misspelled words.
Then write the correct spellings on the lines below.

Dear Tomas,
    You would not believe the things we have
(sean) on our trip. We went to a place where potters make
clay (boals) big enough to sit in! Can you imagine being
(seeted) in a pot? Each pattern (meens) something different.
If a (crowe) is painted, it is for good luck. I hope the town
(keaps) making the pottery so you can see it someday.
                        Manny **(6 points)**

1. **seen (1)**   4. **means (1)**
2. **bowls (1)**   5. **crow (1)**
3. **seated (1)**   6. **keeps (1)**

Unscramble the letters to write a Spelling Word.

7. angro   **groan (1)**
8. weo   **owe (1)**
9. despe   **speed (1)**
10. leanc   **clean (1)**
11. stoar   **roast (1)**
12. rowng   **grown (1)**

Spelling Words

Basic Words
1. seated
2. keeps
3. speed
4. seen
5. means
6. clean
7. groan
8. roast
9. bowls
10. crow
11. owe
12. grown

Review Words
13. green
14. snow

Read directions to children.
Spelling
© Houghton Mifflin Harcourt Publishing Company. All rights reserved.
229
Assessment Tip: Total 18 Points
Grade 2, Unit 6

Irregular Verbs

Underline the correct verb to finish each sentence.
Use the clue that tells when the action happens.

1. We (give, gave) reports today.   **Now (1 point)**
2. I (take, took) the topic of Ben Franklin.   **Past (1)**
3. Sara and I (eat, ate) lunch.   **Past (1)**
4. The teacher (say, said) I could give my report first.   **Past (1)**

Read this story about something that happened last
week. Write the underlined words correctly. Use verbs that
tell about the past.

    I eat lunch with my sister. She give me a library
book. It was about Ben Franklin. She say she liked it.
I take the book to my room. It was a good book. Ben
Franklin give the world many things. It take me just a
little while to read the book.

    I ate lunch with my sister. She gave me a library book. It was
about Ben Franklin. She said she liked it. I took the book to my
room. It was a good book. Ben Franklin gave the world many
things. It took me just a little while to read the book. (6 points)

Read directions to children.
Grammar
© Houghton Mifflin Harcourt Publishing Company. All rights reserved.
230
Assessment Tip: Total 10 Points
Grade 2, Unit 6

Adjectives and Adverbs

- **Adjectives** tell more about nouns.
  He heard the loud thunder.
- **Adverbs** tell more about verbs.
  He prepared his equipment carefully.

Write *noun* or *verb* to tell about the underlined word.
Then circle the adjective or adverb in ( ) to correctly
complete the sentence.

1. It rained (heavy, (heavily)).
   verb (1 point)

2. ((Bright), Brightly) lightning lit up the sky.
   noun (1)

3. Ben Franklin had a ((bold), boldly) idea.
   noun (1)

4. His plan was ((dangerous), dangerously).
   noun (1)

5. His experiment worked (perfect, (perfectly)).
   verb (1)

Read directions to children.
Grammar
© Houghton Mifflin Harcourt Publishing Company. All rights reserved.
231
Assessment Tip: Total 5 Points
Grade 2, Unit 6

Name _____ Date _____

Unit 6
READER'S NOTEBOOK

Exploring Space Travel
Segment 1
Independent Reading

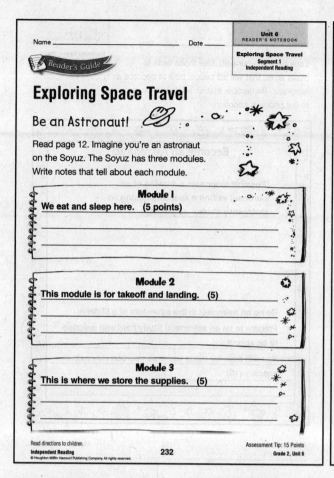

Exploring Space Travel

Be an Astronaut!

Read page 12. Imagine you're an astronaut on the Soyuz. The Soyuz has three modules. Write notes that tell about each module.

Module 1
We eat and sleep here. (5 points)
_____
_____
_____

Module 2
This module is for takeoff and landing. (5)
_____
_____

Module 3
This is where we store the supplies. (5)
_____
_____

Read directions to children.
Independent Reading
© Houghton Mifflin Harcourt Publishing Company. All rights reserved.
232
Assessment Tip: 15 Points
Grade 2, Unit 6

Name _____ Date _____

Unit 6
READER'S NOTEBOOK

Exploring Space Travel
Segment 1
Independent Reading

Use the picture on page 12 to help you draw a diagram of the Soyuz spacecraft. Then write the module numbers and use your notes to tell how the astronauts use each module. After you write, draw a line connecting the writing to each module.

(Students should draw the spacecraft and use their notes from the previous page to complete the writing. A line should connect each section of writing with the corresponding module in the drawing.)
(15 points)

Module _____
_____
_____
_____
_____

Module _____
_____
_____
_____

Module _____
_____
_____
_____
_____

Read directions to children.
Independent Reading
© Houghton Mifflin Harcourt Publishing Company. All rights reserved.
233
Assessment Tip: Total 15 Points
Grade 2, Unit 6

Name _____ Date _____

Unit 6
READER'S NOTEBOOK

Exploring Space Travel
Segment 2
Independent Reading

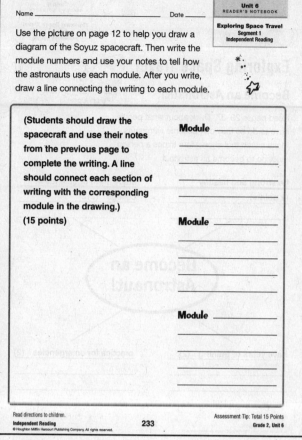

Exploring Space Travel

Make Checklists

Wow! Astronauts have a lot to remember. Complete the table to help the astronauts remember when to wear their special suits and clothes. Use the text, photos, and captions in Chapters 3 and 4 to help you.

When	What to Wear
During takeoff and landing	flight suit (2 points)
On spacewalks	space suit (2)
In the spacecraft when working	regular clothes (2)

Read directions to children.
Independent Reading
© Houghton Mifflin Harcourt Publishing Company. All rights reserved.
234
Assessment Tip: 6 Points
Grade 2, Unit 6

Name _____ Date _____

Unit 6
READER'S NOTEBOOK

Exploring Space Travel
Segment 2
Independent Reading

There is no gravity in the spacecraft. Objects and people are weightless. Make a checklist to remind astronauts how to stay safe without gravity. Add details to tell them why.

When	What to Do
Eating	Strap down the food so it does not float away. (2 points)
Sleeping	Strap the sleeping bag to the wall or chair so you do not float around all night. (2)
Working	Use footholds so you stay in one place. (2)

Read directions to children.
Independent Reading
© Houghton Mifflin Harcourt Publishing Company. All rights reserved.
235
Assessment Tip: 6 Points
Grade 2, Unit 6

Name _____ Date _____

Unit 6
READER'S NOTEBOOK
Exploring Space Travel
Segment 3
Independent Reading

Exploring Space Travel

Become an Astronaut!

Read pages 29–37. Think about what people have to do so they can become astronauts. Make a web that shows four things a person must do to become an astronaut.

be strong and healthy
(2 points)

study math or science in college (2)

Become an Astronaut!

have years of training   (2)

practice for emergencies   (2)

Read directions to children.
Independent Reading
© Houghton Mifflin Harcourt Publishing Company. All rights reserved.
236
Assessment Tip: 8 Points
Grade 2, Unit 6

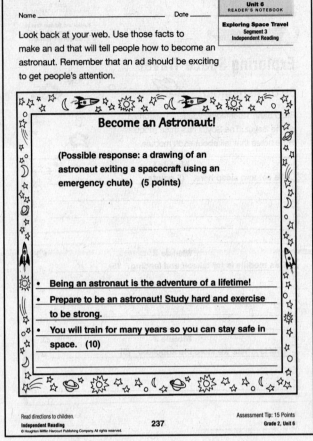

Name _____ Date _____

Unit 6
READER'S NOTEBOOK
Exploring Space Travel
Segment 3
Independent Reading

Look back at your web. Use those facts to make an ad that will tell people how to become an astronaut. Remember that an ad should be exciting to get people's attention.

Become an Astronaut!

(Possible response: a drawing of an astronaut exiting a spacecraft using an emergency chute)   (5 points)

- Being an astronaut is the adventure of a lifetime!
- Prepare to be an astronaut! Study hard and exercise to be strong.
- You will train for many years so you can stay safe in space.   (10)

Read directions to children.
Independent Reading
© Houghton Mifflin Harcourt Publishing Company. All rights reserved.
237
Assessment Tip: 15 Points
Grade 2, Unit 6